Our Race Problems

A Study of Racial Evolution and Conflicts from Ancient History to the Modern Day

By Henry Ferdinand Suksdorf

Published by Pantianos Classics

ISBN-13: 978-1-78987-098-5

First published in 1911

Contents

Preface v

Chapter I - The Laws of Man's Social, Political, Religious, Intellectual, Economic and Ethical Evolution 9

Chapter II - The Factors of The Problems 27

    1. The Prehistoric Man 27
    2. The American Indians 29
    3. The Chinese 32
    4. The Egyptians 38
    5. The Chaldeans, Babylonians and Assyrians 43
    6. The Semitic Race - The Jews 48
    7. The Aryan Race 59
    8. The Hindus 61
    9. The Iranians. 69
    10. The Greeks 71
    12. The Romans. 81
    12. The Arabs. 88
    13. The Teutons. 95
    14. The Italians. 101
    15. The Spaniards. 108
    16. The French. 115

17. The Anglo-Saxons. 129
18. The Germans. 145
19. The Slavs 166
20. The Japanese. 172
21. The Malays. 181
22. The Negro. 182
23. The Human Race 184

Chapter III - Statement and Solution of Our Race-Problems 193

Preface

RACE problems are as old as the human race. Nearly all nations are of mixed origin, and because of this fact, nearly all had to deal with troublesome race problems at some time in their existence. Whenever two or more races, deeply contrasting in type, character and age, met in the same territory, and were forced to occupy it together, vexing race conflicts ensued. Exhaustive disorders and violent disturbances followed, until fusion of the races, and absorption and assimilation of the weaker race by the stronger, brought homogeneity, order, peace and prosperity.

India, Iran, Mesopotamia, Palestine, Greece, Rome, Italy, Spain, France, England and Japan, are cases in point where nations had their vexatious race problems in early days, which were settled by amalgamation, resulting in homogeneity, of type, character, language, sentiment, ideals and aspirations. In Germany, Russia, Austria-Hungary, the Balkan States and Belgium, a large crop of race problems is yet in full bloom, but promises to result eventually in homogeneity through fusion. Until this is accomplished, strife, disorder and insurrections will be the normal condition. And in the colonies and new states of America, Australia and Africa, where a confluence of streams of immigrants of various races takes place, race problems of greater or less magnitude are germinating and sprouting everywhere.

There are only two solutions of these irritating problems; either a complete fusion of the heterogeneous ethnic elements into homogeneity, or extermination or expulsion of the weaker race by the stronger. As a rule, the race problems of the past were solved by slow and steady amalgamation.

When divers races flow together in a new country, race problems present themselves instantaneously, and imperatively demand a solution. And the whole future of the new nation thus formed depends upon this solution. Every immigrant, every colonist, of whatever race, becomes a factor of greater or less importance in the formation of the new people. If he be of superior quality physically, intellectually and morally, he will aid in the improvement of the new national type and character; if inferior, he will exert a deteriorating influence.

The older nations of the Old World, which settled their race problems definitely long ago, and by that means shaped their destiny, must abide by the result; but the new nations, now in the process of formation in the New World, have it yet in their power to shape their future by the solution of these problems. They can make themselves young or old, progressive or stagnant, superior or inferior in character and endowment it all depending on the fact to what extent they admit, absorb and assimilate, or reject, or eject, young or aged, progressive or ultraconservative, vigorous or decadent, alien elements.

Self-preservation, of nations as well as of individuals, is the first law of nature, and the adoption of a policy that will assure a sound, healthy and normal national development is one of the highest duties which a people owe to themselves and to their posterity. New nations can discharge this duty only when they admit immigrants from such countries only as are progressive, and exclude those from lands that are unprogressive and reactionary. The admittance in large numbers of ultraconservative elements will have the tendency to retard the pace of progress of a highly progressive nation, and bring about its premature decline.

The people of the United States have several of these vexations and menacing race problems on their hands; of which some are in their incipient stage, and others are; older and already assume a threatening aspect. The fate of the Republic is involved in the solution of these problems. By immigration and conquest, we incorporate fragments of all races into our body politic. Each fragment, large or small, becomes a factor for good or evil in the formation of the future American nation, which nation will be the resultant of this parallelogram of forces.

Providentially, the United States was first peopled by a highly endowed and intensely progressive race. The Anglo-Saxons and their kindred from Germany, Switzerland, the Netherlands and Scandinavia, in company with the progressive Celts, laid the solid foundation of our social, political, religious and economic institutions. They achieved phenomenal success and made the country what it is today. No other race could have accomplished it.

The Anglo-Saxons, Germans, Swiss, Dutch, Scandinavians, Celts, French and Japanese and, in a less degree, the Italians and Spaniards, constitute the real progressive people existent on earth today. They have created our modern civilization with its astonishing discoveries and inventions. All the others Mongols, Tartars, Turanians, Hindus, Semites, Slavs, Indians, Malays and Negroes are stationary and have contributed little or nothing to the stock of useful knowledge. All these are either too old or too young; and their transportation to progressive America will not change their ultraconservative nature.

Heretofore all immigration, with the exception of the Chinese, has been welcomed without discrimination. Until quite recently, leaving out of present consideration the Negro, who was brought here against his will, the bulk of immigrants came from the progressive regions of Europe, and represented a superior type of manhood. This class, by itself, could insure continued American progress along the lines staked out by the founders of the Republic.

But this stream of immigration has been ebbing fast during the last two decades, and a strong current of inferior quality has set in from the unprogressive east and south-east of Europe. Divers countries of fossilized Asia are also beginning to send their heavy and swelling contingents. This inferior ethnic element, at the rate of nearly a million souls per year, has entered our ports during the last decade. This bodes no good for the American nation. If this rising flood will continue to pour into this country, and if this undesirable human element will be absorbed and assimilated, American manhood and womanhood, and American civilization, will certainly deteriorate.

By the acquisition of the Philippines we acquired a race problem full of lurking danger. It will be a difficult, yes, an impossible task, to fit harmoniously in our body politic the ten millions of Filipinos, so different from us in race, character, age and aspirations.

Another race question looms up on our southern horizon. It is the manifest destiny of the American Union to extend her sway to Panama, and even beyond the Isthmus. Her expansive power, the character of the people in Central America and the West Indies, and the prevailing political and economic conditions there, will force her to annex or "protect" those countries. And when that occurs, we will have to face the knotty problem of finding a proper and suitable place in our political structure for the Latins, Indians and half-breeds of that part of Latin America.

But overshadowing all other race problems is the question: What shall we do with our colored people? It is an intricate and perplexing problem. For nearly half a century preceding the Civil War, the Negro was the cause of violent political agitation, and when the question of African slavery could not be settled except by the arbitrament of the sword, we sacrificed the flower of American manhood and untold wealth, North and South. And still the problem is unsolved and remains a menace. We are as far as ever from fixing a suitable and generally accepted status for the African in our midst.

It is the plain and solemn duty of our generation to so shape our American policy in regard to alien races, that the future American nation will be strong, vigorous and progressive, physically, intellectually and morally; and firmly united in thought, ideals, sentiments, and aspirations. Upon such a policy, American civilization will depend. It is, therefore, of the highest importance that we should thoroughly comprehend the various race problems that confront us, and when understood, solve them with firmness, courage and dispatch. To be irresolute, to drift with the tide, and to be guided by ill-directed philanthropy, will certainly invite destructive disturbances, exhaustive race wars at home and abroad, premature national decay, stagnation of progress and civilization, and the early annihilation of our liberal institutions.

It is incumbent upon us, for these reasons, to study without prejudice all the factors that enter or may enter into the make-up of the American nation. We must study them in regard to their past, present and future; in regard to their history, character, culture and environment; and in regard to the laws of evolution that have made them what they are. We must learn whether they are desirable or undesirable, suitable or unsuitable, for the enjoyment and perpetuation of our social, political and religious institutions.

The study of these factors is the chief purpose of this treatise. And as members of all races flock here, and become factors of greater or less value, nearly all nations and races, that exist or have existed, have been considered. The value of each factor ascertained, the solution of the problems is comparatively easy.

Preceding the brief biographical sketches of the historical nations and races, some space is devoted to the examination of the causes and laws that control the rise and fall, and shape the character and destiny of individuals, families, tribes, nations, races and all humanity. A thorough knowledge of the eternal, universal and immutable laws that govern the evolution of man, socially, politically and religiously, is of paramount necessity to a proper solution of race problems.

In the study of these laws and in their exemplification, I have ventured into new and unexplored fields. However, to present these ideas in the proper form and support them with convincing facts, would require more time, space, learning and means, than I have at my command. That I must leave to others who are better equipped for the task. I can do little more than point out, suggest and intimate the truth. In this respect this work has no higher ambition than to be considered as only a "blazed trail" in the unexplored domain of historical research. If my ideas be right, others, better endowed and equipped, will follow to widen, straighten and level the path into a broad highway.

And, if in spite of its many defects and shortcomings, of which the author is well aware, this modest volume should open a new field for the study of history, and contribute to the adoption of a policy which will solve aright our race problems, and which will maintain the high character, the progressive spirit, the intellectual force and the noble virtues of the American people for generations and centuries to come, its object will be fully attained.

H. F. S.

Spokane, Washington.

Chapter I - The Laws of Man's Social, Political, Religious, Intellectual, Economic and Ethical Evolution

"THIS world is governed by law" has become the leading dogma of modern civilization, and upon this dogma, as a solid and enduring foundation, true science erects its magnificent temple. Law, eternal, universal and irrevocable, is the very life of science. No science can flourish when any and all the natural laws may be revoked or suspended at any moment. Science cannot admit the existence of a miracle.

This doctrine of government by law made its first conquests in the domain of natural science. Man discovered slowly and gradually that the forces of nature operated with a precision and unvarying results, that could be formulated into laws. The human race, which had been floundering through bogs and quagmires of doubts, beliefs and suppositions for ages, found at last in these laws solid ground to stand on. Something firm, certain and positive, had entered the field of human knowledge; indeed, it furnished the first knowledge worth the name. There is no real knowledge, except what is based upon natural law.

These islets of positive knowledge in a dismal swamp of doubt and surmise were enlarged rapidly during the last three centuries. Strictly speaking, all natural sciences astronomy, botany, zoology, geology, physics, anatomy, physiology, chemistry, philology, meteorology, etc. are modern sciences. Human knowledge, previous to our age, was not scientific. The savants of former ages, theologians, philosophers, physicians, jurists, etc., could only think in surmises of more or less value. Today, all science, all real knowledge, must be based on law. The true scientist labors to discover the law which governs the phenomena, and he will not rest content until he has discovered, demonstrated and formulated the law.

Thousands of such laws have been found and announced during the last three centuries; untold thousands are still hidden from man's view, but from what we do know, we are justified in adopting the dogma of the government of the physical world by universal, eternal and unchangeable law.

But science did not rest with the conquest of the physical world. She invaded boldly the domain of man's intellectual, moral and social nature. She attempts to establish and demonstrate the great truth that man's thoughts, sentiments, and actions, that his form of government, his social institutions, his religions, his art, his science, his philosophy, his literature, his language and his economic institutions were also evolved and rose, flourished and decayed in strict obedience to universal and immutable law.

Man, really, is never a legislator. He can never make a law which is to govern human society. He can only discover and formulate the natural law in accordance with which society acts and develops. No scientist claims more than the honor of discovery of certain laws in natural sciences. Plants and animals grew and died, suns and planets moved in their orbits, the elements attracted and repelled each other, languages developed, religions and states sprang up, flourished and disappeared, in obedience to unchangeable laws, long before botanists, zoologists, astronomers and founders of religions and states, appeared, to discover and formulate these laws. Hero worship, to which human nature is prone, has exalted a Lycurgus, a Solon, a Moses, a Hamurabi, a Kung-fu-tse, a Jesus and a Mohammed, to the position of superhuman and semi-divine law-givers, but critical, iconoclastic science brings them down to the general level of a common humanity, and recognizes in them only wise men who discerned and formulated the natural law, in conformity with which the society of their time and country had silently been built up and developed.

Legislation which is founded upon the natural law is enduring and beneficial; all acts, decrees and ordinances, not so based, are vicious, detrimental to society, and soon become dead letters.

Man, considered as an individual merely, is subject to the laws of nature that govern the organic and inorganic world; he sees, hears, tastes, smells, feels, is born, eats, digests, assimilates food, grows, acts, decays and dies, like all other animals. But as a social being he rises high above his fellow-creatures. Modern science follows him into this higher sphere, and endeavors to establish the fact that, even in the complexity of the genesis, growth and decay of his "social, political, religious and economic institutions, eternal and irrevocable law rules supreme.

To discover these laws we must proceed in a scientific manner. Beginning with man's first arrival on earth, we must collect, sift and arrange all the facts of his existence and his evolution, and from them deduce the general laws that governed his history.

It matters not, for the present inquiry, whether man came into this world by the special act of a Creator, or whether in the general scheme of evolution, he was differentiated and developed by slow degrees from lower classes of organic beings. It is immaterial to our purpose whether the human race sprang from one or more created pairs, or was evolved from ape-like beings; but the exact knowledge of the time and place, when and where man mad-e his advent on earth, and the condition he was then in, is of fundamental importance. A comparison of his original with his subsequent condition will lead us to the discovery of the laws of his evolution.

Man made his advent either as a single pair at one place, or as a number of pairs, at one or divers places; he was introduced at one time or at successive epochs. Whatever the facts may be need not concern us, but as to the physical, social, intellectual and ethical condition of the original man, all the evidence, with the exception of revelation, points unmistakably to the fact that he rose slowly and by almost imperceptible degrees from the lowest possible state to his present high position.

Man has left some record of all the time of his existence and evolution; meagre during the early part of his existence, more plentiful during later times. In skeletons, accidentally preserved and accidentally found; in burial mounds and caves; in tools and implements of stone, bronze and iron; in huts, palaces and temples; in highways and ships; in the social, political, religious and economic institutions, as they were successively evolved; we find the chronicles of the coming and going of nations and races; and from these facts we can deduce the natural laws that wrought these changes.

Very few traces of primitive man are found. They cover long periods of extremely slow growth, which must be measured by tens of thousands of years. However, the discovered records, scanty as they are at present, jumbled together in wild, chronological disorder, as we find them, force us to the unavoidable conclusion that the first man, created or evolved, was but slightly and by an almost imperceptible degree removed from the brute; that he had no home, no tools, no implements, no art, no social order, no religion, no ethics and no language, or, at best, all these only in a very rudimentary state. But he bore within himself a spark of a progressive spirit, and this distinguished him from the rest of creation.

With the first man or men white, yellow, brown, or black intellectually, socially and morally very near the brute began the history of the human race. Man was progressive. Slowly and wearily he plodded onward and upward, and by extremely slow degrees transformed his crude tools ultimately into elaborate machines; his primitive hut or cave into a palace; his rough altar into a magnificent temple; his uncouth garments into the gay habiliments of the courtier; his superstitious awe of nature's forces into refined religious systems; his rudimentary social relations into the complex order of a highly organized state; his rude art into the masterpieces of a Praxiteles and a Raphael; and his few and clumsy exclamations into the splendid diction of a Homer, a Virgil, a Dante, a Shakespeare, a Voltaire and a Goethe.

From our elevated position we can now follow the upward and onward course of humanity from its crude beginning to the high culture of our twentieth century. Like a vast panorama the history of man is spread out before us. A thick haze, blurring all outlines and obscuring all objects, covers the horizon. That is the age of primitive man. Slowly the race emerges from the almost impenetrable gloom. We discern a spasmodic, but, upon the whole, steady advance. The race does not advance in a broad, even front. Here and there, now in the centre, and then on the flanks, a nation or a race dashes energetically forward to higher ground, and then subsides into a state of inactivity and stagnation. Its native energy and progressive force was dissipated, and the leadership was transferred to another nation or race on another part of the field.

Generations after generations, nations after nations, races after races the men of the Palaeolithic, Neolithic, Bronze and Iron ages Indians, Chinese, Egyptians, Chaldeans, Babylonians, Hindus, Semites, Hellenes, Romans, Arabs, Neo-Latins, Teutons and Japanese rose up successively, assumed temporary leadership, led mankind up the rugged path of progress, to become exhausted speedily, and relinquish the office of standard bearer of progress to a younger, more vigorous and more progressive race, and then quietly drift to the rear.

And yet, through the multitudinous and tangled facts and phenomena, marking the sporadic advances, halts and retrogressions, the rise and fall of nations, and races, of civilizations and religions, and of schools of thought and taste; through the ages of stone celts, bronze chisels and steel blade; through canoe, trireme, sailing vessel and steamship; through burial mound, cromlech, cyclopian wall, pyramid and suspension bridge; through hut, cottage and palace; through stone altar and marble temple; through polytheism and monotheism; through patriarchism, tribalism, nationalism and humanism; through chieftainship, kingship and democracy; through monosyllabic, agglutinative and inflective speech; through pictorial writing, hieroglyphs and phonetic alphabets; through folk-song, epic, lyric and drama; in fact, through all that man has thought, felt and wrought, in all ages and on all continents, looms up the great lummous truth, that causal chains link facts arid phenomena together, and that immutable law, and not chance or arbitrary power, controls the destiny of man as a social being.

It is therefore of paramount importance that we should discover and formulate the laws, in obedience to which nations, races, states, religions, arts, literatures, customs, industries, trade and commerce, have been called into being and developed.

Prof. John William Draper, one of the keenest and most advanced thinkers of the last century, has, in this respect, rendered to humanity highly valuable pioneer service. In the first chapter of his "History of the Intellectual Development of Europe," he lays down some laws or rules of man's social evolution, in terms so terse, clear and precise, that I can do no better than insert them verbatim.

In that celebrated work he says:

"Man is the archetype of society. Individual development is the model of social progress.

"All mundane events are the results of the operation of law.

"The march of individual existence shadows forth the march of race-existence, being indeed, its representative on a little scale.

"Groups of men, or nations, are disturbed by the same accidents, or complete the same cycle as the individual. Some scarcely pass beyond infancy, some are destroyed on a sudden, some die of mere old age. Of such groups, each may exhibit, at the same moment, an advance to a different stage, just as we see in the same family the young, the middle-aged, the old.

"So in a family of many nations, some are more mature, some less advanced, some die in early life, some are worn out By extreme old age; all show special peculiarities.

"To the death of particles in the individuals, answers the death of persons in the nation, of which they are integral constituents.

"A national type pursues its way physically and intellectually through changes and developments answering to those of the individual, and being represented by Infancy, Childhood, Youth, Manhood, Old Age and Death, respectively.

"If from its original seats a whole nation were transposed to some new abode, in which the climate, the seasons, the aspect of nature, were altogether different, it would appear spontaneously in all its parts to commence a movement to come into harmony with the new conditions.

"Or, by interior disturbance, particularly by blood admixture, with more rapidity may a national type be affected, the result plainly depending on the' extent to which admixture has taken place. This is a disturbance capable of mathematical computation.

"The origin, existence and death of nations depend thus on physical influences, which are themselves the results of immutable laws.

"The life of a nation thus flows in a regular sequence, determined by invariable law."

To which may be added the following laws and rules:

The first great law that strikes us as we survey the history of mankind may be stated as follows; families, clans, tribes, nations, races and even the whole human race, are not ingeniously constructed mechanisms, but are true living organisms, and, as such, are subject to the laws which control the birth, development, decay and death of all living organisms.

It is not difficult to grasp this idea, when we reflect that all living organisms are composed of innumerable, isolated, infinitesimal cells held together by strong vital forces. In the same manner are the detached individual units bound together by the ties of love, patriotism, common interests, descent, tradition, history, language, cult and culture, in the larger organisms of nations, states, races and humanity. And when we speak of public opinion, public interest, public conscience and public spirit, we already have in view the opinion, interest, conscience and spirit, in the aggregate, of all the individuals who compose the state or nation or race.

The individual is built up by living cells, and tribes, nations, races and humanity are formed by individual units, organically united. All these organisms renew themselves in the same manner. Cells continuously appear, mature and die in the individual, and individuals are incessantly born, flourish and perish in the larger organisms of the nation, race or humanity, but the identity of the greater organism is not affected by this unceasing change.

The life of the individual is the prototype of the life of the tribe, the nation, the race and of all humanity; the one is measured by years, the other by centuries. In all we recognize the same successive phases of infancy, childhood, youth, manhood, old age and death, each phase in every one of these organisms being characterized by certain physical, intellectual and moral traits or features.

Babe, child, youth, man and sage, form the family; families group themselves into clans and tribes; clans and tribes into nations; and nations and races, representing the various phases from infancy to dotage, compose the grand organism of humanity. At any given time do we find tribes, nations and races, some in their infancy, some in their youth, some in their prime of manhood, and others in the decay and decrepitude of old age. Humanity is but a large family of nations and races, in which every phase of life is represented.

One phase of life, in individuals as well as in nations and races, merges imperceptibly into the next succeeding. There is no sharp line of demarcation between the phases. To aid man's comprehension, arbitrary classification was resorted to; and hence the division of life in the phases of infancy, childhood, youth, manhood and old age. The characteristic features of a phase vanish slowly, to give way to the traits of the succeeding phase. These characteristic features are mainly of a physical nature in the individual, but preeminently intellectual and moral in the organisms of nations and races. These characteristic traits furnish us with clues to the age of individuals, nations and races.

The characteristics of infancy, childhood and youth are: an exuberant and creative imagination, lack of cool reason, excessive credulity, faith in authority, curiosity, a ready belief in fables, legends and miracles, inconsistency in opinion and aspirations, strong enthusiasm, cheerful optimism, great but spasmodic energy, fertility of plans and schemes, fondness of play, sport, music and poetry, marked imitativeness, emotional temperament, impulsiveness, proneness to symbolism, fickleness in love and hate, vacillation of purpose, intense egotism, cruelty, improvidence, want of perseverance and steady application, pliancy of character, rapid change in habits, inconsistency in plans, motives and ideals, inquisitiveness, and quick adaptability to new surroundings.

In manhood calm, sober reason has superseded a vivid fancy; doubt and criticism have supplanted blind faith and credulity; clear insight has dissipated a world of phantasms; men and events are taken more at their true value; hero-worship vanishes; originality, strong creative and inventive force, steady purpose and persevering industry succeed the imitativeness, the jerky energy and the vacillating methods of youth; the optimism of youth is balanced by the pessimism of old age; the romantic love of poetry, music and the creations of luxuriant fancy, give way to a desire for calm investigation after plain truth; the pliant character of childhood hardens into firmly formed habits; the intense, narrow egotism of youth is transformed into a broader sympathy which embraces family, tribe, nation and race; the adaptability to new environment diminishes it is the period of greatest originality, strongest creative and inventive power, self-consciousness and expansiveness in the life of a nation.

As the typical symptoms of old age we find: a general physical, intellectual and moral decadence; a deterioration of originality, invention and creative force; an impotency to produce or accept new ideas; inability to adapt itself to new conditions and to changes in the modes of life and thought; diminution of energy; the sterility, stagnation and fossilization of thought; growing pessimism; resigned submission to authority; reminiscence and garrulity.

The characteristic intellectual and moral features of infancy, youth, manhood and old age are generally the same in individuals, tribes, nations and all humanity.

The individual, in his anatomical and physiological organization, conforms himself to the phase of life of the nation or race or humanity of which he is a member. The age of the larger and higher organism, be it that of youth, manhood or dotage, is stamped upon his character. In the young nation or race all individual members, from the babe to the sage, manifest a juvenile spirit; all the units of a nation or race in its prime partake of the traits of vigorous, original, creative and inventive manhood; and with nations and races in their decline, every individual member bears the imprint of old age in physical appearance, mental force and moral character.

Thus, for instance, the sage Socrates was old as an individual, in the prime of manhood as a Greek, and young as a member of the human race; or, an Indian papoose is young as an individual, in full maturity as a part of the great unit of humanity, and in its dotage as an Indian both partaking simultaneously of the triple character of infancy, manhood and old age.

Man, contemplated as an individual and as a social unit, thus assumes a status quite complex as to his age. He may be young, middle-aged or old, and so may be his nation or his race or all humanity, but in each case he participates in the age of the higher and larger organism of which he is a member.

Comparatively few individuals enjoy a normal life from infancy to old age. Most of them die prematurely from external or internal causes. The same is true with nations. Most of them suffer annihilation in infancy, youth and manhood, through conquest, absorption, amalgamation, epidemics, extravagance, luxury and vice, and only a very few pass through all the phases of life to a serene and ripe old age.

There never was a general, simultaneous advance of the whole human race. Progress, at any given time, was confined to one or a few nations. The others remained stationary or followed sluggishly. The races of the Stone

Age, the Indians of Mexico, Central America and Peru, the Chinese, the Egyptians, the Babylonians, the Hindus, the Greeks, the Romans, the Italians, Spanish and French, the Anglo-Saxon and Germans, and the Japanese, successively created and developed civilizations, adapted to their national and racial character and the phase of life of humanity then prevailing. They followed each other as temporary standard-bearers of culture. The light of a luminous civilization was kindled and maintained for a time by various nations and races, at various times and on different continents, while the surrounding world shone only by reflected light. One nation, one race after another, yellow, brown, black or white, took the lead in building up a civilization, and yet, the role played by each was not assigned to it accidentally, but fitted harmoniously in the grand drama of the human race.

A nation or race, like buds in winter, may remain in a dormant state, through centuries and millenaries, but when, in the general advance of the human race, its springtime arrives, it begins its national or racial life and, once begun, will not cease advancing and developing until its course is arrested by disaster or old age.

A nation or race cannot rejuvenate itself. Old age, with its decay and decrepitude, and finally death, is as unavoidable with nations and races as with individuals.

However, a nation or race, advanced in years, may be rejuvenated through amalgamation or fusion with a younger and more vigorous nation or race. The new nation, thus formed, is a resultant in accordance with the law of the parallelogram of forces. It begins its national or racial life at an age and with a character, resulting from the fusion of ethnical elements, differing in age, numerical strength, physical, intellectual and moral force. If, for instance, one very young and another quite aged race, should become fused into a new homogeneous people, the new nation, resulting from the merger, would be neither young nor old, but, clearing infancy, childhood and youth at a bound, begin its national existence at the prime of manhood.

This is a very important law. Nearly all great historical nations have been formed by the fusion of different ethnical elements, and the character and history of such nations can only be fully understood, when we consider the nature of the mixture. The great variety in age, numerical strength and character of the different ethnical elements flowing together, render it a complicated problem, but when the values of the different factors are obtained, even if only approximately, we are in a position to determine the age, character and future history of the new nation.

Many nations have sprung from colonization; but such a nation, while new is rarely young. A colony begins its national existence at exactly the stage or phase of life at which the mother country stood at the time of separation; it will keep pace, rise, flourish, grow old and perish with it. Transplantation of a nation to a new country does not seriously affect its normal development.

When two or more ethnic elements, differing in age, character and numerical strength, meet in a colony, the law of the parallelogram of forces steps in at once and determines the age, character and destiny of the new nation thus forming.

Two or more nations or races, however strongly they may contrast with each other physically, intellectually and morally, cannot occupy the same territory without thorough fusion eventually taking place. They may, and generally do arrange themselves at first into upper and lower social strata, but, in spite of the spirit of caste, stringent laws and strong race-antipathies, they will merge and a new, homogeneous nation will ultimately result from the amalgamation.

The capacity for assimilation is stronger in young than in old nations and races. Juvenile people are easily absorbed, and readily absorb foreign, ethnic elements. Aged nations and races, having grown obdurate, ossified and petrified in ideas, speech, customs and manners, tenaciously resist assimilation and absorption.

Only homogeneous nations, only those where rights, privileges and duties, are fairly, equally and justly distributed, are capable of the highest social, political, intellectual and economic attainments. Slavery, serfdom, peonage and caste, always associated with people in a state of uncompleted fusion, are drags on national progress.

Every nation or race possesses its own distinct national or racial character, and in conformity to it will create and evolve a civilization characteristically its own. In the larger frame of the civilization of a common humanity, there is abundant room for national and racial diversity and peculiarities. Every nation or race succeeds best in creating a civilization in full harmony with, and growing out of its own character. The result is always disastrous if an alien culture, even if of a higher order, is forced upon a people. It must be suited to the character and age of a nation.

There is a comparatively short period in the life of every organism of plants in their efflorescence and of animals at their full maturity which is marked by an extraordinary display of energy, activity and expansion of vital forces. This is the time when the organism fulfils its real mission. The same is true in regard to the great organisms of the nation, the race and humanity. The life of a nation extends over many centuries; but its greatest political expansion and power, the utmost activity of its social forces, its boldest inventions and creations, and its highest achievements in art, literature, science, war, commerce and industry, are compressed within the narrow limits of a few centuries at or near its zenith. This is the short epoch when nations really make history and accomplish what is assigned to them.

The duration of the life of a nation or race or of all humanity is in proportion to their respective size and mass.

The successive phases of infancy, childhood, youth, manhood and old age, in the lives of nations, races and of all humanity, are well marked by corresponding changes in social institutions, forms of government, religion, ethics, art, philosophy, literature and language. Each phase has its characteristic traits.

Climate, environment, religion, form of government and civilization, exert but a slight influence on the rise and fall of nations. Nations have risen and fallen in the temperate and tropic zones, on sea coasts and inland, in arid and humid countries, on plains and tablelands, but the ascent and descent took place under unchanged conditions.

All organic life begins with the simple cell, and is built up by differentiation. A tendency to pass from the simple to the complex, from the general to the special, from the homogeneous to the heterogeneous, may be observed throughout nature. New organs are continuously evolved to conform to new conditions, and new functions of the organs are constantly added to meet new demands.

The earliest forms of life on our globe were of the simplest structure. A constant differentiation ensued to keep pace with the changes in the environment. From the earliest forms of life to man, the latest and most perfect, there is a continuous and marked increase ID the heterogeneity of structure.

Law, order and a general plan is clearly discernible in the evolution of organic life on earth. All organic life is built up in obedience to a few simple laws working in manifold variations. Species succeeded species in the rising scale of perfection; but the embryonic life of every species presents a brief synopsis of the history of all organic life preceding it.

In man's social and political evolution we find a similar condition. Individualism, patriarchism, tribalism and nationalism, mark the successive phases of man's social and political development down to the present. Every nation, no matter of what phase in the life of humanity it is a representative, must pass through all the earlier stages of social and political evolution. Every civilized modern nation has reached the stage of nationalism, but in its early infancy and youth ,each had to pass successively through the individualistic, patriarchal and tribal phases.

Primitive man was but slightly differentiated from the brute creation. No social ties restrained him. His desire, his will was his law. He knew no family, no home, no tools, no religion, no language and no society. He stood on the individualistic, the lowest stage of social evolution. But, as the primitive man could leave scarcely any records behind him, we know very little of his condition.

When man stepped into the early dawn of history we find him already advanced to the second or patriarchal phase of social and political development. He had organized the family. His social relations had become more complex. The family was then the highest social unit, and man found himself both as an individual and as a member of a higher organism, the family.

That was the early infancy of the human race; the age of stone and bronze; of burial mounds, dolmens and cromlechs, of monosyllabic speech, crude pictorial writing and patriarchal forms of government. Its representative nations and races, with the exception of a few scattered remnants in inaccessible regions, have disappeared through absorption or extermination.

The family grew into a tribe. Another rung in the ladder of social and political progress had been mounted. By that man's social relation grew still more complicated. He became conscious of the fact that now he was simultaneously an individual, and a member of a family and of a tribe. He acquired new rights and assumed new duties. Three social units individual, family and tribe laid claims upon him, . and worked together in harmony. Differentiation in occupation continued. New germs of civilization sprouted and flourished. More orderly and permanent forms of government were instituted. New inventions made easier the acquisition of food, raiment and shelter. Iron superseded stone and bronze. Agriculture began to displace the hunt and the herd. Religious myths coalesced and were systematized. Isolated speech grew into agglutinative, and pictorial writing into hieroglyphics. The patriarch or head of the leading family became the war-chief, judge and priest of the tribe.

It was the juvenile or tribal age of humanity. It was an era of wild and luxuriant imagination, of heroic adventure, of bold grandeur in art, of gigantic monuments, and of mighty tribal deities in religion. The true representatives of this stage were the American Indians, the Egyptians, the Chaldeans, the Chinese, and the Semites. These nations or races never developed their social, political and religious institutions beyond the tribal stage, Powerful chieftains might occasionally weld a number of tribes into a mighty kingdom, but it remained always tribal in its structure, and when the cohesive force of a common and strong ruler relaxed, the empire disintegrated immediately into the original tribal units.

In the course of time man ascended to a still higher level of social and political organization. Tribes merged into nations having an organic structure. Man was still an individual, but at the same time, a member of a family, a tribe and a nation; and his relations to his fellowmen became correspondingly more intricate. The social units individual, family, clan, tribe and nation were harmoniously united in the larger organism. Each unit claimed rights and assumed duties which had to be adjusted by rulers, priests, judges and legislators.

It is the national stage, the phase of youth and early manhood in the life of humanity. It prevails today among all the civilized nations. The true nation, the organic union of individuals, families, clans and tribes into the greater organism of the nation, is strictly a modern growth. Antiquity knew nothing of it. Even the Greeks and Romans, otherwise far in advance of their contemporaries, could only make tentative and futile attempts at nationalism. The modern civilized nations of Europe, America and Asia, are the true representatives of nationalism, and of the manhood phase in the life of the human race. National speech, religions, literatures, arts, interests, traditions, aspirations and policies, are the characteristic political and social features of our age.

Throughout the civilized world the nation is today the highest social and political unit. The principle of nationalism is the predominant destructive and constructive social and political force at present.

The next level to be mounted by man in his social and political ascent, will be that of race, and beyond that, and still higher, that of a common humanity. But both of these steps belong to the future.

Religious development ran a course parallel to that of social and political evolution. Individualism, patriarchism, tribalism and nationalism are also the successive phases through which religions were evolved.

Individualistic religion characterized the early infancy of mankind and of nations. It was emphatically polytheistic. To the primitive man, as to a child, all nature was animated. Super-human demons, spirits or gods, dwelt in all objects and phenomena of nature, and from amongst them each individual selected his tutelary deity, whose favor to gain and whose wrath to appease, he worshiped. Abject, superstitious fear of these supernatural beings was the soul of all primitive religions.

When the family was organized the tutelary divinity of the head of the family or patriarch was naturally promoted to the position of the family god. The other individual tutelary deities ranged themselves around the family fireplace according to the rank and importance of their worshipers. The patriarch was war-chief, ruler, judge and priest, in one person. His god was supreme and was worshiped by all and, frequently, after his demise, his tutelary divinity and his soul, merged into one deity, and led to the worship of ancestors.

Man never worshiped anything but spirits, whatever may be understood by that term. Genuine idolatry never existed on earth. Images of wood, stone and metal, from the crudely fashioned fetish of the Congo Negro, to the artistic marble divinities of Greece, Rome and Babylon, and to the sacred miracle-working statues and pictures of Christian saints, were nothing but symbols, which were not worshiped, but within or behind which the devout worshiper fancied the spiritual deity, to whom his prayers, incantations and sacrifices, were addressed.

As the family expanded into the tribe, the patriarch became the chieftain and, corresponding to this social change, his and his family's tutelary deity was elevated to the position of chief tribal god. The concentration of power and importance in the tutelary deity of the chief degraded the tutelary deities of the other families and members of the tribe to subordinate positions, and many suffered annihilation from lack of praise, prayer and sacrifice.

Again man climbed to a higher level of social and political progress, and his religion underwent a corresponding change. A number of tribes merged into a nation. The leading tribal chief became an elected and, subsequently, an hereditary king. The other chiefs were reduced to the state of vassals and courtiers. The gods imitated their worshipers. The struggle for existence and supremacy between individuals, families, clans and tribes on earth, was duplicated among the gods in heaven. The exuberant imagination of the youthful race of man, like a magic lantern, threw a picture in miniature of man's terrestrial affairs, magnified to gigantic dimensions, on the blue, celestial screen above. Heaven was only a faithful, but much enlarged copy of earth. The hierarchy of the celestial empire was modelled after the social and political organization on earth; and in the metamorphosis from individualism to patriarchism, from patriarchism to tribalism and from tribalism to nationalism, the gods followed suit. The tutelary divinity of the despotic and ambitious king soon monopolized all prayers, adoration and sacrifice, and the other deities were subordinated to the rank of servants and messengers, or were eliminated entirely. An autocrat ruled above as well as below.

In the fierce battle for existence and supremacy, the spirits, demons and gods who dwelt in the most striking and awe-inspiring objects and phenomena of nature, had the advantage decidedly and came out triumphant. The spirits inhabiting the thundercloud, the lightning-riven mountain, the celestial bodies, the fire-emitting and earth-shaking volcano, the frowning sea, the hot, ills-curing spring, the poisonous snake, the colossal, uncouth dragon, the mysterious cave or a famous hero, naturally and gradually became the supreme deities of some tribes or nations.

Such is the genesis of all the great gods who ever existed. They all had their beginning as the tutelary deity of some primitive man, dwelling in some striking object or phenomenon of nature. They rose or fell, flourished or perished with the fortunes of their worshipers. Frequently, however, they manifested greater tenacity of life, and survived the individuals, families, tribes and nations that had created or adopted them, and, in a changed form became the deities of alien successors. Thus, the huge and terrible saurians, doubtless the contemporaries of primitive man, retained their place as powerful, sinister and evil deities in the form of dangerous dragons, long after the species had become extinct.

The religious idea kept pace with man's social and political advance. The national idea, verging upon the racial, is paramount today, and all great religions take the same stand; they are all national or racial in character. As a general rule, Shintoism is confined to the Japanese, Confucianism to the Chinese, Buddhism to the Mongols, Judaism to the Jews, Islam to the Semites, Hamites and Turanians, Christianity to the Aryans, Catholicism to the Neo-Latins and Celts, Protestantism to the Teutons and Greek Orthodoxy to the Slavs. The exceptions are due to force. In spite of the zeal of missionaries and the proselyting activity of conquerors, the advance of the religions came always to a halt at the boundaries of races. Race and blood determine the permanent, terrestrial borders of the empires of the gods. The dream of a universal religion will only be realized, when the human race, in its further progress, has reached the summit of a common humanity.

All the gods, great or small, whom man has ever worshiped, were and are anthropomorphic. They were no realities. They were and are conceptions of the human imagination; figments of the human brain. They were the vain attempts of the limited human understanding to comprehend and personify the cause of the existence and of the government of this vast universe.

The power that governs the universe and man's conception of it are two entirely different things. The former is absolutely incomprehensible to the finite mind; the latter, a product of the human fancy and reason, is subject to the laws of evolution like all human creations, and must be dealt with scientifically. These conceptions, these god-ideas, vary with man's age, race, environment and civilization.

In this sense, man created his gods; and as he knew nothing superior to himself, he created them after his own image; in form mostly; in thought, feeling and action, always. It is conceded by all that the great deities of former ages, - Zeus, Athene, Osiris, Iris, Ptah, Merodach, Baal, Indra, Jupiter, Mars, Wotan and a myriad of lesser divinities, now long vanished into nothing, were mere phantoms, although their worshipers firmly believed them to be realities. What is true of them is true of those yet extant. This plain truth, when once generally adopted by all thoughtful men, will perceptibly increase tolerance and materially diminish hypocrisy and religious strife and persecution.

As a rule, the gods were and are ideal men; men magnified to infinity. And as the god-idea and religious conceptions sprang from the innermost nature and character of man, the great historical gods were ideal Indians, Egyptians, Chinese, Babylonians, Hindus, Jews, Greeks, Romans, Arabs and Teutons. Indeed, all religions took a national or racial form and coloring, from the same cause which brought forth national or racial languages, arts, and literatures.

Human nature is practically the same at all times and all places, and all its creations conform to general types. Nations and races can produce only slight variations and modifications of these types. The gods, consequently, whether they were created by Mongols, Malays, Tartars, Semites, Aryans, Indians or Negroes, were all essentially human, and bore a strong family resemblance. Indeed, the conceptions are so profoundly alike, that we can take almost any hymn, prayer or invocation, to a god of any cult, and substitute the name of any other deity from any other cult without changing the effect.

Man's conceptions of a god improved and became more refined with the intellectual and moral advance of the nations and the race.

From the genesis of the gods, it is evident that polytheism was and is the universal rule. A pure monotheism never existed. All religious conceptions must be treated alike. We must not classify one religion as polytheistic and another as monotheistic, when, in fact, there is scarcely a difference between them. We cannot draw an arbitrary line of demarcation in the scale of supernatural and divine beings or conceptions, from the fetish of the barbarian to the God of the Christian. If the hosts of demons, ghosts, tutelary spirits, manes, nymphs, hob-goblins, fairies, imps, kobolds, gnomes, undines, elves, sylphs, etc., and all the greater divinities of the heathen religions, are to be rated as deities of low or high degree, truth and justice and fairness demand that Satan, devils, angels, archangels and all the miracle-working patriarchs, prophets, apostles and saints of the so-called monotheistic religions, should be placed in the same class.

The great contrast between the Orient, where autocrat and subject were separated by a wide gap, and the more democratic Occident, where a greater equality and a more intimate intercourse existed, led to the false classification of religions into monotheistic and polytheistic. The religions of the Semitic East reflected terrestrial autocracy and despotism; and those of the more democratic Occident mirrored a condition where rulers were only the first among peers.

Religious conceptions and creations, like social, political, literary and philosophic ideas, as they sprang up, flourished and disappeared in various climes, ages and races, are subject to scientific inquiry. Science aims to learn the laws that govern the birth, growth, change and decay of religious thought and practice.

The evolution of ethics kept pace with the progress of social institutions. Primitive man stood alone and knew of no ethics. Ethics appeared with the foundation of the family, and its field widened as man made his social progress through family, clan, tribe, and nation. Every upward step in social progress brought new rights and duties, and increased the complexity in the relations existing between the individual man and the other social units of the family, tribe and nation, and in the relations between these units. The love of family, tribe, nation, race and of all humanity, is egotism after all, but an egotism refined, broadened and ennobled in the social and ethical advance.

Ethics adjusts the rights and duties of all the social units, as they arise in the progress of the nation or race. Ethics is a natural product of society, and keeps pace with it in its march from barbarism to civilization. Society is built up in obedience to immutable natural laws; and it is the office of students of ethics, legislators and judges, guided by necessity, to find and formulate these laws.

Ethics is not an off-shoot of religion. Each sprang up independent of the other. Ethics deals exclusively with the relations of man to man and to society; religion concerns itself with the relation of man to the deity he has created. The welfare of the individual and of society is the object of ethics; to gain the favor and learn the will of the deity is the aim of religion. Primitive religions, therefore, had nothing to do with questions of moral conduct. The gods only demanded worship, submission and loyalty. Piety, therefore, is erroneously designated as a virtue. The relation existing between man and the god he has chosen or created, does not touch his moral nature. A man may be, and frequently is, a pious man and a scoundrel combined. Worship of his god does not make him good or bad. But when piety is ranked high as a virtue, it leads to hypocrisy. Ethics is the pioneer that explores new territory in the dominion of morals, and blazes the trail for the advance; laws and customs follow to level and pave the highway. Ethics is the restless stream of moral progress, but in its quiet eddies, coves and bays its deposited sediment hardens into laws, customs and usages. Ethics is universal; religion is local, personal, tribal, national or racial.

But ethics and religion became almost inextricably interwoven, as soon as the human race had passed through the phase of infancy. Kings and rulers needed the sanction of religion to insure the obedience of their subjects. The oracles of the gods were influenced to command what potentates and priests desired. With an awe-inspiring "thus sayeth the Lord" did Hammurabi in Babylon, Zarathustra in Iran, Moses on Sinai, Mohammed at Mecca, the prophets in Israel, and many others, proclaim their own version of what was right and wrong.

This alliance of throne and altar has always retarded ethical progress. Society is incessantly advancing, and ethics must keep pace with it; but laws, decrees, edicts and ordinances, promulgated by kings and priests, at the behest of the deity, must stand immutable, and, though originally suited to the condition of society then prevailing, must become inconvenient and tyrannical, and impede ethical and social progress in the end. The classic books of Confucius crystallized Chinese thought, the Koran renders the Moslem world unprogressive, and the Pentateuch has become a stumbling block in the upward path of Aryan nations.

The literature of a nation reflects its progress from infancy to old age. Infancy, childhood and youth, with their blind credulity and lively, exuberant imagination, delight in myths of the gods, tales of herpes, legends of giants, sorcerers and monsters, narratives of miracles and folk-songs. Epic poetry, such as the Mahabarata, the Ramanya, the Song of Nimrod, the Iliad and Odyssey, the Edda, Beowulf, Gudrun and the Nibelungen song, is almost exclusively the product of juvenile nations.

In the prime of life vivid fancy vanishes and is superseded by clear, calm, sober, searching and calculating reason. Originality of thought, creative and inventive genius, and bold investigation of science are characteristic of this phase of national life. Poetry, especially epic poetry, is at a discount. History, the drama and scientific literature, being in full accord with the prevailing spirit, flourish.

At the approach of old age originality ceases; creative and inventive force is on the wane; feeble criticism is indulged in; commentaries, imitations of great ancestors, compilations, memoirs and reminiscences, comprise the favorite productions of the authors of a nation growing old.

Of all the great and prominent men of a nation, its literary men are the best representatives of its progress through the successive phases of its life.

In regard to form of government, patriarchism, chieftainship, kingship, democracy, Caesarism and imperialism, mark the successive steps in a nation's political development. That form of government, which, for the time being, suits the age and character of a nation, is for it the most beneficial. Patriarchism is fitted for infancy, kingship for youth, democracy, the keystone in the arch of national life, for manhood, and Caesarism and autocracy again for old age. The change of form must correspond, and, under normal conditions does correspond, to the nation's advance in age.

Humanity, considered as an organic whole, also had its infancy and youth, reached its prime in the present age, and in the future, will experience the approach of old age with its decadence, fossilization and decrepitude. Each phase in the life of humanity manifested its characteristic features in language, writing, art, religion, science, literature and form of government; and every stage of evolution was represented by some particular nation or race.

Monosyllabic speech, folk songs, pictorial writing, and patriarchal cults and forms of government, were associated with humanity's childhood. Agglutinative languages, tribal religions and governments, epic poetry and the gigantic in art, were associated with mankind's youth. And inflective speech, phonetic alphabets, grace and beauty in art, national and rational religions, national governments, democracy, highly refined ethics, the drama and an extraordinary development of science, accompany the phase of manhood in the life of the human race.

In treating of the different nations and races that, in the various ages, have filled the proud position of humanity's representatives, we must speak guardedly of superior and inferior nations and races. A people's physical, intellectual and moral capacity, depends, at any given time, upon the phase of their own national life in which we find them, and upon the stage in the life of the human race, of which it is a representative.

In the family of nations the same order prevails as in the family at the fireside. Here the babe, the child, the youth, the man and the sage, surround the same hearth. The man dominates the domestic circle by reason of his superior physical and mental vigor. A score of years pass by and the scene shifts. The babe has grown into a lusty youth; the youth is now in his prime of manhood and rules the family; the man has passed into dotage; the sage has sunk into his grave; and a new generation fills the cradle. And so it continues without intermission for centuries. Superiority and rule are only temporarily coupled with manhood; inferiority and obedience are associated with childhood, youth and old age.

Nations and races rise, flourish, decay and perish, in a similar manner in the great family of nations, which we call humanity. There were always, at any given time, nations and races which stood on the stage of infancy, youth, manhood or old age; but that nation which at that particular time enjoyed the prime and vigor of full manhood, assumed leadership, and the others, young or old, followed voluntarily or through compulsion. This hegemony of one nation, however, was never of long duration. The approach of old age sapped the vital forces of the leader and champion; youthful, more vigorous and more progressive nations rose to snatch the ensign of leadership from the nerveless hand, to carry it upward and onward to higher levels, and to share the same fate later.

Mankind is like a tree. The process of germination and sprouting was hidden in darkness that was the age of original man. The twigs of the young sapling grow, mature, decay, die and disappear one after another, as the plant grows that is the age of prehistoric races who have all vanished. The sapling expands into a tree; the limbs and branches spread symmetrically in all directions; the tree has reached its time of maturity, of greatest vital activity and expansion; that is the period in which we live, when moral and intellectual forces exert themselves to the utmost, and when Mongolians, Malays, Hindus, Semites, Aryans, Indians, and Negroes, must be regarded as the limbs extending symmetrically in all directions from the trunk of the tree of humanity.

Chapter II - The Factors of The Problems

1. The Prehistoric Man

It will now be necessary to examine every ethnic factor that enters or in future may enter into the formation of the American nation, both as to its character and value. As practically every race and nation is already represented here, it will necessitate a review of all that ever existed on this globe. For even those nations and races that have been absorbed by others, have not lost their influence as factors. Their blood will tell. But the consideration given to each factor must be in proportion to its value.

Man's history, in a larger sense, began with the existence of our earth. The history of our globe, and of its organic life, anterior to the coming of man, is but an introductory chapter to the special history of humanity. We cannot fully comprehend man unless we consider him in connection with his environment and his fellow creatures. We can readily understand that any marked deviation from the size and weight of this planet, its position in the solar system, amount of light and heat received from the sun, its seasons, its climate, its atmospheric conditions and its distribution of land and water, would have produced a marked change in its organic life and in man, its crowning product.

The successive appearance, as geology reveals it to us, of invertebrates, fishes, marine plants, land plants, amphibians, reptiles, birds, mammals and man, marks the steps in the evolution of organic life. Man came logically at the time and manner he did. His existence fits harmoniously into the general scheme of creation. Without man's presence, organic life would be but a torso, an arch without a keystone.

We cannot, even approximately, fix the time of the advent of man. Certainly it was tens of thousands, perhaps hundreds of thousands of years ago.

Physically, intellectually, morally and socially, the primitive man was only slightly removed from the brute. All reliable evidence points conclusively to this fact.

He was progressive, but his progress was extremely slow. Only the anatomical structure of some buried remains accidentally preserved and discovered, throw some light on the general condition of our earliest ancestors.

The man of the Palaeolithic age lived in caves, subsisted on hunting and fishing, did not till the soil, domesticated no animals, worked with chipped flint, utilized fire, buried his dead in mounds and probably had created a very rudimentary language.

It must be assumed, from an analogy with historical races, that these Palaeolithic people rose, flourished, decayed, and perished, and passed through the phases of infancy, youth, manhood and old age.

A wide gap extends between the Palaeolithic and Neolithic ages of Europe. The Palaeolithic race had apparently passed the meridian of its racial existence and sunk into the decay and decrepitude of old age, when the younger, more vigorous and progressive Neolithic people invaded the continent and subjugated or exterminated them. The men of the Neolithic age were of a new race of higher capacity. It is unreasonable and unscientific to suppose that the Palaeolithic race should be progressive for a long period, invent tools, build up a primitive civilization, sink into the condition of deterioration and, after a long age of stagnation, rejuvenate itself, again become progressive, and erect a new culture of a different and more advanced type on the ruins of the old.

The Palaeolithic man was the representative of humanity's early infancy, and as such created the first rudimentary civilization. His mission accomplished, his race grew old, decrepit and stagnant, and gave way to others.

The Neolithic people were at first only hunters and fishers, and in point of culture stood below their Palaeolithic predecessors. They were progressive, however, and adopted much of the higher civilization of the decadent race which they conquered, annihilated or absorbed. They began to domesticate dogs, cattle, pigs and geese. They used implements of polished stone, invented bows and arrows, and erected gravemounds, stone altars, cromlechs and dolmens.

They believed in the immortality of the soul; they made hammers, axes, chisels, spears, knives and plows of stone. Later, after a period of progress, they cultivated wheat, barley and millet; spun hemp and flax; wove cloth, planted fruit trees and manufactured amber ornaments.

This swarthy, round-faced race, of short stature, evidently of Asiatic or Turanian origin, advanced to a patriarchal, probably to a tribal form of government, executed great public works, created a religion with ancestral worship, an organized priesthood and an elaborate ritual, formed a higher type of speech, lived in villages, tilled the soil, built homes for the family and carried on trade with distant lands. Humanity owes to this race very many new and important inventions.

When this race had passed through the phases of progressive, inventive and creative youth and manhood, it grew feeble, sterile and decadent from old age and, in its turn, was conquered, annihilated or absorbed by a younger, bolder and abler race.

The transition from the Neolithic to the bronze age was sudden. The conquering race, young, gifted, energetic and progressive, adopted the culture of the subjugated race to a large extent, and engrafted upon it its own racial ideas and ideals. The civilization which they unfolded, though still quite primitive, was much superior to that of their predecessors. They were Aryans, probably, the remote ancestors of European and American nations.

Such, briefly, and in dim outline, is the history of prehistoric man in Europe. Three civilizations, each superior to the preceding, each created by a distinct race, succeeded each other at longer or shorter intervals. The Palaeolithic and Neolithic races, which laid the crude foundation of European culture, have vanished. Each one rose, flourished, decayed and perished; each accomplished its modest mission; each played its assigned part in the first act of the grand drama of humanity. They represented mankind in its early infancy.

Traces of Palaeolithic and Neolithic man found on other continents indicate that the evolution of mankind pursued the same course everywhere.

2. The American Indians

Out of the night of prehistoric times we step into the dawn of history. Even the early age of the historical period is devoid of a written history. The life of the earliest historic nations and races is recorded in mounds, pyramids, hieroglyphics, temples, tools, and implements. From them we can learn what the men of antiquity thought, felt and achieved.

The Indian race of America has undoubtedly a glorious past behind it, and some day an interpretation of the mounds on the Mississippi and the Ohio, and of the ruins and inscriptions of Mexico, Central America and Peru, will reveal its history in full.

The civilization of the Indian, as evolved in Anahuac, Yucatan and Peru, is of a very high antiquity, but whether it antedates those of the Nile, the Euphrates or the Pei-ho or not, is still a mooted question. The institutions of the Indians show in some respects a more archaic character than those of the early Egyptians, Chaldeans and Chinese, and in other respects manifest a more advanced type.

The Indian is possessed of great fortitude, dignified reserve, stoic apathy and loyalty to his tribe. He is gloomy, stern, proud, taciturn, suspicious, phlegmatic, vindictive, averse to steady and regular labor, incapable of continuous process of reasoning on abstract subjects and destitute of the inventive faculty.

His social and political institutions never advanced beyond the patriarchal or tribal state, and his language stopped short at the agglutinative or polysynthetic stage. He remained essentially a nomadic or semi-nomadic hunter and fisher; cultivated very few fibrous and food plants; domesticated only a few animals; invented no iron implements and only utilized bronze, copper, silver and gold for tools and ornaments. The great mass of the race, from the Arctic Sea to Cape Horn, remained in the Stone Age down to the arrival of Columbus.

His religion is still individualistic, patriarchal or tribal. A multitude of spirits and demons dwell in the objects and phenomena of nature, and the tutelary deities of the individual, the family and tribe are worshiped in a shamanistic fashion. He has become absolutely unprogressive; his ideas, customs and laws are fossilized; the contact with progressive and superior races makes no impression upon him; he cannot adapt himself to new environment and stolidly resigns himself to the fate of extinction. The race has reached its dotage.

The Indian race is a true representative of humanity's infancy. It, also, lived through the phases of infancy, childhood, youth and manhood to old age. Its zenith must be placed long anterior to the Christian era. The civilization which surprised the conquistadores of Mexico, Yucatan and Peru, was only the aftermath of a much higher culture which preceded it by many centuries. It was the last feeble flickering of a notable civilization, that had shed its lustre over two continents in the dim and remote past.

The old myths and legends of the Indians, and the layers of relics which successive waves of civilization have deposited in the forests of Central America and on the plateaus of Anahuac and Peru, where each higher and later stratum points to an inferior culture than the one underneath and older, indicate unmistakably that the race crossed the meridian of its life thousands of years ago, and that it has been on the down grade many centuries.

Man's social development in America was analogous to that of Europe and Asia. The Indian's culture began with low, primitive and rudimentary conditions. The race did not spring fully equipped from the hand of a creator like Pallas Athena from the head of Zeus. On the contrary, it began life at a very low stage, rose gradually to its point of culmination in the course of many centuries, and then commenced its descent to the stagnation and petrifaction of old age. This race, like all others, had its phases of progressive, imaginative childhood and youth, of bold, vigorous, inventive and creative manhood, and of sterile, feeble, decadent and ossified old age.

It is quite probable that a Palaeolithic race occupied this continent at a very early age, ran through its phases of life, created a primitive civilization, and when grown aged, weak and unprogressive, was conquered, annihilated and absorbed by the young, vigorous and progressive Indian race.

This race, after having subdued, exterminated or absorbed the aboriginal race and adopted its cultural achievements, spread in a homogeneous mass over both continents, and evolved a civilization quite adapted to its racial character and to the phase of infancy in the life of humanity.

The advance of the race was not steady and simultaneous in all parts of the continents, but spasmodic; periods of progress, stagnation and retrogression succeeding each other regularly in different sections. Tribes rose, flourished and perished in the larger life of the race. At different times and in various localities particular tribes would push ahead of the others, assume the lead, expand their political power, enrich the inherited culture by new inventions and original ideas, grow old and decrepit, and hand over the banner of leadership to another tribe, younger and more progressive. In the long ascent and descent of the race, many tribes came to the front, and successively represented the infancy, childhood, youth, manhood and old age of the whole race.

Like the rising flood of the incoming tide, where each succeeding wave reaches a higher point on the shelving shore until high-water mark is attained, so rose the civilization of the Indian during its progressive period, until it reached its point of culmination in Mexico, Central America and Peru.

The era when the Indian race stood at or near its zenith cannot as yet be fixed. The myths, fables, legends and traditions point to a grand, golden age in the distant past, when giants, demigods and divinities founded states, originated religions and civilizations, invented hieroglyphics and useful implements, and built cities, temples, palaces and roads. Native chroniclers placed Votan and Zamma, the reputed founders of Maya civilization, in the tenth century, B. C. Quetzalcoatl, according to aboriginal sources, arrived about 174 A. D.

Of the rise of Indian civilization we know but little; nearly everything we find belongs to the area of decline and deterioration.

Indian culture reached its highest point in Peru, on the shores of Lake Titicaca. The ruins of that region indicate that three or more waves of civilization swept over the land successively at long intervals, and left their deposits in as many strata. There is very strong evidence of the existence of a Palaeolithic race. It was succeeded by a race which erected burial mounds and cromlechs. A people which attained a comparatively high degree of culture preceded the Incas. They ruled over an extensive empire; they erected cyclopean edifices, temples, palaces and massive fortresses, and adorned them with symbolic sculptures, highly artistic and of great antiquity; they tamed the llama and alpaca; cultivated maize, potatoes, cotton and fruit trees; elaborated a religious system and a complicated political administration; com structed marvellous highways and bridges; evolved a comprehensive literature, consisting of epic and lyric songs and history; and made a notable advance in medicine, astronomy, chronology, industrial arts, agriculture and civil government.

The Incas were only imitating epigoni; devoid of originality, inventive force and progressive spirit. They represented the Indian race in its decline, as did the Aztecs of Mexico and the Mayas of Central America.

The native chroniclers claimed that the Incas came to Peru in 1240 A. D. and that the superior race which preceded them and which evolved the Peruvian civilization, began its career in 470 B. C. Whatever value we may attach to these chronicles, this seems to be the truth: that the aboriginal culture of these people is very old; that it had its beginning thousands of years since; that it passed through long ages of slow growth, progress, invention and discovery, before it reached its zenith centuries before the commencement of the Christian era; that many tribes successively participated in its upbuilding; and that it has been on the downgrade for two thousand years or more.

Nearly all the myths, legends, traditions, relics and ruins of the Indian race, the stratified deposits of Indian civilization in Mexico, Peru and Central America, give evidence of the race's period of decline; very few speak of the era of rise and progress that preceded it. The rise and fall of Indian culture and power in Mexico and Central America is analogous to that of Peru.

The life of the Indian race covers a period of many thousands of years. It had its poetic childhood, its progressive youth, its creative and expansive manhood, and its unprogressive, impotent old age; and each phase was represented by a different tribe or nation. It represented humanity in its infancy. From very low conditions it advanced to patriarchal and tribal government, to tutelary deities of individuals, families and tribes, to agglutinative and polysynthetic speech, and to the manufacture of implements of polished stone and bronze, and then it became stationary, stagnant and crystallized in thought and habit.

Its racial life has been normal. It attained a high age because broad oceans protected it from the aggression, conquest, extermination and absorption by young, progressive, expansive and aggressive races until quite recently. It is now doomed to speedy extinction except in Latin America. No external or internal force can cause its revival. No new civilization, no new, alien religion, no new, foreign code of ethics, no new, economical condition, can regenerate it. It may be rejuvenated to some extent by a fusion with the Latin and Negro race in tropical and subtropical America, but that rejuvenation will be only evanescent, as the Latins themselves are on the decline, and the Negro race is numerically weak.

The Indian race is almost extinct in the United States, the census of 1900 shows only 266,760 souls and it can hardly be considered a factor in the building-up of the future American nation; but as it is the manifest destiny of the Union to extend its sway to Panama and beyond; and as the blood in the veins of Mexicans and Central Americans is three-fourth Indian, the race with its age, character, ossification and idiosyncrasies, may become an important factor, at least in a large section of the future "Greater America."

3. The Chinese

The Chinese, according to the census of 1900, number only 119,050 souls in the United States of America, exclusive of its insular possessions, and nearly all of them are adverse to assimilation. They cannot be considered a factor of any value at present, but as about 400,000,000 of them are crowded in a limited territory beyond the Pacific, and as our appetite for conquest is likely to increase, and as this race may acquire a good footing in territory already in our possession or to be acquired later, such as the Philippines, the Hawaiian Islands, Mexico, Central America, etc., we may have to deal with it in the future as a very important factor.

The history of the Chinese is unique and highly interesting, as it presents a record of a nation, or rather of a race, extending over a period of nearly five thousand years.

Protected by the sea, high mountain ranges and forbidding deserts, surrounded by inferior barbarians, and inhabiting the fertile valleys of the Hoang-Ho, and the Yangtse-kiang, this gifted and interesting race began its racial or national life long before the dawn of history. So far as we know it had no foreign tutor to guide it during infancy, childhood and youth. It evolved a civilization characteristically its own, and was exposed to foreign influence only after it had crossed the meridian of its national life, and when national character, modes of thought, customs and habits had become rigid, firm and unyielding from age.

The Chinese is *par excellence* the autodidact, the self-made nation in the human family. Its civilization, in all its parts, in form of government and society, in art, religion, literature and industry, is essentially its own creation.

Its chronicles and literature cover a space of upward of forty centuries; but its recorded history began when its political, social, religious and economic institutions were already fully developed, and when it stood in its zenith. Of its formative period, of its most interesting epoch of growth from infancy to manhood, from barbarism to a high culture, there is very little reliable record. An impenetrable fogbank of myths and legends rests on China's days of childhood. China stepped into the light of history, a full-fledged nation in the prime of manhood.

The chronicles, annals and popular poetry of the ancient Chinese inform us that at a very early date, or about 2500 B. C. they had already organized a complete and complex administrative system; had divided the realm into provinces, departments and cities; had the land surveyed and classified for purposes of taxation; had invented sun-dials, and calculated time, eclipses and the movements of the planets; had constructed paved roads, lined with shade trees; had drained marshes, built dykes and dug canals; had built seagoing vessels; had made tools and utensils of iron, bronze, gold and silver; had cast bells and statues; did travel per boat, ship, sedan-chair, cart and wagon; built huts, villas and castles; resided in villages and walled cities; wore woven cloth, embroidered silk and leather shoes; cultivated bamboo, barley, beans, hemp, indigo, melons, millet, pepper, wheat, cherries, chestnuts, mulberries, pears and plums, practiced music on flutes and drums; sent out mailed warriors to battle, besieged fortified towns with movable towers; made education general; created an extensive literature; elaborated a religious system with a comprehensive ceremonial; developed a code of law, defining right and wrong; and evolved letters from pictorial writing.

China, at that early time, enjoyed a civilization which was, in most respects, not inferior to that of Europe in the seventeenth century.

All writers, native or foreign, on Chinese history and conditions, are unanimous in their verdict, that the social, political, religious and economic life of the Chinese people, has not materially changed since the days of their great emperors, Hwang-ti (2650), Yaou and Shun (2357 to 2205) and Yu (2200 B.C). Ossification of all national institutions had already set in at that early date. The nation had crossed its meridian and was on the down grade toward the degeneracy of old age. With the exception of an occasional brief revival of intellectual activity, through the impulse given by an unusually intelligent and progressive ruler or reformer, the history of China presents nothing but a picture of stagnation, fossilization and slow deterioration.

As infancy, childhood and youth precede manhood in the life of a nation as well as in that of the individual, many centuries of slow growth and progress must have passed ere China reached the height of its civilization. The ascent resembles the descent. We now know fairly well how long it took the Greeks, Romans, Italians, Spanish, French, Anglo-Saxons and Germans, to climb to the point of culmination in their respective national lives, and, by reasoning from analogy, and bearing in mind the law that the duration of a nation's life is in proportion to its size and mass, and that in this respect the Chinese nation far exceeds any one of those named, we can safely fix the time of the beginning' of its infancy at six or seven thousand years before the beginning of the Christian era. The nation had to pass through a long period of infancy, childhood and youth, of progress, invention and discovery, before it reached its zenith of manhood, about 2000 to 2500 years before our era.

As said before, the Chinese had no foreign teachers in their childhood. They had to invent everything they used. They had to domesticate wild animals; improve wild cereals and fruit; devise plans for castles, cities, canals, roads and ships; organize the various individual, patriarchal and tribal cults into a national system, and build up an orderly society and all without a model.

It is possible, however, and evidence of the fact is accumulating, that races of the Palaeolithic, Neolithic or bronze ages, preceded the Chinese, and, successively evolving rudimentary civilizations, as elsewhere, laid the foundation of Mongolian culture. Be that as it may, the civilization of China is essentially Chinese in character.

The age of the great emperors, Hwang-ti, Yaou, Shun and Yu (2650 to 2200 B. C), the "Golden Age" of China, was evidently that people's era of progress, growth, originality, creative force, inventive genius and great expansion of political power.

Three dynasties ruled after them down to Kung-fu-tse, or Confucius (557-479 B. C). It was an era of reaction, following an age of great intellectual and moral exertion. The annals of this age are meager, unreliable, and distorted by a mass of myths, fables and legends. Books were rare and learning was confined to a few. The age bore the stamp of stagnation, decadence and impotence. The popular poets were silent, the inventors died out, no original thinkers rose, the central power was on the wane, and the empire disintegrated into a number of semi-independent, feudal principalities.

The latter part of this period and the beginning of the next experienced a great intellectual and literary revival. Kuan-tse (650), Sun Wu (514), Kung-fu-tse (551-479), Lao-tse (500), Tso-Kin-Ning (476), Chu-Shu-Nien (299), Meng-tse (372-289 B. C.), and many other poets, philosophers and historians, illuminated that age, and their thoughts left an indelible impress on the Chinese character. This revival is probably due to the fact that a younger tribe or branch of the Chinese race rose to power at that time and superseded and to some extent rejuvenated the decadent older tribe or nationality which had created China's original civilization.

Kung-fu-tse outranked all his contemporaries, and became an absolute authority in politics, morals, manners, and religious thought, to his people. This sage, however, was not a founder of a new religion. He possessed no originality, no creative nor inventive genius, and never claimed it. He was only a collector, compiler, interpreter and commentator of what had come down from China's real classical age. He was a true representative of a decaying, crystalizing, aging people. He strove to arrest the downward course by a return to the social, political and religious conditions of the ancient prosperous, vigorous, virtuous, progressive and happy China under its great emperors.

Kung-fu-tse, with this end in view, collected, sifted, edited and arranged the voluminous literature which had Accumulated down to his day. The result was a number of books constituting the Chinese classics. They contain essays on symbols, cosmological treatises, histories and popular folk songs. These songs, written at the time of the great emperors, and even anterior to that age, mirror faithfully the thoughts and sentiments of a courageous, optimistic, independent, aggressive and progressive spirit, such as the Chinese of that era possessed.

Confucius was no originator of a new faith or a code of ethics; he was not even a reformer, but only a restorer. His social, political and religious ideal was ancient, patriarchal China, ruled by great emperors, as a father governs his family; all held together by the ties of filial love and respect and a strong sense of duty; and where propriety, sense of order, industry, frugality, honesty, truthfulness, equanimity and ancestral worship were the cardinal virtues.

He was a true representative of his people on their way to the decadence, unprogressiveness and petrifaction of old age. For that reason his work was a great success. He crystalized for a long time, perhaps forever, the ideas, ideals and customs of his nation. He supplied a far larger number of men with a standard of correct thinking and living than any other founder or reformer of religion.

The emperor Chi-Hwang-ti (221 B. C), vigorous, forceful and revolutionary, endeavored in vain to arrest the general downward trend. He destroyed feudalism, reunited the country, built the great wall and inaugurated many reforms. Opposed strenuously by the ultraconservative literati, he ordered books and authors to be burnt.

The Han dynasty, the "Pride of China" ascended the throne in 206 B. C. A revival of the literary, scientific, political and military spirit ensued. Great libraries were established. All the books that had escaped fire were collected. A bright constellation of poets, historians, philosophers, statesmen and scientists an inferior aftermath rose suddenly above the horizon; but they were only imitators, compilers and commentators. Through all this extensive literature, and all that was produced subsequently, we look in vain for the bold, optimistic, natural, independent, aggressive and progressive spirit that animated the poets and thinkers of the classic age. Originality, creative and inventive force had vanished long ago. Hoary, feeble, imbecile, unprogressive, unproductive and ossified old age had settled upon the "Flowery Kingdom" for good. The literati represented the decline of their nation.

One event, however, world-wide of importance and consequences, transpired during the reign of the Han dynasty. The wild nomadic Hiong-nu or Huns, were pressing hard against the northern boundary of China. The great wall was constructed as a defense against their raids. The Hiong-nu were at last signally defeated and forced westward. The savage Hunnic hordes reached successively the Caspian, the Volga, the Euxine, the Baltic, and even the regions beyond the Rhine and Danube. They forced the eastern Germanic tribes from their homes on the Vistula and Oder to seek new settlements to the south and west. The victory of a Chinese army shortly before the Christian era thus became the cause of the Great Migrations, the destruction of the Roman empire and the creation of the new Gothic, Vandal, Frank, Lombard and Anglo-Saxon kingdoms. The shock administered to the Huns of Manchuria was transmitted from tribe to tribe, until its force was finally dissipated on the shores of the distant Atlantic.

Buddhism was introduced into China at this time. It spread rapidly. It influenced art, architecture and literature to some extent, but it made no deep and enduring impression on the Chinese mind and soul; on the contrary, it had to accommodate itself to the Chinese spirit, character and culture. Old age had made the Chinese obdurate and any attempt from within or without at reform or change proved futile.

And so it remained to the present age. Chinese history, during the last seventeen centuries, is uneventful and monotonous. Mongols, Tartars and Manchus came, conquered and ruled the country in succession, but all these external changes left the folk-soul of the Chinese, their ideals and manners, intact. Deterioration continued. Brief, spasmodic revivals occurred at long intervals, but they were speedily followed by periods of more pronounced decay and degeneracy.

China has remained essentially unchanged for four thousand years. Character, mode of thinking and manner of living are stereotyped. The nation, and especially the literati, who breathe and live in the atmosphere of the old classics, are hostile to all reforms and innovations. The people are ultra-conservative. Guided by Kung-futse they go back to the age of Yaou and Shun for wisdom and standards of life. They build vehicles, construct furniture, utensils and tools, erect houses, temples and palaces, cultivate the soil, write poetry, philosophize, decide cases, administer public affairs, and worship and fear deified ancestors, tutelary deities and an innumerable host of demons, spirits and gods, in the same style and manner as did the subjects of Yaou and the contemporaries of Confucius.

This people, self-sufficient in its culture, isolated from the rest of the world, immune from the assault of younger, more progressive and expansive races, did survive all other nations of antiquity. Like an anachronism, this fossil representative of humanity's infancy, rises mysteriously in the midst of the stirring, progressive, modern life.

This hoary race passed through its phase of hopeful, progressive, imaginative childhood and youth anterior to the third millennium, B. C, and reached the meridian of its racial existence, its epoch of originality, invention, creative force and greatest political activity, power and expansion during the third millennium, B. C., at a time when mankind, considered as a living organism, was still in its infancy, and had not passed beyond the stage of monosyllabic or isolating languages, patriarchal forms of government, picture writing, and widest polytheism. Having arrived at its point of culmination, decay and decline set in, and as a result of approaching old age, its social, political, religious and economic institutions became stagnant, stationary and crystalized.

The social, political, and religious life in China never rose above the primitive, patriarchal stage. The family is still the social, religious and administrative unit, and the state is but a large family ruled by one head. The family is the prototype of the state. The emperor is patriarch, ruler, supreme judge and high priest in one person. China, in its evolution, remained stationary in the patriarchal phase, and never attempted the ascent to the higher level of the tribal and national stage.

Fossils give us a glimpse of the animal and plant life of remote epochs of the past; and in the petrified thoughts and manners of the present China, we can study man's ideas, habits and customs during humanity's childhood. There we find yet the primitive, monosyllabic speech, patriarchal form of government, pictorial writing, slightly modified, and the very ancient religion, with its army of spirits and demons dwelling in every striking object and phenomenon of nature, whose favors have to be gained by praise, prayer and sacrifice, and whose will must be learned through signs, oracles, dreams and magic.

The long era of complete isolation which shielded China from intrusion, and permitted the full development of a normal racial life, covering at least seven thousand years, has come to an end. The young, ambitious, aggressive nations of the earth, with their progressive ideas, are pressing through the gates of the Flowery Kingdom. It is a critical moment for the empire, China, the still hearty and robust sage among the nations of the world; China, which can look back upon nearly fifty centuries of glorious history; China, which saw India, Persia, Assyria, Babylon, Egypt, Greece, Rome and Arabia rise, flourish and fall, and which observed Italy, Spain, France, England, Germany and Japan, grow from infancy to manhood; China, which like a garrulous grandam, can regale us with charming nursery tales of mankind's childhood; this China must now choose between extermination and progress. She must choose the former. She cannot regenerate or rejuvenate herself. She is too far advanced in age. She may consent to the adoption of an alien civilization superficially; and may be forced to partial reforms and innovations in her institutions. Such a change may even bring about a temporary revival of intellectual and moral life, but a more general and lasting reaction and decadence will follow. Young Aryan civilization engrafted on the decaying Mongolian trunk will produce neither flower nor fruit; disintegration will only be hastened thereby. China can only be rejuvenated by a strong infusion of young Japanese or Malayan blood.

The extensive introduction to and the absorption of such an ethnic element by the people of the United States could only be detrimental in its effect. It would deteriorate intellect, morals and manners. In our insular possessions of the Pacific, however, the effect would be otherwise, but of that we will treat later. Fused with the American nation in considerable proportion, this element would hasten the approach of the decadence of old age. Nations must protect themselves from known danger. The Chinese Exclusion Act is a wise, statesmanlike measure.

4. The Egyptians

It seems quite impossible that the descendants of the ancient Egyptians, Babylonians, Persians and Hindus should ever come to the territory of the United States in such numbers as to become a factor of any value in the formation of the American nation. But as the lives of these nations also exemplify the laws and rules of evolution laid down in a previous chapter; and as it is deemed best that all historical nations should participate in this general review, in the chronological order in which they appeared, a comparatively brief sketch of the lives of these nations is inserted.

The explorers of the year 3000 B. C, if such there were, would have found four great centres of a high civilization, located on the Nile, on the Euphrates, on the Hoang-Ho and in tropical and subtropical America, respectively. Here were the foci of human intelligence, culture and power at this date. Of these civilizations the American and Chinese were the most archaic in character. The culture of the Egyptians and Chaldeans indicates an advance to a higher level. China and America represented the early, Egypt and Babylonia the later infancy of the human race.

The Egyptians transformed a monosyllabic language, partially at least, into an agglutinative; introduced phonetic elements into their pictorial writing; made the tribe, instead of the family, the predominant social and political unit, raised art to a higher level, differentiated the priest from the ruler, and reduced religion to a system.

The Egyptians were not autochthonous in the valley of the Nile. They were invaders, and probably came from the Euphrates at a very early date, so that even tradition, of a very retentive memory, had forgotten the fact.

A Palaeolithic and a Neolithic race preceded them on the banks of the Nile. These Neolithic aborigines belonged to a copper-colored race with thin legs, large feet, prominent cheek bones, and large lips, evidently a race of inferior physical organization and intellectual development. They were a chiefly pastoral people, but also produced pottery of a highly artistic quality, manufactured flint implements of a high order and finish, and carved elegant bowls and vases out of hard rocks. This race which in the course of many centuries had built up a primitive, Neolithic civilization, was conquered by the young, invading race, and reduced to servitude. These Neolithic people had had their infancy, youth and manhood, and were probably sinking into the decline of old age, when the young and progressive Egyptians conquered the valley. Those that survived the sword were absorbed and assimilated; conquerors and conquered slowly merged into a new and homogeneous people. The infusion of old blood hastened the progress of the invaders, who erected a newer and grander culture on the ruins of the old.

The date of this invasion is lost in the obscurity of prehistoric times. We can only discern objects dimly through the fog of legends and myths.

About 4000 B. C. the Egyptians debouch into the twilight of history. Menes, placed by some historians as far back as 5700 B. C., was a legendary personage. With the first and second dynasties, whose monuments are identified, and who ruled about the beginning of the fourth millennium, B. C., authentic history begins in the valley of the Nile.

A brighter light reveals to us the life of these people during the reigns of the fourth dynasty and its immediate successors, from about 4000 B. C. downward. It was an era of great progress. The race passed from youth into early manhood. The great pyramids, an evolution of the ancient *mastaba* or burial mound of earth or brick, and colossal temples were constructed, and social, political, religious and economic life unfolded itself in grand style. It was an age of daring originality, bold invention and strenuous creative power.

The monuments of that time reveal a highly developed art, bold and sublime in its conceptions, and noble in its execution; an ingeniously organized government and civil administration; an elaborate system of theology; a full code of ethics, indicating a complex and refined social condition; a voluminous literature, conserved by an advanced system of writing; and private life greatly differentiated and articulated. The mural paintings in the tombs of the ancient kings furnish a faithful picture of public and private life.

Two types of men are represented by these ancient paintings and sculptures; one, tall, muscular, with large, full eyes, receding forehead, oval face, straight or aquiline nose, dark to light brown complexion, wavy or curled hair, distended nostrils, full lips and scanty beard, evidently that of the governing aristocratic caste of the invaders; the other, the common people, originally the subjugated aborigines, squat, dumpy and heavy, with long, retreating skull, coarse features, distended nostrils, round cheeks, and thick lips. A strong admixture of Ethiopian blood is evident. Complete fusion of the two races had not yet taken place at that time.

The paintings, inscriptions and sculptures point to the unmistakable fact that the Egyptians, as early as 3000 to 4000 years before our era, had domesticated goats, sheep and asses; raised twenty different kinds of grain and fruit; operated mills; baked bread; cultivated the soil with hoe and plow; made wine and beer; spun and wove; modelled in clay; carved wood, stone and ivory; organized the various trades into guilds; made butter and cheese; surveyed the land and recorded the boundaries; regulated irrigation by the construction of canals, dikes and reservoirs; manufactured tools and implements of iron or bronze; adorned the homes of the wealthy with shade and fruit trees, trellised arbors and fish ponds; evolved architecture, sculpture and painting to a then unparalleled height of bold and simple grandeur; regulated weights and measures; practiced music; promoted science, especially medicine, astronomy and geometry; calculated time; wrote chronicles, prayers, hymns, formulas of sorcery, poems, tales, rituals of the tomb and mythical treatises, such as "The Book of the Dead"; and enriched civilization by a large number of practical inventions.

The Egyptians carried their social, political and religious institutions to a higher level than the Chinese and Indians. They passed from the patriarchal to the tribal stage. The *nome,* which was the enlarged family, became the predominant social and political unit. Each nome had its own chieftain, capital, civil administration, army, navy and religious cult. Each sovereign chief had his feudal vassals, serfs, soldiers and priests.

Political and religious institutions were developed along parallel lines. Individual, family and tribe, in their evolution, found a counterpart in the individual, familiar and tribal gods. When the head of the family became the chief of the nome, his or the tutelary deity of his family became the chief god of the nome; and when a nome grew uncommonly wealthy and powerful, and subjected other nomes to its dominion, the divinities above followed suit; the tribal deity of the ambitious, conquering nome assumed supreme rank and reduced the gods of the subjugated individuals, families and nomes, to inferior rank and subordinate positions in the celestial hierarchy. When through inter-marriages or treaties two or more nomes were united on terms of equality, the gods conformed to the situation and formed combinations of equals. The celestial kingdom above was a much magnified copy of social and political Egypt. The anthropomorphic gods of the Nile valley, being idealized Egyptians, thought, felt, acted and ruled like their worshipers.

When Memphis, Heliopolis, Thebes, Abydos, Denderah, Sais, Thinis and Edfou, the old Nome capitals, successively became the great centres of wealth, power, learning and influence, and attained to the hegemony of the Nile valley, their gods participated in the change. They rose, fell, merged, were naturalized or totally eliminated, according to the political fate of their nome.

It is almost impossible to obtain a clear, comprehensive view of the religion of Egypt. Religious ideas and rituals Were in a continuous fltix. Gods, myths and religious worship varied with every political change like pictures in a kaleidoscope, or like the forming and dissolving clouds. Nomes, with their capitals, incessantly rose, flourished and subsided, and with them their gods, their myths and their religious ceremonials. When capitals like Memphis, Thebes, Abydos, etc., attained more enduring prominence, their deities, mythologies and rites experienced a corresponding lasting supremacy. Thus, Pthah of Memphis, Ra of Heliopolis, Amun of Thebes, Osiris and Isis of Philae and Abydos, Hathor of Denderah, Uit of Sais, Shu of Thinis and Harshuditi of Edfou, were successively the tutelary deities of an individual, of a family and of a nome, and rose to high rank and enduring fame, because their nome, with its capital, had secured vast and permanent wealth, power and influence. The rank of the god depended upon the wealth, learning, military power and political prestige of his worshipers.

Egypt never developed into a true nation. The realm of the Pharaohs was never an organic whole, but, at best, only a bundle of nomes, welded together by the power of a nome, a city or a ruler. The tribal character remained distinct and uppermost. Social, political and religious evolution stopped and petrified at the tribal stage.

Of the Egyptian, as of other people of antiquity, we are only acquainted with the story of its prime and decline. Of its infancy, childhood, and youth, of its formative age, of its rise and growth, we know little or nothing. It is a long, weary road from barbarism to a high civilization, and many centuries must have passed while the nation advanced from infancy to manhood, but this interesting period is hidden from our view.

The Egyptian nation stood at its zenith about 3000, B. C. It was then in the prime of its life. It maintained itself at or near this height from the 4th to the 12th dynasty, or from about 4000 to 2500 B. C. This era witnessed the culmination of Egyptian civilization. Architecture, sculpture, painting, literature, science, government, agriculture, religion and the mechanical arts were developed to as high a perfection as the people were capable of giving them at that time. The pulse of national life beat strong. It was the epoch of invention and creative force; of the builders of the great pyramids, temples, palaces and tombs, and of the great sculptors and painters who adorned them. It was an era when a well organized priesthood, the custodian of learning, elaborated religious systems which, for their solemn rites, their chants, prayers and sacrifice, their mystical mythologies, their faith in the immortality of the soul and final judgment, and their magnificent temples, secured the admiration of the world for many centuries.

Marked deterioration set in about 2500 B. C. The center of political, religious and industrial life shifted from Memphis to Herapolis and thence to Thebes. Political and religious disintegration set in. Feudal barons undermined the central authority. Boldness of conception and vigor of execution in the arts was on the wane. Artists, architects and poets became mere imitators of their great ancestors. The great pyramids and temples of Cheops, Kephren, Mykosinos and Papi, looked contemptuously down upon the pigmy creations of decadent generations. The age of originality and progress had passed. Thought, ideals and manners became stagnant and ossified. The inevitable decline had begun, and the nation sank deeper and deeper into the decay and decrepitude of old age.

The 12th dynasty (2380 to 2136, B. C.) ushered in an ephemeral revival of arts, industry and commerce at Karnack, Luxor and Thebes.

The Hyksos, a pastoral, barbarous, Semitic people from Asia, conquered and occupied the regions of the lower Nile about 2000 B. C. They overcame easily the aging, degenerating, Egyptian people. They ruled the land about four hundred years. Few monuments remain of this period. The intellectual and moral life of the nation was at a low ebb.

The 18th dynasty, (1591-1443, B. C.) expelled the Hyksos, and once more revived the national spirit. This regeneration culminated in the reign of Rameses, the Great, (1388-1322, B. C.). This prince carried his victorious arms into Asia repeatedly, united the land, revived learning, and covered the banks of the Nile, from its mouth to the second cataract, with monuments, palaces, temples and royal tombs. He could only arrest the downward drift momentarily. The nation was aging rapidly. The revived national spirit was soon dissipated again. Reforms and innovations ceased. Artists were mere copyists. Poets, priests and scholars submitted to absolute authority. The warlike spirit fled, and national life glided along like a sluggish stream. Mercenary troops were invited to fight the battles of the Egyptians. Ethiopians, Ionians, Berbers and Semites crowded into the cities, destroying the homogeneity and national character of the people, and accelerated decadence.

Egypt was rapidly growing old and feeble. The younger, vigorous and progressive Greeks, Persians and Romans threatened her existence. She was forced out of her isolation. Old and decrepit, she could not resist the onslaught of energetic and expansive and aggressive neighbors. She could not regenerate or rejuvenate herself. Her mission was accomplished. Her day of leadership in state-craft, art, theology and learning was past forever. Her sun had set. Evening twilight spread over the valley. Her nerveless arms, palsied with age, could not ward off the foe. Resigned, she bowed her hoary head under the yoke of Persians, Greeks, Romans and Arabs, successively. Egypt ceased to exist as an independent nation.

5. The Chaldeans, Babylonians and Assyrians

The civilization on the Euphrates rose simultaneously with that of the Nile. There is little evidence that the two mutually influenced each other to any large extent. But, when we observe that the two peoples rose, reached their zenith and declined about the same time, and that their social and political organizations, their religions, their artistic conceptions, and their native characters, bear a strong family resemblance, we are forced to the conclusion of kinship existing between them.

They belonged to that great race which created a primitive civilization in southern Europe, northern Africa and western Asia; a race which, as compared with the Mongolian, represented an advanced stage of human progress; a race, whose agglutinative language had superseded the monosyllabic; whose tribal government had displaced the patriarchal; whose hieroglyphics and cuneiform script crowded out pictorial writings; whose worship of family gods had given way to tribal cults; and who erected megalithic monuments in all the lands over which it had sway.

It is quite probable that the two people separated at an early date; the Chaldeans remaining on the Euphrates, and the Egyptians migrating to the Nile.

There is some evidence of the fact that Palaeolithic and Neolithic races preceded the Chaldeans, and laid the crude foundation, upon which the magnificent Chaldean civilization was reared later.

As with all nations of antiquity, the infancy, childhood and youth, the formative period, the age of growth, progress, originality, invention and creative force, of the Chaldeans, is covered by the night of prehistoric times. Some historical facts are undoubtedly encysted in the myths, fables, legends and traditions of gods, demi-gods, heroes and monsters, in which Chaldean literature abounds; but they cannot furnish us with a faithful picture of early life on the Euphrates. When the morning twilight of history drove murky night from the valley, the civilization of the Chaldeans or Sumerians was already fully developed. This people entered the arena of history when they were in the prime of manhood. Their authentic history is only the history of their decline. We are made acquainted with their noon and evening, but not with their morning and forenoon.

Sargon, the Elder, and Naram-Sin, his successor, (3800 to 3700 B. C), were the contemporaries of the great Pharaohs, who built the great pyramids. Their people at that time stood at or near the zenith of their national life. Little is known of these rulers.

The art of recording events in their chronological order is of a much later date. Official annals, speaking of successions, wars, conquests, constructions of temples, palaces and canals, by illustrious rulers, exist; but they throw little light on the cultural condition of the people.

True history, however, is less concerned about the tedious lists of kings, dynasties and wars, than in the growth and decay of the intellectual and moral life of a nation. We desire to know how a nation, at the successive phases of its life, thought and felt, and realized its ideals in government, society, art, religion and literature.

Fortunately, the Chaldeans have left behind them a most complete and authentic record of their public and private life during the centuries when they stood at or near the point of culmination of their national existence. They did not use brush and chisel much, but they wrote diligently, and their writing has been preserved. They had evolved the cuneiform script from the ancient pictorial writing. Stilus and clay tablets were to them what pen, ink and paper are to us. Those tablets served as letters, records and archives.

Millions of such tablets are now brought to light from the ruins of old Babylon. Science has learned to decipher the cuneiform inscriptions. They furnish us with a picture of photographic faithfulness of the private and public life on the Euphrates four and five thousand years ago. These buried libraries reveal many new truths, correct many deep-rooted errors, and shed new light on antiquity, and on the evolution of man.

From these tablets we learn that in the age of Sargon, the Elder, and his successors, or from about 3800 to 2000 B. C, the Chaldeans and Babylonians evolved a civilization of a high order. They built imposing temples on high artificial mounds; surveyed the land, and classified it for the purpose of taxation; drained swamps; inaugurated a rational system of irrigation; carried agriculture and horticulture to a high state of perfection; invented the cuneiform system of writing; founded archives and libraries; recorded surveys, deeds, leases, marriages, mortgages, decrees, judgments, etc.; made a signal advance in astronomy, geometry, chronology and arithmetic; divided time into years, months, weeks, days, hours, minutes and seconds; were acquainted with the signs of the zodiac; used the lunar cycle of 223 months, and the great cycles of 60,600 and 3600 years, in their calculations; and devised a system of weights and measures, which was adopted as the standard by the surrounding nations.

They created a comprehensive literature composed of epics, songs, chronicles, cosmogonies, prayers, hymns, formulas of sorcery, liturgies, etc. The epics of Gilgamesh and of the descent of the goddess Ishtar to Hades, are works of great merit. They much resemble the grand epics of the Greeks, the Germans and the Norse. They treat of the deeds and adventures of gods, heroes, giants and monsters, and originated in the childhood and youth of the nation, when an unrestrained, luxuriant imagination dominated intellectual activity, and when the people believed in vast hosts of ghosts and demons inhabiting all the impressive objects and phenomena of nature. Many of the ideas and speculations of the Chaldeans have become permanently imbedded in the legends, sciences and cosmogonies of other nations, down to the present day.

The Chaldeans, in their social, political and religious evolution, had passed from the patriarchal into the tribal phase, and tentatively made the attempt to climb to the higher level of nationalism and true kingship. The city-states Eridu, Uru, Larsa, Uruck, Lagash, Nippur, Borsippa, Babel, Kishu, Kuta, Agade, Lippara, Erach, Isiu, Maru, Calah and Tarbat, like the nomes of Egypt, formed the dominant political units. Their chiefs frequently assumed the title of kings.

The fierce battle for existence and supremacy between families, clans, tribes and cities, resulted in the subjugation, extermination, absorption and assimilation of the weaker, and in the centralization of wealth, power and culture at a few capitals.

The religious evolution, as everywhere else, kept pace with the political. The celestial struggle for existence and hegemony among the gods was analogous to the terrestrial battle among the city-states. Each city-state had its own divine hierarchy. The supreme deity at Erech was Anu; at Calneh and Nippur, Bel; at Ur, Sin; at Larsa and Lippara, Samach; at Kuta, Nergal; at Caleh and Nineveh, Cidal; in lower Mesopotamia, Bilit; and in Borsippa, Nebo. There was nothing permanent in the political and religious organization of the Chaldeans. City-states and their dynasties rose, flourished and fell, and with them their tutelary deities.

It does not appear that foreign rulers conquered Chaldea in this age, and forced alien gods and worships upon them. All their gods were ideal Chaldeans, created by the Chaldean mind; products of home industry.

It seems that the Chaldean nation crossed the meridian of its life, and its civilization reached its point of culmination about thirty centuries before our era. It was the age of its greatest intellectual activity, power and expansion; of invention, originality and creative force. It stood near its zenith, and in the prime of manhood for probably a thousand years. We have but little authentic history of that period, and must depend on inference. When all the discovered tablets have been deciphered and arranged, they will supply us with a complete record of that epoch.

Authentic history of Chaldea begins at the close of the third millenary, when Hamurabi, (2200 B. C), ruled. This famous potentate promulgated a code which, in regard to ethics, refinement of reasoning and the administration of justice, is a unique monument of that early age. And as law, ethics and culture advance shoulder to shoulder, the laws of that code supply us with a good insight into the high social and moral development of the nation.

The age of Hamurabi gave indications of decay. Hamurabi and his contemporaries could only collect, restore, compile, imitate and codify the work of their more original and progressive ancestors. The nation was decadent and began to age. Inventions, discoveries, reforms, and innovations, the touchstones of progress, grew scarce. Chaldea was on the downgrade to old age.

But instead of sinking slowly and helplessly into the imbecility, sterility and senility of old age, the Chaldeans, Sumerians or Akkadians, as they are variously called, enjoyed the good fortune to be repeatedly rejuvenated by fusion with younger, more energetic and more progressive people.

The early inhabitants of the valleys of the Euphrates and the Tigris were ethnically not a homogeneous people. The Chaldeans were of pure blood and probably belonged to the Turanian race. They occupied the lower part of the valley, where their civilization originated and flourished. Further up a strong admixture of Semitic blood took place. In the lower valley the Chaldeans predominated; in the middle, Chaldeans and Semites merged into more equal parts; and in the upper regions, towards the sources of the rivers, ruled the Semitic Assyrians.

The Semitic race, of which we shall treat in the next section, was a younger race and reached its zenith a thousand years or more later than the Chaldean., The effect of the amalgamation of the two races was the rejuvenation of the Chaldean; it gave it a new lease of life. Babylon, occupied by a now fairly homogeneous people of mixed descent, led in the revival, and became the illustrious center of wealth, power and intellectual life, while the old Accadian city-states, Eridu, Erech, Uru, Agade and others, pined away from old age and sank into ruin.

This transfer of the seat of wealth, power and culture to Babylon, did not materially modify the original Chaldean civilization. Babylon merely inherited a civilization; it could not create one. Babylon spread Sumerian civilization over a larger territory, reformed and changed it superficially; but form of government, social institutions, literature, architecture, sculpture, mechanical arts, laws, the gods, religious myths and worship everything that the Chaldeans, in the course of many centuries, had invented, discovered, acquired and created, remained essentially the same as the Babylonians found it.

The Babylonians passed rapidly through the phases of childhood and youth. The fusion of the two races, while it regenerated the Chaldean, hastened the advance to manhood and old age of the Semitic element. The new Chaldeo-Semitic people practically began their national existence in the prime of life and, consequently, always manifested a lack of originality, creative and inventive genius. They were imitators only.

Babylon reached its point of culmination about 1600 B. C. Then the decadence of old age, with its concomitants of ease, luxury, effeminacy, corruption, stagnancy and feebleness, set in, Babylon, which had furnished the world with a brilliant revival of Sumerian civilization, in its turn entered the phase of sterile, weak and ultra-conservative old age.

Meanwhile a young, sturdy and energetic people, largely of Semitic origin, had grown up from infancy to manhood in the upper valley of the Euphrates and Tigris. The infusion of old Chaldean blood had accelerated the development of the Semitic Assyrians. The Semitic race character is very pronounced in the physical, moral and intellectual traits of the Assyrians. The Assyrian nation was now ready for its mission to conquer and absorb the Chaldeans and Babylonians, and conjointly with them to build up a great world power.

Babylon, grown old, unprogressive and decrepit, was too impotent to resist the furious attack of the youthful Assyrians. The Assyrian king, Tiglath Pileser, (1120 to 1100 B. C.) conquered city and state and made Babylon and Chaldea Assyrian provinces.

The change of rulers, however, did not affect the character of Chaldean civilization to any large extent. The conquerors adopted the religion, art, literature, customs, manners, social and political institutions, of the conquered almost bodily; they even used the ancient Sumerian language in the prayers, hymns, invocations, liturgies and formulas of their worship. They only installed a few of their native, tribal deities in the Babylonian pantheon. They did not improve Chaldean culture; on the contrary, they were content with an inferior copy of it. The Assyrians, like nearly all Semites, were skillful in war, state-craft and commerce, and in the adoption and utilization of the products of foreign civilizations; but were deficient in originality, invention and creative genius.

The Assyrians shifted the focus of civilization from Babylon to Nineveh. They founded a world-empire, and transplanted the seeds of Chaldean culture to Egypt, Susiana, Persia, Armenia, Syria, Judea and Phoenicia. That was their mission. They were no creators, no originators, but merely traders in goods, ideas and institutions. Chaldean myths, legends, cosmogonies, ideas and cultural achievements were transmitted by the Assyrians to Palestine and thence to the whole Christian world.

Assyria also had its day. It rose, flourished and perished. It stood at or near its zenith in the eighth century before Christ, during the reigns of Shalmaneser, (727 B. C), Sargon, (722-705 B. C), and Sennacherib (705-681 B. C.). Then the descent began. Opulence, profligacy, ossification of ideas, ideals and manners, and all the vices and evils which beset a nation in the grasp of old age, appeared. In 625 B. C. proud Nineveh, and with it the empire, fell under the combined assault of Medea, Babylon and Susiana. The conquerors divided the booty and Assyria was no more.

Once more, however, the Chaldean civilization flashed up at Babylon in a brilliant but short-lived flame during the reign of the highly gifted Nebuchadnezzar. Once more the famous city on the Euphrates rose to an ephemeral, commanding position of wealth, power, learning and influence, and the throbbing pulse of its strenuous life was felt throughout the then known world. But, the rejuvenation of Babylon by the Assyrians could only suspend but not arrest permanently the downward course. The aging and aged nation lacked the vigor for a sustained effort. The symptoms of decay and imbecility multiplied on all sides; and when the aggressive, juvenile Persians, under Cyrus, swept across the border in 538 B. C. the enervated, senile sage of the Euphrates tottered to the ground, to rise no more. Hoary Chaldean civilization, the admiration and model of western Asia, perished with the people that had created it.

And then came long centuries of desolation. Persians, Greeks, Romans, Parthians, Tartars, Arabs and Turks, dashed successively across the once fertile plains, destroyed temples, palaces, cities, roads and canals, until the valley of the Euphrates became a dreary desert. Even history and tradition had almost forgotten the glorious past of the highly gifted Chaldeans when, during the last century, the pick and shovel in the hands of investigating Aryans uncovered it again.

Three great nations of antiquity the Chaldeans, the Babylonians and the Assyrians successively made the valleys of the Euphrates and Tigris, the arena of their exploits. The Chaldeans originated and built up a civilization of a high order. In their old age and decay they were rejuvenated through fusion with the younger Babylonians, who revived the sinking Chaldean civilization. When old age and decrepitude approached again, the young and vigorous Assyrian came to the rescue and, blending with the aged and decadent Chaldean and Babylonian, galvanized them once more into an evanescent intellectual life. After that short revival dotage claimed these nations permanently. Greek, Roman, Tartar, Arab and Turkish hordes swept across the deserted lands since then, but they found only the silence of the graves of perished nations.

6. The Semitic Race - The Jews

The Jews, although weak in numbers and intellectually rather inferior, have acted a leading part in the great drama of humanity. We cannot speak of the Jews as the creators of a civilization peculiarly their own, as we speak of the Chinese, Egyptians, Babylonians, Hindus, Greeks, Romans and even of American Indians. The Jews were never original, inventive or creative in art, science, literature, philosophy or statesmanship. Scarcely an original idea, discovery or invention of great importance, can be traced back to them. And yet, in spite of all that, are the mediocre works of Jewish rulers, poets, historians and prophets, more extensively known and more highly appreciated throughout the civilized world than the masterpieces of all the other nations and races of antiquity.

The Jews belong to the Semitic race which, since prehistoric times, occupied the territory bounded generally by the Mediterranean, the Red Sea, the Persian Gulf, the Iranian plateau and the Armenian Mountains. It is a race of mixed origin. The geographical position of its home favored fusion with alien races. By a kind of endosmose and exosmose it communicated with Africa by the way of the isthmus of Suez and the strait of Bab-el-Mandeb. To the east and north the country was open to invaders.

The purest race-type developed in the central region, in northern Arabia, Palestine and Syria. Turanic and Aryan admixture is evident in the East and North and Ethopian in the South.

These contrasting, heterogeneous, ethnic elements were slowly fused into a mass, fairly homogeneous in language and physical, mental and moral characteristics. But the diversity of origin prevented a complete union, and the race always lacked a solidarity in aims, ideas and aspirations. But this composite character assigned to the Semitic race its peculiar place in history.

Some Semitic tribes or nations, such as the Assyrians, Syrians, Phoenicians, Jews and Arabs, rose to the rank of civilized people, but they were devoid of originality, and inventive and creative genius, the true test of genuine civilization. They could only appropriate, modify and utilize the cultural products of other races. Human civilization owes them but little. They were good borrowers and imitators, but rarely inventors or creators. They shone with reflected light. The Assyrians adopted the civilization of the Chaldeans; the Phoenicians followed in the wake of Egypt; the Jews borrowed from all their neighbors; and the Arabs were pronounced eclectics in religion, art, philosophy and government.

The Semites fill a low, intermediate gap between the Chaldean and Aryan civilizations. What with languages quite archaic in their development; with an intellect that could not grasp nor express abstract ideas, nor construct philosophical systems, nor create organically built-up epics and dramas; and with social, religious and political institutions invariably stopping short in their evolution at the patriarchal or tribal stage; this race was a true representative of humanity's childhood days.

The Semitic race also had its infancy, childhood and youth; its long centuries of slow growth. Considered as an organic whole, it stood at or near its zenith when the Assyrians under Shalmaneser and Sargon, (727705 B. C.); the Jews under David and Solomon, (about 1000 B. C.); the Carthaginians in the age immediately preceding the Punic wars; and the Phoenicians under Hiram, as the representatives of the race reached their highest altitude in civilization. After that age came the inevitable decline. The Arab episode represented only a Semitic aftermath.

With one exception history knows little of the Semites of antiquity; that exception is the Jews. Meager are the chronicles of the Assyrians and Phoenicians, and of the hundreds of Semitic tribes and kingdoms, that rose, flourished and perished in Asia Minor, we know scarcely the name of a score.

By a singular fate, through the extension of Hellenic culture and Roman power, and through the efforts of a new religion, rising out of the disintegrating Judaism, were the myths, legends, traditions and writings of the Hebrews preserved and transmitted to posterity. If the early Christians had not faithfully preserved the Jewish chronicles and literature, oblivion would have buried them long ago, as were those of hundreds of peoples of antiquity.

Much of the ancient Hebrew literature is undoubtedly lost, but in what is left we have, or rather we have what pretends to be, a fairly complete history of the life and the achievements of that nation.

How much is true of that history and based on actual fact, is a problem upon which a host of able, diligent and fearless inquirers is engaged. The world now demands the plain, unvarnished truth; it wants to be informed of what in those remote clays actually transpired on the Jordan as well as on the Nile, the Euphrates, the Ganges and on the Hoang-ho, in antiquity.

History, until quite recently, was quite one-sided, partial and prejudiced. The myths, fables, legends, traditions, annals and chronicles of the Chinese, Hindus, Egyptians, Babylonians, Greeks and Romans, were subjected to the closest scrutiny and a keen, merciless criticism; but when the works of the Hebrews were to be considered, they were declared to be sacred and divine, and an awe-inspiring "taboo" silenced the critics.

But a radical change has come. The age of childish credulity is passing away, and the age of calm reason supersedes it. More and more, men begin to entertain the view that for nearly two thousand years the works of the Jews have been given undue prominence, far above their merit, over the achievements of the so-called heathen nations of antiquity. The demand that the accomplishments of the Hebrews, be it in poetry, history, science, art, theology or prophecy, should be judged with the same courageous and unprejudiced impartiality, and measured by the same standards that we apply to the works of the Egyptians, Babylonians, Hindus, Chinese, Greeks and Romans, is now generally sustained, except by the clergy.

Approaching the subject matter in that spirit, we find that the authentic and reliable history of the Jews begins with Samuel, Saul and David. Everything anterior to that date is myth, legend, fable and untrustworthy tradition, although some historical truths lie unquestionably encysted in them.

The story in Genesis of the creation, sabbath, paradise, the snake and the temptation, the fall of man, Cain and Abel, demigods, giants, the flood, the tower of Babel, etc., are nursery tales and pure myths such as cluster around the cradle of all nations, and possess very little historical value. They even lack originality. They form a conglomerate composed of fragments of Egyptian and Chaldean cosmogonies and legends.

Dawn approaches with Abraham, and persons and events loom up in faint, nebulous outline. The myths of the patriarchs point to an early migration of a Semitic tribe from the Euphrates to the Jordan. Its god-idea, religious customs and social and economic institutions were crude and primitive.

The Hebrews, like nearly all their Semitic contemporaries, were a nomadic, patriarchal people, depending upon their herds, living in tents, enjoying only the rudiments of culture, and worshiping tutelary deities of individuals and families. Around their camp-fires they told weird, fantastic tales of the adventures of gods, demons, demigods, heroes and monsters. It was the phase of infancy in the life of the people.

We have seen that the Hyksos, a pastoral, nomadic, Semitic race, invaded Egypt and remained there nearly five hundred years. They acquired some of the Egyptians' learning and customs. It is quite probable that the Hebrews of Canaan were forced to participate in the migration. The Hyksos were expelled from Egypt and the Israelites returned to their home on the Jordan.

The Jews, led by the semi-legendary Moses, an educated Egyptian Hebrew, wandered slowly through the desert, and at the foot of sacred, tempest-tossed, thunder-swept Sinai, received from him a rudimentary social, political and religious organization, which was undoubtedly modelled after the Egyptian. In this organization, given by Moses and added to and modified much in later times, the tribal had already displaced the old patriarchal state.

The so-called Mosaic law belongs to a much later date. It was. a collection or codification of the customs and laws that had sprung up spontaneously among the people and become fixed. The influence of the higher Egyptian and Babylonian civilizations upon this code is evident. Its ethics point to a highly educated people and not a rude, nomadic horde, as the Jews of that day were.

The Hebrews, after a long sojourn in the desert, conquered Palestine, expelled, exterminated or absorbed the natives, divided the land among the tribes, and began their career as a distinct people. An age of violent disturbances, of wars between the Israelites and the Canaanites, and of internal strife between the tribes, followed the conquest. It was the heroic, romantic age of Israel; an epoch full of youthful optimism, sudden hope and despair, vacillating purposes, daring enterprises and bold adventures. Everything was in a state of chaos. Constant rivalry and friction prevailed among the tribes. Ideas and institutions were in continual commotion and flux. The center of political and religious power shifted from place to place, but abided nowhere long enough to procure for it the hegemony in Israel. It was the formative period, the phase of stormy youth of the Hebrew people.

The religious was analogous to the political condition. The anarchical state below was reflected on the celestial vault above. The vague conception of the thunder-god Yahweh, probably carried with them from lightning-riven Sinai, had not yet been condensed into a national deity. A host of demons and spirits dwelt yet in trees, hills, caves, fountains and groves. The tutelary deities of persons, families and clans, had not yet been eliminated. Even the gods of neighboring nations or tribes were recognized. The weaker gods succumbed to the stronger. The tutelary deities of the most forceful chiefs, clans and tribes, especially Yahweh, the thunder-god, triumphed finally in the battle for existence and supremacy. Religious conceptions, ideas and rites, grouped themselves about the surviving divinities. Zion, Gilgal, Gibeon, Sichem, Mizpah, Bethel, Dan and Gilead became centers of tribal cults.

The religious belief of the Israelites, at the time of the judges, was not monotheistic. Elohim and Sabaoth carry with them the sense of plurality. Their books speak of demigods, angels, cherubim, ghosts and demons; and the deities of their neighbors, Baal, Camos, Milcom, Astoreth, Moloch and others, were recognized as gods, and frequently worshiped. All these were superhuman and divine beings in the eyes of the ancient Hebrews. If such conceptions are treated as deities among the heathen, it is but just and fair to accord them the same treatment among the Jews.

The Jewish gods were anthropomorphic. They could not be anything else. The god-idea, the conception of a supernatural, divine being, springs from the inmost nature of man, and must be his own image. The gods of the Hebrews were ideal Hebrews, much magnified; they thought, felt, talked, acted, loved and hated like their worshipers. The Israelites stood culturally on the same level with their Semitic neighbors, and the gods of all these tribes bear a strong family resemblance.

A notable change occurred when Samuel and Saul established kingship. The turbulent, anarchic age of youth came to an end, and the people entered the phase of manhood. Saul, David and Solomon endeavored to weld the tribes into a nation, but failed in the attempt; the people soon sank back into the tribal relation.

Israel advanced with rapid strides during this era. It was its age of originality, creative force and expansion. Writing was introduced; annals were written; a national administration was established; a national literature was inaugurated; folk-songs, hymns, legends, myths and traditions were collected; the fragments of the epics "Legends of the Patriarchs" and "Legends of the Wars of Yahweh" were fused into a connected narrative; and the diverse god-ideas and cults were fused together, centralized and nationalized. Yahweh, the special tutelary deity of the leading tribe, was proclaimed to be the supreme deity of Israel. A national priesthood and a national worship of Yahweh were organized. The seat of the national worship was located at Jerusalem, the newly created national capital, and the old centers of tribal cults, Ramah, Nob, Gilgal, Shiloh, Bethel, Sichem and others, dwindled into insignificance.

Israel's national life culminated under David and Solomon, and maintained itself at this height for about three centuries. The nation was in its prime of manhood. Whatever progress the people made, either from their own initiative or by assimilation of imported ideas, was condensed into this period. David was the real motive force that raised Israel to the pinnacle of power, fame and culture and, strange to say, if the personal description of him may be believed in, this famous ruler was no Semite, but a blond descendant of Hellenic colonists.

The national idea had taken root in the minds of only a few more progressive men. Public opinion never rose above the tribal phase. The tribe remained the dominant political unit. David and Solomon held the tribes together by force, but the fissure between the northern and southern tribes, temporarily closed, opened again under Rehoboam in a deep, broad, permanent chasm.

The secession was probably due to ethnical changes. The northern tribes, now collectively called Israel, had not exterminated but absorbed the aboriginal population, and had lived in close proximity to the highly civilized people of Tyre, Sidon and Damascus. The southern tribes, now designated as Judah, remained comparatively pure in blood. The North manifested a keen susceptibility to foreign influence in art, science, literature and religion, and, as a consequence, was imbued with a liberal, tolerant and progressive spirit; but the South remained exclusive and impervious to alien ideas.

Israel continued to be the center of Hebrew intellectual life for two centuries after Solomon. Whatever of merit the Jews produced in art, literature and science, came almost exclusively from the North. There the folk-songs, epics, idyls, myths and legends were collected, edited and put into more artistic forms. There arose prophecy, a distinguishing feature of Jewish life; nearly all the great prophets came from the North.

Orthodox Judah remained stagnant and reactionary during this time. A fanatic, zealous and unprogressive priesthood ruled at Jerusalem. The literature of the North, the Elohistic version of Hebrew mythical and legendary history, the product of popular, enthusiastic poets in close touch with the higher intellectual life of Tyre, Damascus and Nineveh, permeated slowly to the capital of Judah, and was here transformed into the dry, unromantic, Yahvistic version by an exclusive, narrow-minded and pedantic priesthood.

Israel stood at its zenith about the time of Ahab (960 B. C.), and remained at its height until about the reign of Hiskias (760 B. C). The nation's intellectual force and creative power was in the ascendant until the era of the great prophets.

The books of the prophets constitute the only really original work of the Jews and are a mirror of their times. Egypt, Babylon, Assyria, Phoenicia and the petty Semitic kingdoms, were all on the down grade of approaching old age, and the young and rising nations of Hellas and Rome were unknown to the Jewish authors. All around them the prophets witnessed the spread of profligacy, luxury, effeminacy, poverty, corruption and oppression, the concomitants of national decadence and dotage. They observed how their own people became infected with the germs of decay, and attributed the decline in morals to the pernicious influence of foreign gods, cults and civilizations, and strenuously advocated a speedy return to the isolation, the simple life and faith of their ancestors. They were bitterly opposed to all progress and culture coming from abroad. The prophets were the last active, native, intellectual force in the formation of the national character. They fostered an extraordinary pride of race, compiled and edited the canon of sacred books, and moulded the religious thought of the nation.

Their forecasts of future events are of no more value than the oracles of the pagans. It is easy and safe to predict calamities to nations in the physical, intellectual and moral decomposition of old age. History is full of such predictions. Many of their prophesies are vague and may be interpreted to mean most anything. Others were evidently written after the events happened. This is a favorite trick of literary men, in illustration of which, the prophecy of Cranmer in the last scene of Shakespeare's Henry VIII, may be cited. The hope of a Messiah, who should come and redeem and raise up his downtrodden nation, is not peculiarly Israelitish. Messianism is a quite common feature in the history of mankind. The prophets were the earnest, fearless, eloquent, passionate and zealous tribunes of the people against their oppressors, and undoubtedly did much good, but their claim of divine inspiration must be rejected, as we reject such claims made by the Pythias, augurs, sybils and magi of other lands.

Then the decline began. Symptoms of approaching old age multiplied. Creative and inventive genius vanished. The literary work produced during the era terminating with the return from captivity, was performed by mere compilers, commentators, and expounders.

The North was the first to feel the effect of age. Court and people after Ahab sank deeper and deeper into the mire of degeneracy. Weakened intellectually and morally, the ten tribes fell an easy prey to Sargon of Assyria. They were conquered and deported, and in 721 B. C. disappeared forever.

Judah maintained a precarious independence about a century and a half longer. The change wrought in Judah after the deportation of the ten tribes was remarkable. The northern poets and authors were silenced, and the priesthood at Jerusalem became the sole custodian of the national literature, traditions, ideals, aspirations and religious conceptions. All the existing books were collected, sifted and edited by the sober, fanatic and intolerant priests of Yahweh. The Pentateuch received its finishing touches. Ritualistic service predominated. Yahweh, angry, cruel, vindictive, vacillating, partial, loving only the Jews and hating all the rest of mankind, now became the supreme god of the one tribe. The gods reflect the physical, intellectual and moral state of their worshipers. Like people, like gods, Yahweh was the idealized Jew of the era of the prophets.

The symptoms of intellectual and moral decadence in Judah increased after Isaiah and Hezekiah. Isaiah was one of the last representatives of the classical epoch. After him there was a steady deterioration in thought and style. The later prophets lack the fierce, manly vigor of ideas, and the terse, penetrating style of the earlier ones. Jeremiah, Ezekiel and their contemporaries, about 600 B. C., are much inferior to the earlier writers, both in the wealth of ideas and the form of expression.

The conquest of Judah by Nebuchadnezzar in 588 B. C. and the exile hastened the downward course of the Jews. The captivity wrought a radical change in their thoughts and manners. The returning exiles were a much transformed race. Their religious ideas were remodelled under the influence of their Persian and Babylonian masters and friends.

The Hebrews had brought with them, or imported later, many religious rites from Egypt. The circumcision, the ark as the favorite abode of the deity, the oracle, the consecrated loaves, the symbolic serpent, the cherubim, the music and dance, Thummim and Urim, the superstitious regard of the name of the deity, and the sacredotal vestments of the priests, were of Egyptian origin. Their cosmogony, the institution of the Sabbath and other feasts, were imported from Chaldea.

The southern orthodox Jews, from the conquest of Canaan down to the captivity, resisted strenuously any influence from abroad, but to the gentle sway of the Medean Magi, and the priests of Ahura Mazda they succumbed without protest. Their theology, while retaining the central figure of Yahweh, was strongly tinctured by Zoroastrianism, during the exile.

Yahweh, as one of the numerous tribal deities of the Semites, was originally the idealized and deified patriarch of a nomadic family or clan, and later, when the tribe became the prominent political unit, developed into an autocratic, despotic, oriental tribal god. In this evolution he kept pace with the social and political growth of the Jews. The exile suddenly broadened the intellectual horizon of the Hebrews, and Yahweh experienced a corresponding change. They were now members of an enlightened and tolerant world-empire, where many races and religions dwelt in peace side by side, and Yahweh was remoulded in imitation of Ahura-Mazda, the chief deity of the Persians.

The immortality of the soul, the last judgment, future reward and punishment, the coming millennium, messianism, the celestial court with its archangels, angels and messengers, the fall of the angels, the revolt and intrigues of Satan became tenets, more or less pronounced, of Israel's faith, after the captivity. They were of Iranian origin. The spirit of the Zend-Avesta penetrated and leavened Jewish theology.

Indeed, nearly everything pertaining to Hebrew civilization can be traced back to Egypt, Chaldea, Babylon, Assyria, Iran and Phoenicia. Zion was a junk-shop, where well-worn, second-hand garments from Thebes, Memphis, Babylon, Nineveh, Susa and Tyre, were exhibited and offered for sale as homemade goods. And as such the Christians have worn them for nearly two thousand years.

Decadence continued unabated in Judah during and after the captivity. No writers of originality appeared. Their prophets were silenced. The Talmud, with its superstition and casuistry, took its place beside the Thorah. Rabbis commented upon and expounded the so-called Mosaic law. Creative energy was dead. The literary force was exhausted. Art, literature and science disappeared from the banks of the Jordan. Profound silence ruled in Israel from about 400 to about 200 B. C. Old age was at hand.

Alexander overthrew the aged Persian empire. Hellenic culture followed in the track of the conquerors and spread over the Orient. It, too, was decadent at that time, but it enjoyed a revival in the East, especially at Alexandria and Antioch. This revival also galvanized Israel into a renewed literary, religious and political life. The sacred books were translated into Greek. The apocryphal books, Proverbs, Ecclesiastes, Daniel, the books of Enoch and the sibyl, and others, appeared in rapid succession during the last two centuries before the Christian era.

This revival was aided by an internal cause. Palestine, after the deportation of the ten tribes, was largely peopled by colonists from the Assyrian, Babylonian and Persian realms. These heterogeneous elements gradually fused with the surviving Jews into a new homogeneous people. The law of the parallelogram of force applied. The new nation differed materially from the former Jews in character, language, religion and customs. Young, alien blood from abroad rejuvenated the aged nation to some extent. During the process of amalgamation, intellectual life was at a low ebb, but when a fair degree of homogeneity had been attained, a new efflorescence took place.

The last revival of Jewish national life, caused by fusion with younger and progressive ethnic elements, and by contact with regenerated Hellenic culture at Antioch and Alexandria, was of short duration. The approach of old age was retarded but not checked. Intellectual energy ebbed rapidly. One after another the lights of poetry, history, theology and science went out. The gathering gloom of evening twilight settled upon the valleys and mountains of the "Promised Land." The Romans took possession. Jerusalem was destroyed in A. D. 70, the Jews dispersed, and Israel ceased to exist as an independent nation.

The history of the Jews, like that of the Edomites, Ammonites, Hittites, Amaleckites and hundreds of the petty tribes and kingdoms of Asia, would have been buried in oblivion if at the very close of it certain events had not occurred at Jerusalem and on the shores of the Galilean sea. These events riveted the attention of the civilized world to everything pertaining to the life of Israel.

The Hebrews filled only a modest and very obscure niche in antiquity's temple of fame. Contemporary writers, down to the Christian era, ignore them almost entirely. They had contributed nothing to the world's stock of real learning. No useful, epoch-making invention; no original, creative idea in art, science, literature, law and philosophy, can be traced to them. They rose, flourished and perished, like scores of puny Semitic nations of their neighborhood, and with them stopped at the same cultural level. If, at the close of their life, the mentioned events had not transpired, they would have been exterminated and absorbed like the others, during the turbulent, anarchic centuries that followed; only fragments, if any, of their literature would have survived; and Yahweh would have shared the fate of the other tribal gods of the Semites.

But Israel, ignored and despised, rose to an exalted position at the hour of its dissolution, not by its merit, but through foreign aid and a peculiar conjuncture of forces.

All the nations of that part of the world, Egyptians, Babylonians, Assyrians, Persians, Hindus, Syrians, Jews, Phoenicians, Greeks and Romans, had at that time crossed the meridians of their national lives respectively, and were rushing with accelerated speed into the decadence, corruption, disintegration, impotency and unprogressiveness of old age. They were all in a moribund condition. Amid this universal degeneracy and decomposition, a new religion, destined to conquer the civilized world, sprang up in Galilee.

This new religious movement at first appeared in the nature of a revival of the old prophetism. If it had been confined to the Jews, it would have vanished without leaving a trace behind it. But it soon lost its specific Jewish and Semitic character. Paul, a Hellenized Greek, and Roman citizen, placed the infant religion in the charge of Greek and Roman nurses. That decided its fate. The philosophers of decadent Hellas formed the creed of the new religion, and the Jurists of Rome moulded its form and internal and external organization, after the model of the Latin state. Its soul was Hellenic, its body Roman. The Semitic Yahweh became an adopted and naturalized Greek and Roman god.

As soon as the metamorphosis of the new religion, from a Semitic into an Aryan, had taken place, the Jews and the other Semites changed their friendly into a hostile attitude toward it. Christianity spread , with unexampled rapidity throughout the Aryan world, but lost its hold on the Semitic. Jesus and his disciples were genuine Jews, but the intellectual and moral nature attributed to them by the Greek and Latin Church fathers, was essentially Aryan. Judaism, pure and simple, as taught by Moses and the prophets, could never have made an impression on the Aryan West. The Jews refused to follow the new and alien gods. Race instinct determined their position.

Christianity adopted Judaism as its parent, and all the writers of the Old Testament were considered inspired. This gave the Jew an undue and unmerited prominence among the Christian nations of the world. And it has been a curse and a blessing to him. The undeserved, fulsome and extravagant praise of his ancestors has generated in him the belief in his superiority, and, in his own estimation, made him the aristocrat par excellence in the human family.

The unstinted praise for two thousand years by the leading nations that the Jews were God's chosen people, and peculiarly endowed to redeem a wicked world, has made the Jew proud, haughty, exclusive, egotistical and self-conscious to an extraordinary degree.

He stubbornly resists absorption and assimilation by the peoples among whom he has cast his lot. With him race and religion are conterminous. His race claims his first allegiance everywhere. He forms a state within a state. And for this he is feared, despised and hated. Anti-Semitism is but the spasmodic effort of a sound organism to eject an indigestible morsel from the system.

Dispersed throughout the world for nearly two thousand years, leading a parasitic life, and subsisting upon the substance of other political organisms, the Jew has lost all capacity for self-government. In culture he adapts himself to the people among whom he has his temporary abode. If he shines anywhere and in anything, it is by reflected light. His race is in its dotage. It has lost the power to invent, create and originate, long ago. If the Jews could be gathered together in one country, be it Palestine or some other land, and were made to shift for themselves, they would soon drop to the level of the other Semitic nations of Asia and Africa.

The number of Jews in the United States is estimated at two millions, and this number is swelled annually by a strong immigration from Europe, especially from Russia, Poland, Roumania and Austria. If they would permit themselves to be absorbed and assimilated, like all the other nations and races flowing together on this continent to build up the great, homogeneous American nation of the future, they would be a factor of some value and significance. But, true to their traditions, they will remain isolated and, like the Parsees of the Orient and the Gypsies all over the world, form a sort of nation within a nation, and prefer a mechanical to an organic union with the rest of the people.

But as they shun manual labor; as they are rarely found on the farm, in the workshop and in domestic service; as they cling to the towns and cities; as they crowd into the store, the office and the learned professions; and as a sentiment of solidarity and mutual assistance aids them materially in life's battle, they must be considered an important factor for good or bad in the economical and ethical development of this nation.

But when this critical, investigating, rational and iconoclastic age assigns to Israel, ancient and modern, her proper place in history; when the words and deeds of the Jews of the Old Testament are removed from under the magnifying microscope of Christian theology; when Christian divines cease to pervert history; when a universal standard of merit is adopted, and all the heroes, statesmen, poets, seers and savants of antiquity, Christian, Jewish or pagan, stand out in just and full proportion, then will Israel submit to absorption and assimilation, and silently pass away.

The Semitic race, considered as an organic whole, crossed its meridian about the beginning of the last millennium before Christ and stood in the full vigor of manhood at or near its zenith for several centuries. It was the age when the Semitic capitals of Nineveh, Tyre, Sidon, Carthage, Jerusalem and Damascus flourished; when David, Solomon, Hiram, Ahab, Shalmanezer and Sargon, ruled. The race, as such, represented a primitive stage in the development of the human race and forms a connecting link between the civilizations of the oriental Egyptians and Chaldeans and the western Greeks and Romans. Its languages stopped growing at an early stage; its governments remained patriarchal and tribal; its religions were imitations of terrestrial autocracies; its gods were idealized oriental chiefs and despots; its art and science were inferior copies of those of Egypt and Babylon, and its literature consisted of songs, lyrics, anecdotal tales, proverbs and annals strung together without organic cohesion. It could not create organically built-up epics, dramas or philosophical systems. The race manifested little originality, invention or creative power.

The decline of the race set in about the seventh century B. C. The descent was rapid. Old age, with its sterility, weakness, and fossilization of ideas and manners, had overcome nearly the whole Semitic world at the time of Alexander and Cato. The aged Semitic nations offered but a feeble resistance to the Greek and Roman conquerors. They were exterminated or absorbed and assimilated by the victors, with the exception of the Jews, who maintained their nationality in the dispersion, and the Arabs, who were destined for a final but brilliant revival of the race.

7. The Aryan Race

A new race now enters the arena of history. The Palaeolithic and Neolithic races, the Indians, the Chinese, the Egyptians, the Chaldeans and the Semites which, so far, have passed in review, represented the phase of infancy, childhood and very early youth in the life of humanity, but the Aryans, now coming to the fore, were destined to be the representative of mankind's youth and manhood.

The Aryans, in conformity to this high mission, wore the badge of superiority from the very beginning of their career. They had already passed through the early, primitive phases of social and intellectual development at the time of their first appearance in history. When nature determines to issue an improved edition of organic life, she prefaces it with a resume of her previous work. The foetus of the higher animals shows, in miniature, the evolution of organic life on earth; and the higher developed human races, in a like manner, repeat in compressed form, during the early stages of their existence, the previous development of humanity.

The Aryans, when they stepped upon the stage of history, had left the phase of monosyllabic and agglutinative speech behind them, and used inflective languages to communicate ideas of a higher order. They had discarded the patriarchal form of government for the tribal, and made preparations to ascend to the higher level of nationalism. Their religions and mythologies kept pace with their social and political evolution, and their tutelary deities became successively their individual, familiar, tribal, national and even racial gods. Genuine kingship had superseded chieftainship, to be displaced later by the democratic republic, the highest culmination in the political evolution. They were the first to recognize order and the rule of impersonal law in the universe, instead of the absolute, arbitrary and capricious will of a despotic ruler of the state or the universe, such as was the political and religious conception of the Mongolian, Turanian and Semitic people. They were the first to create systems of philosophy and organic and articulated epics and dramas, in place of the anecdotal narratives, folk-songs and epigrammatic productions of oriental literature.

The Aryan is physically distinguished from the other races by a fair complexion, blue eyes, blond hair, and usually a tall stature. That is the distinctive Aryan type. Where darker shades occur, accompanied by Aryan speech and culture, they point to an amalgamation with darker races. The Aryan, whether found in India, Iran, Europe or America, has always looked upon blond hair and a fair skin as the characteristic marks of his race.

This race played a prominent part during the last four thousand years, and acted the leading role during the last twenty-five centuries in the world's drama. The civilizations which rose and flourished successively on the Ganges, in Bactria, on the Aegean Sea, on the Tiber, Ebro, Seine, Thames, Rhine, Hudson and Mississippi, bear the impress of Aryan genius.

No other race has achieved as much for human culture; none has so revolutionized the world's social, political, religious and economic institutions; none experienced such an extraordinary expansion in numbers, power, wealth and dominion. Limited originally to a narrow home on the shores of the Baltic and North Sea, it developed an irresistible expansive force and founded the powerful and progressive empires of India, Iran, Hellas and Rome, in dim antiquity; established the kingdoms of Italy, Spain, Portugal, France, England, Germany and Scandinavia in the early part of the Middle Ages; and, in modern times, extended its sway over America, Australia Africa and a large part of Asia. It dominates the world today.

Where stood the cradle of this race? Students of comparative philology and of comparative theology, noticing the marked affinity of language and religious myths of the Hindus, Iranians, Hellenes, Latins, Teutons, Slavs, and Celts, came to the conclusion that all these nations were descendants of the same Aryan ancestors, and that the original home of this race must be sought for on the banks of the Oxus and Jaxartes, whence successive migrations found their way to India, Greece, Rome, Sarmatia and northern Europe.

That theory must be discarded now. It is a physical impossibility that this race should have sprung up in Central Asia. What the divers races are physically, intellectually and morally, they became under the influence of the climate, topography, flora and fauna, of their homes, exerted incessantly upon them through thousands or tens of thousands of years. It is inconceivable that a fair-complexioned, blond-haired and blue-eyed race should have been evolved on the arid, sunlit plateau of Asia. Crisp, dry air and an abundance of sunshine favor pigmentation and must invariably produce a dark or colored race. Pale colors are associated with absence of light. A race with bleached hair and skin could only be evolved in a moist, mild, cloudy climate with super-abundant shade.

The only region of large extent on our globe with conditions favorable for the evolution of a fair skinned race, is to be found in north-western Europe. There clouds, fogs, shady woods, moist and mild breezes, long, dark winters, much twilight and short summers with mellow sunlight, prevail ideal conditions for the production of such a race. Under the murky sky of this sombre region stood the cradle of the Aryans.

Furthermore, if Bactria or the tableland of Iran had been the home and radiating point of the Aryan race, the purity of race-type would necessarily increase with the approach to that center. This is not the case; on the contrary, the fair complexion has almost totally disappeared from that region. And race-types maintain themselves in any region with tenacious persistence, in spite of conquest, subjugation and migrations, as long as climatic conditions continue unaltered.

The hypothesis that north-western Europe is the home and radiating center of the Aryan race, is supported by all the known facts. The blond type predominates in Scandinavia, north-western Germany, the Low Countries and England. It diminishes in proportion as we go south or east until it is almost completely lost among the brunettes of the Mediterranean, the Black Sea, and of the steppes of eastern Russia.

Hindus and Iranians, Hellenes and Latins represent prehistoric migrations from the old Aryan home. Internal and external causes, probably a strong pressure from the aggressive, expansive and more civilized race of the south of Europe, split off the eastern tribes from the main stock, and forced them to the east and southeast, where, after long wanderings, they secured new, permanent homes in Iran, India, Hellas and Rome.

The detached tribes began a separate national existence, and commenced to build up a typical Aryan civilization in their new homes. Their gradual amalgamation with an aged and aging aboriginal people of the conquered countries accelerated their development, modified their race-type, colored their civilizations and directed their course. The hastening process through fusion with old races caused Hindus, Iranians, Greeks and Latins, to pass through all the phases of national life, from infancy to old age, before those who remained at the original seat reached the age of youth.

Everywhere, be it in India, Iran, Hellas and Rome, in antiquity; be it in Italy, Spain and France at a later date, did the blond, conquering Aryan lose his characteristic race-type in an unfavorable climate and among the more numerous, swarthy, conquered natives. The pure type renews and maintains itself perennially only in the countries that border on the Baltic and the German Ocean.

8. The Hindus

Yielding to the irresistible pressure of the older and more advanced people of the South of Europe upon the young and backward North, the Aryan Hindus and Iranians had been detached from their kindred on the Baltic. They wandered through the Scythian steppes and around the Caspian, and secured a new and more permanent home in Bactria, on the banks of the Oxus and Jaxartes.

They constituted one people, or at least two closely related tribes. They dwelt together in harmony for some time, but, owing to some disagreement, religious, political or ethnical, they separated in anger; the Iranians remaining and the Hindus migrating through the mountain passes of Cabul to the valley of the Indus.

It is quite probable that these Aryan tribes, on their long journey from the Baltic to the Oxus, and during their sojourn on the plains of Iran, had conquered, absorbed and assimilated some foreign ethnic elements, encountered on the way or in their new home. This mixture ^produced a marked change in type, myths, customs and languages. This seems to have been particularly the case with the Iranians. The result was much friction and finally separation. The Hindus maintained their purity of blood.

The time of the Hindu invasion cannot as yet be fixed with any degree of certainty. Unreliable Hindu chronicles place the date of the invasion at 3100 B. C. The Hindu was always deficient in chronology, and this was especially the case during the infancy of this highly imaginative people. His unrestrained fancy ruled everything. He had no sense for sober facts and chronology. His literary work lacked order, and resembled a pathless, tangled jungle of luxuriant growth.

The oldest Hindu literature consisted of songs and hymns addressed to the tutelary deities of the tribes, which were composed by popular poets on the march and at the camp fire during the conquest, and sung at the sacrifice. They were produced at divers places and during many centuries, and were finally collected and compiled in the form of the classic Rig-Veda. They are not arranged in the chronological order of their first appearance. Some are more archaic in form and thought than others, and reflect faithfully the primitive ideas and institutions of the Hindus in the early days of the conquest. If the Vedic hymns could be systematized and arranged in chronological order, their style and contents would mirror step by step the conquering march from Cabul to the Ganges, and the steady progress made in government, religious conceptions, society, language, literature and economic life, during the Vedic age.

The Aryan conquest of India was not led by great captains, commanding vast armies, subjugating extensive territories, and dividing them in a feudal manner among their followers. It was rather an armed immigration, an immense raid by families, clans and tribes, without a unity of plan, and resulting in much fierce and desultory fighting with the slowly retreating natives.

Many generations passed away before the Aryan invaders reached the lower Ganges. It was the heroic age, the phase of Hindu childhood, the epoch of buoyant hope, fervent faith, vivid imagination, daring enterprise and epic hymns of great merit addressed to the tribal gods.

When we reflect that the evolution of a people is a very slow process; that every phase of a nation's life consumes centuries; and that a notable progress is perceptible in the culture of the Hindus between the early and the later parts of the Vedic period; we come to the conclusion that the Hindu historians are not so very wrong, and that the invasion, and the beginning of Hindu national life on the Indus and Ganges, can be placed in the middle of the third millenary before the Christian era.

The civilization which the Hindus evolved during the earlier part of the Vedic period was one of no mean order. The tribe was the dominant social and political unit. The heads of families and chiefs of tribes, were each ruler, judge and priest in one person, but these functions began to be segregated. Social equality, a concomitant of patriarchal and tribal conditions, was universal. There were no social castes, no feudal grades, no priesthood. The people dwelt in isolated homesteads, villages and walled towns. They raised wheat, barley, fruit and vegetables, and used plows, flails, sieves, and hand-mills to grind the corn. They spun and wove. They constructed roads and drove iron-tired vehicles over them. They had domesticated cattle, horses, goats, sheep, geese and dogs. Carpenters, wagon-makers, goldsmiths, saddlers, blacksmiths and potters, plied their vocations. Upon the whole, it was a civilization much resembling that of the Germans of the age of the Merovingians.

The Aryan invaders encountered an inferior race in India. The Vedic poets speak contemptuously of it as dark, ugly, flat-nosed, filthy, without gods, worship, law or society, and in aspect, culture and manners, deeply contrasting with the fair invaders. The aborigines were of low physical, mental and moral development; spoke monosyllabic or agglutinated languages, knew of no writing, used stone implements, and adhered to shamanism and the worship of fetishes. It was a very primitive race and represented humanity's early infancy.

These aborigines of the Indus, the Jumna and the Ganges were exterminated, enslaved or driven to the almost inaccessible mountains of the Himalayas or the Deccan, by the Aryan invaders. Their posterity dwells there today and has not changed much; a vast conglomerate, wherein are imbedded fragments of Palaeolithic, Neolithic, Turanian, Negroid, Mongolian and Tartar races. The earliest progress of mankind, in its early phase, can be studied among the hill tribes of India, on living specimens and representatives of every stage of development.

The Hindu people were in their childhood when they arrived on the banks of the Indus. The transition from the Vedic to the Brahmanical literature some ten centuries later, indicated the passage from childhood into youth.

The conquest was complete about 1500 B. C. The sword of the conqueror was sheathed and the people settled down to cultivate the arts of peace. A notable change had already taken place during the latter part of the Vedic epoch, (about 2000 to 1500 B. C.). The warlike spirit had diminished; tribes had coalesced into greater organisms, resembling nations; kingship had superseded tribal chieftainship; a well organized priesthood, the custodian of worship and learning, had arisen; feudalism, with its castes and classes, had supplanted the former social equality; the spontaneous, natural and popular poetry of the old Vedas had given way to the more elegant, artistic and refined verses of the learned priests; and great strides in advance had been made in the industrial arts.

The Mahabarata, a grand epic, worthy to be placed alongside the great epics of other nations, and ascribed to the thirteenth century, before our era, furnishes us with a faithful picture of the Hindu life of that age. As compared with a former period progress had been astonishing. Rice, beans, flax, hemp, cotton, peas, melons, pumpkins, sugarcane, bananas and cocoanuts, had been added to former productions. Tools, implements, utensils and textile fabrics had been much improved. Hereditary kings ruled in magnificent capitals. The royal courts were crowded with chamberlains, lackeys, musicians, dancers, cooks and gladiators. Merchants imported foreign goods to gratify the luxurious tastes of a refined society. It was the glorious phase of the vigor, originality, invention, creative force, power and expansion of youth.

The religious thought advanced parallel with the political. The tribe was the prominent political unit when the Hindus descended into the plain of the Punjab, and their tribal gods accompanied them. The early phase when all nature was animated by ghosts and demons, and the later phase of personal and familiar tutelary deities, they had outgrown before they entered the passes of Cabul.

The Vedic age was filled with the rivalries and the struggle for existence and supremacy among families, clans and tribes, and tribal gods participated in the interminable contests. Every Vedic poet, while recognizing the existence of the other tribal deities and even the more prominent divinities of the subjugated aborigines, elevated his local and tribal tutelary god to the position of a supreme deity in the Hindu pantheon. Hence the utter confusion in the rank of the Vedic gods. It was an age of numerous gods but no general or national cult. Varuna, Indra, Agni, Ushas, Surya, Savitar, Pushan and others, originally personal, patriarchal and local deities, assumed their rank as supreme or subordinate divinities in accordance with the power and influence of the poet's tribe. One poet or priest addressed Varuna as the chief deity, another Agni, another Indra, still another Ushas, and so forth, down to the end of the list.

Indra, the god of the thunder cloud like the Sinaitic Yahweh, Olympian Zeus and Teutonic Thor, gradually gained the ascendency over the other divinities and eventually secured almost universal and enduring supremacy.

Tribes merged into petty kingdoms, but no king was able to centralize all political power at one point; and no Hindu deity could completely destroy its rivals and focus all religious thought and cults at a common center. The many independent tribes and puny kingdoms sustained polytheism. True national monarchy and its twin sister monotheism, never secured a firm footing in India.

The Vedic religion points to a high ethical advance of the people. The belief in a future judgment, and reward of virtue and punishment of evil, was general. Their conceptions of gods were noble. They were idealized Hindus. Their gods were their friends. The worshipers approached them with love and confidence, and not with awe, fear, trembling and mortal dread, as did the Turanians and Semites. Their deities endeavored to establish and improve social order; praised and demanded purity, truthfulness, honesty, bravery, benevolence, hospitality, justice and the sacredness of life, property and marriage, and condemned and prohibited pride, avarice, dishonesty and falsehood. The worship was simple, and devoid of cruelty; sacrifice being usually confined to flowers and the juice of fruit and plants. Ethics is an unfailing gauge of civilization, and the refined ethics of the Vedic Hindus indicate a comparatively high culture and a complex and refined state of society. Indeed, the Hindus of this age, like all people destined to play a leading part in history, were strong, noble, virtuous and progressive in the phase of their youth.

A remarkable transformation of the social, political and religious life of the Hindus took place at the close of the Vedic period, or in the first part of the succeeding epoch. Down to that time everything, society, religion and literature, bore the true Aryan stamp. The swarthy, subjugated natives had taken no part in building up the civilization. Now the numerous aboriginal element began to assert a growing influence; it became a strong, ever increasing factor in shaping national thought and life. The social barriers which had been erected between the fair conquerors and their dark-skinned subjects, and which led to the rigid division of society into castes, proved ineffective. The two races fused in spite of strong race-animosities, prohibitions and draconic legislation against amalgamation. Members of the lower castes, invariably native slaves or serfs, acquired wealth, learning, power and influence and rose to positions among the higher, aristocratic castes of the Aryans. The Mahabarata speaks already of native kings as the peers and social equals of Aryan princes, and of frequent intermarriages between the two races.

The Aryans had established and maintained themselves as a ruling aristocracy. They lost their native vigor and energy and became effeminate and enervate after the conquest, through a long season of prosperity and luxury. The despised aborigines, confined to the toil of the farm and the shop, the places of national regeneration, numerically weak in the Punjab, stronger in the Midland Provinces and predominant on the lower Ganges, rose slowly, and in the course of centuries gained the ascendancy. With them ascended their gods. The dark, gloomy, fierce, uncouth and bloodthirsty deities of the downtrodden, brutish natives, Krishna, the shepherd god of the mountain, Ahi, the serpent god; Vala, the cave dweller; Rudra, the sinister storm god; Siva, the terrible; Kali, his cannibal consort; Vritra, Vishnu, and a host of demons, ghosts, nymphs, giants, and monsters, took their place by the side of the bright, cheerful, kind and noble Aryan divinities; crowded them out of the temples, and eventually expelled them from the sacrificial altars. The two races changed their relative positions, and so did their gods.

The early Vedic gods were anthropomorphic. They were idealized and deified Hindu heroes. They represent the youthful, heroic age of the race. The learned priests of the later Vedic period converted them into metaphysical beings, who personified night, dawn, day, moon, earth, sky, storm, the intoxicating soma, fire, etc. As such vague, nebulous beings they relaxed their hold on the popular mind, and slowly vanished in the hazy distance of speculation. The gods of the aborigines, more anthropomorphic, took the popular fancy and pressed to the front. The ordinary human mind wants something tangible, concrete and personal for his deities. All the old Aryan gods, with the exception of Indra and Mithra had already passed away when the Mahabharata was written.

The Hindu nation crossed the meridian of its life some time between 1200 and 1000 B. C. The era when the nation stood at or near its point of culmination was one of great intellectual activity, during which the Brahmanas, the Upanishads, and the great epics Mahabharata and Ramayana all masterpieces were produced. It was an age of exceptional originality, invention and creative genius. These people had nothing to build upon or to copy from. They had to create everything.

The chronological order of the numerous and meritorious poetical, philosophical, legal and scientific works of this period, can only be established by internal evidence from their contents. Every representative national masterpiece, in its conception, ideas, form and style, bears the impress of the nation's age; be it that of infancy, childhood, youth, manhood or old age. The Vedas, with their simple faith, their grand, anthropomorphic deities, their optimism, their sublime imagination, and their picturesque and majestic language, represent the youth; the bold speculations of the Brahmin philosophers, the codes of law manifesting great legal acumen, and the praiseworthy works of scientists, represent manhood, when strong, calm, sober, calculating reason had superseded airy, unrestrained, exuberant fancy. But as a true representative of humanity's childhood age, India, young or old, was always highly imaginative.

A rapid decline of the national spirit and intellectual force set in during the last part of the Brahmanical period. The era of progress, invention, originality, creative power and literary masterpieces, came to an end; the bright, noble Aryan divinities made room for the fierce, cruel deities of the aborigines; the old simple worship deteriorated into an elaborate, symbolical and shamanistic ritual; true kingship was converted into despotism; imitations, compilations and commentaries, succeeded the original creations of the Vedic and Brahmanical era; and the ideas, manners, laws and institutions of the people grew hardened, rigid and petrified. Old age with its imbecility, unprogressiveness and sterility, approached.

The nation would have grown old, sooner or later, in obedience to the laws of nature. The decline, however, would have been deferred for generations and centuries, and the Hindus would have achieved greater things, if they had been able to maintain their purity of blood. The solemn grandeur of the Vedic hymns, the grand, masterly built-up epics Mahabharata and Ramayana, and the deep and daring speculations of the Brahmins, promised grander accomplishments, if the people could have lived a normal national life.

But decadence was hastened and premature old age came through fusion with an inferior and much aged race. The effect of the mixture of the two races was to accelerate the downward pace of the Aryan, and to rejuvenate slightly the aboriginal race. A new, fairly homogeneous people, inferior to the Aryan, but superior to the native races, sprang from the merger, The aborigines, far outnumbering the Aryans, became the dominant factor after the amalgamation, and gave to the intellectual work and the social and religious institutions of the new nation its character. Henceforth, whatever the Hindus thought and accomplished, was not typically Aryan, but bore the impress of the aborigines' native character.

In this era of Aryan degeneracy arose Buddhism. The new religion was in the nature of a popular revolt against the rigid clericalism of the Brahmins, against the absolute authority of the Vedas, and against the inhuman order of caste. The Buddhistic movement inaugurated by Gautama in the sixth century before the Christian era, was a rising of the oppressed and despised natives against the arrogant, aristocratic Aryans. The low castes and common people, aspiring to higher social positions, welcomed the new doctrines of equality.

Several general councils, especially the last one held at Patna in 244 B. C, formulated the teachings of Gautama, "the Buddha," into a dogma. The masses were now Buddhistic, and King Asoka raised Buddhism to the rank of a state religion in his realm. The high-caste Aryans still adhered to Brahminism.

History is almost mute in regard to the affairs of India during the long interval between the age of Gautama and about the year 1000 A. D. The rejuvenation of the aborigines through fusion with the Aryans caused only a short-lived Buddhistic revival. The general down-grade march was soon resumed again. Intellectual life was ebbing incessantly. The Buddhistic revival had not infused much new life into letters, science or philosophy. The general trend was toward a lower level. The two religious systems existed side by side for upward of a thousand years. Both were tolerant and decadent. The people sank deeper and deeper into the impotency, sterility and decrepitude of old age.

Buddhism, meantime, was proselyting very successfully among Mongolian and Mongoloid nations. It became strongly mongolized in its character and, as a result of the change, was eliminated from India and found refuge in Mongolian countries, a fate similar to that of Christianity.

The steady absorption and assimilation of the Aryan element by the native, and the general decay and disintegration of religious and social institutions, caused Brahminism to adapt itself slowly to the ideas and ideals prevailing among the common people. The primitive beliefs and customs of the native races reasserted themselves and found recognition.

A compromise between the warring religious systems was the final result. Out of the fragments and debris and muck of the decomposing religions modern Hinduism was constructed. It was adopted generally about 1000 A. D. and seems to suit most of the people. It is a conglomerate of the primitive fetishism and shamanism of the aborigines, decadent Brahminism and some Buddhistic tenets and usages.

The conquest of India by the Islamite Arabs caused a notable intellectual revival. It was evanescent, however. What was achieved in art and literature is owing chiefly to the Arab invaders. But the infusion of young Arab blood into the gigantic Hindu mass was too weak to rejuvenate the aging body.

The Anglo-Saxons have endeavored during the last one hundred and fifty years to regenerate India. Their efforts were futile. They could introduce railroads, telegraphs, newspapers, machines, orderly government and a host of missionaries, but their work was superficial. The unprogressive, aged folk soul of the Hindu was not touched. Neither Islam nor Christianity was able to arrest permanently the downward course to dotage and decrepitude; their successes were only ephemeral.

India is a helpless sage. It is incapable of reform, innovation and progress. It has had its day. It had its stormy, buoyant, progressive youth when the splendid Vedic hymns were written, about 2500 to 1500 B. C. It enjoyed its manhood and age of reason, invention and creative power, when, between 1500 and 600 B. C. it produced the grand epics Mahabharata and Ramayana and the Brahmanas, Upanishads, law codes, and theologic-philosophical systems. It had its decline after that. Decadence, and steady deterioration in art, science, government, morals and religious beliefs and usages, has been the rule since "the Buddah" first tried to reform India's society. Final extinction or, possibly, absorption and assimilation and rejuvenation by a strong, young race, is the fate that awaits the Hindu people.

The Hindus are undesirable immigrants. The low caste laborers, mechanics and farmers, from whom emigrants are chiefly recruited, belong mainly to the inferior aboriginal stock, carry but little Aryan blood in their veins, and are fossilized and ultra-conservative in their ideas, ideals and habits. Their presence in large numbers would have a deteriorating influence on the formation of the American nation of the future.

9. The Iranians.

The twin tribes of the Hindus and Iranians, as we have seen, left their old Aryan home on the Baltic in prehistoric times, and after a long journey settled in their new home on the plains of Bactria.

After a joint occupancy of Iran of some duration, they separated. The Hindus migrated to the plains of the Indus and the Ganges. The Iranians remained on the banks of the Oxus and the Jaxartes.

The cause of the estrangement and secession is unknown. It was probably ethnical. From several things known about them, we can infer that the Iranians were imbued less with race-pride than the Hindus, and suffered amalgamation with alien peoples. This worked a differentiation in speech, form of government, society, myths, legends, religion, manners and finally complete rupture,

The Iranians, although the contrast and enmity between the fair invaders and the swarthy natives is mentioned in their books, merged with their Turanian and probably Semitic neighbors into a new, homogeneous people. They built up a civilization which, in the main, bears the impress of Aryan genius, but manifests strong traces of Turanian and Semitic influence. The bright, warlike anthropomorphic Aryan gods, for instance, whom the two tribes originally worshiped jointly, and whom the Hindus took with them to the Indus, were metamorphosed by the Iranians into demons and evil, sinister deities, after the separation. New divinities of a more national, spiritual and metaphysical nature, and partly of Turanic and Semitic origin, displaced the Aryan gods in Iran. The two tribes, at the time of the separation, possessed in common a highly developed inflective language, the promising rudiments of a literature, an advanced social organization, and a religion which, in its evolution, had already passed the personal and patriarchal stage into the tribal.

The Zend-Avesta was the sacred book of the Iranians. Savants assert that it existed in its present form as late as 1200 B. C. Like the Vedas and most sacred books, it is the work of many authors, and was composed in the course of many generations. It is evidently only a fragment of a comprehensive religious literature. It was probably contemporary with the Vedas of India, but in its present form shows indications of maturity and even decadence. The youth of the Iranian people had created, but manhood and old age of the race had modified it.

A long phase of childhood and youth; of growth, progressiveness, luxuriant fancy, originality and creative force, preceded the age when the fragmentary religious works of the Iranians were cemented together into the Zend-Avesta.

The nation stood in the prime of manhood at the time when the Zend-Avesta was completed in its present form. It was an era of centralization of political power. Kingship had superseded chieftainship, and, in accordance with this change, did the gods reconstitute their hierarchy above the clouds. Ahura Mazda, the tutelary deity of the person, family and tribe of the autocratic king, became the absolute ruler above, and around his throne; the other gods had to content themselves with subordinate positions. The Zend-Avesta with the good god Ahura Mazda and the evil deity Angro-Mainyus, and the hosts of angels and archangels on either side, mirrors an oriental, despotic government of that age, with its autocrat, vassals, ministers, satraps, messengers and plotting rebels and pretenders.

The noble ethics of the Zend-Avesta point to a high and sound moral condition of the Iranians in their youth and prime of manhood. The conception of a just, benevolent and spiritual supreme deity; the belief in the immortality of the soul; in the last judgment held by the Messiah; in the reward of virtue in heaven and in punishment of crime in hell; in angels as the executors of the will of the Supreme Being; and in the final triumph of good over evil, were valuable ethical treasures which found their way from Iran via Babylon, Jerusalem and Alexandria to Rome and the West. Much of the ethical and philosophical teachings of Zarathustra, or Zoroaster, was embodied in the tenets of Judaism and Christianity.

Three or more waves of intellectual activity swept over Iran at irregular intervals, since the day when Zarathustra compiled and edited the Zend-Avesta, and when his people had begun the descent to old age Each wave was a revival.

The Iranian Medes and Persians rose up and erected a powerful world empire, with Susa, Ecbatana, Perseopolis and Babylon, as the centers of power, learning, art and literature. They revived the sinking intellectual life of western Asia during their rule from the fall of Nineveh in 622 to the battle of Arbela in 331 B. C.

Five centuries of decadence, impotency and decay in Iran followed the downfall of the Persian empire. The dynasty of the Sassanidae resuscitated the people (218 to 636 A. D.). Persia again became a great political power and developed much intellectual activity, especially in the collection, compilation and restoration of the old Iranian myths, legends, traditions, literature and religions.

A period of decadence again intervened between the short revival under the Sassanidse and the Arab conquest of the country.

The youthful, daring and vigorous Arab race regenerated aged and aging Iran once more. An epoch of splendor dawned upon Persia in the ninth century, and its effulgence continued until the 14th. An army of illustrious poets, theologians, philosophers, historians and scientists, of whom Firdusi and Hafiz attained world-wide fame, arose.

Since then all is silent in Iran. Old age with its sterility, ossification and weakness has secured a final triumph. Another regeneration is not in sight.

These repeated alternations between intellectual revivals and eras of decadence were undoubtedly due to ethnical changes. No nation can regenerate itself, and live through a past phase of life again, after it has once entered upon the downgrade to old age. The cause must have been external. Everyone of these rejuvenations of Iran must have been caused by the infusion of young, active and progressive blood.

Extensive transpositions through conquests, deportations, colonizations and migrations took place in that turbulent region. And when we consider the fact that everyone of these successive revivals was accompanied by an abrupt and radical change in language and thought; that the classical Zend gave way to Old Persian at the time of Cyrus and the Achaemenides; that the Old Persian was supplanted by the Pehlevi of the Sassanidae; and that the Pehlevi was superseded by the New Persian of Firdusi and Hafiz, we infer that these regenerations were caused by repeated fusions of the aged Iranian with younger and more vigorous races.

This certainly was the case with the last revival. The youthful, energetic, optimistic and enthusiastic Arabs conquered Persia in 636 A. D. Hosts of Arab soldiers, traders, officers, preachers and teachers rushed to the plains of Iran; mingled and fused with the natives, and furnished the new homogeneous nation, springing from the amalgamation, with the intellectual and moral leaven which was to bring forth a new and splendid outburst of life in poetry, history, philosophy, science, war and statesmanship.

Semitic Arabs and Iranian Persians merged into one homogeneous people. The fusion was fairly complete in two centuries after the conquest. Then the intellectual revival began. It culminated in Firdusi (916 to 940 A. D.), and ended in the fourteenth century with Hafiz. The new civilization evolved was neither Semitic nor Aryan, but Perso-Arabic in character; the joint product of the two races after their fusion. The young Arab had rejuvenated the aged Iranian.

The history of Iran furnishes us with good examples of repeated revivals or rejuvenations of aged nations through a blending with young elements. The Medes and Persians rejuvenated the old Iranians of Zarathustra. When the Persians became decrepit from old age, an influx of new blood from Parthia and Armenia brought about the intellectual revival of the Sassanidae. And when the symptoms of approaching old age made themselves manifest again in old Iran, the sturdy, young and progressive race from Arabia brought rejuvenation once more. The youth and manhood of the new Persian nation was of short duration; it lasted only from the seventh to the fourteenth century. Since then sterile, unprogressive, feeble and decrepit old age again ruled in Iran.

10. The Greeks.

When the Greeks invaded Hellas, they encountered a race of dark complexion, small stature, simple habits, unwarlike disposition, sea-faring, quite intellectual, able to erect massive works of stone, to construct canals and dams, and which worshiped its gods at Dodona in Epirus, at Delphi and other sacred places. The Greeks called this people the Pelasgians.

Three ages the Palaeolithic, the Neolithic and the bronze succeeded each other at irregular intervals in the countries around the Mediterranean, and extending far into Asia. Three races rose, flourished and perished successively in that region before the advent of the Greeks. Each race carried culture to a higher level than the one immediately preceding it. Finally, a race, using implements of polished stone and bronze, occupied the land. It covered the country with huge, massive, cyclopean structures; erected burial mounds, cromlechs, dolmens and stonehenges, and at different centers evolved an advanced civilization. It was the Pelasgic race.

It is not to be assumed that each conquering race exterminated its predecessor. The conquered people were enslaved to a large extent and, in the course of centuries, through absorption and assimilation formed a new, homogeneous race with the conquerors. Where the people of the bronze age remained comparatively pure, they carried civilization to a higher level than did those who had absorbed a large percentage of aged and inferior races. The Pelasgians belonged to this latter class.

Into the dominions of the Pelasgians who inhabited the shores and islands of the eastern Mediterranean, the Graeco-Italian invasion swept like an inundation. The aging Pelasgians, who had already crossed the meridian of their racial life, could not resist the onslaught of the young, vigorous, aggressive, invading race. The aged Pelasgian race, of superior culture, was reduced to servitude and subordinate social position and, as always in such cases, became the tutors of the victors.

The Hellenes were Aryans of pure type. This is evident from their earliest writings. Homer, for instance, describes nearly all his gods, goddesses and heroes as of fair complexion, blond and blue-eyed. Where the dark type appears, as with the oldest gods Zeus, Poseidon and Hephaistos, they were of Pelasgic origin and only Hellenic by adoption. As the gods are the personified ideals of their worshipers, we infer that the fair deities of the Greek pantheon were of Aryan and the dark divinities of Pelasgic origin.

The ancient home of the Hellenes was on the Baltic shores. Forcibly torn loose from their kindred, they wandered through the Sarmatian plain to the Euxine, and thence southward to the coasts and islands of the Aegean Sea.

In the long march from the Bosporus to Sicily, continuing for centuries, the pure Aryan type became more or less adulterated by the native Pelasgian element. It remained purest around the Aegean, where subsequently Hellenic civilization of the highest perfection was unfolded. At the periphery of Aryan influence and power, in northern Hellas, in southern Italy and in the hinterland of the Greek colonies of Asia Minor, the colonizing energy of the invaders soon spent itself. The numerical preponderance of the Aryan diminished in proportion to the distance from the centres of intelligence and power on the Aegean. New national types, indicating a fusion of Aryans and Pelasgians in varying proportions, arose in different sections. Language, ideas, ideals and manners bore the Aryan stamp where this race predominated numerically; but where the Pelasgic element was in the majority, a corresponding modification of speech, thought and customs is quite discernible. The Dorians of the north and west could not conceal the strong admixture of Pelasgic blood; the inhabitants of "Greater Greece" showed the strong effect of fusion with the aborigines of southern Italy and Sicily; the Aeolian type exhibited strong traces of Semitic, Egyptian and Pelasgic influence; and the Ionians only preserved the purity of race to a large extent. They became the standard bearers of Hellenic culture; they only made Greek history.

The infancy of the Hellenic people lies hidden in the obscurity of prehistoric times. A part of that phase was spent at the old Aryan home on the Baltic; a part on the sojourn in the steppes, and on the shores of the Black Sea; a part in the conquest and colonization of the new home; and another part in the formation of a new nation out of the fusion of Aryan and Pelasgic elements.

A fair degree of homogeneity in speech, social and political institutions, religions, customs and aspirations, had been attained by Ionians, Dorians and Aeolians in particular, and by all the Greeks in general, as early as 1500 B. C.

The childhood of Hellas is still obscured by the mist of morning; but through these mists we begin to discern shadowy, migratory movements, and the heroic deeds and daring adventures, and the fantastic, gigantic forms, in dim outline, of gods, demi-gods, heroes and monsters.

How much truth lies encysted in the beautiful myths and legends of Deucalion, Cecrops, Codrus, Perseus, Theseus, Heracles and the Argonauts, will never be revealed. The Hellenes were then in their childhood, and their wild, vivid and unrestrained imagination exaggerated everything, gave all beings a romantic and picturesque character, and magnified them to colossal dimensions.

With Homer and Hesiod about 900 to 850 B. C. Greece stepped from childhood into early youth. Luxuriant fancy swayed the soul of the young nation, and the grand epics, the Iliad and Odyssey, and works of a similar nature were produced. It was the poetic and heroic age of youth.

The Pelasgic race, and to some extent Egypt and Babylon, had been the early tutors of young Hellas. Many fructifying ideas, many germs of a higher civilization, many intellectual impulses, percolated through to the Aegean Sea from the centers of culture on the Nile and the Euphrates; but the Hellenic pupil knew of no slavish obedience. To every imported and naturalized idea, be it in art, philosophy and religion, he gave the cast, form and coloring of his individual, national and racial genius. He developed a strong individuality from the very first. He would take the raw material and the crude fabrics of oriental culture, and transform them into masterpieces of a grandeur, beauty and majesty far surpassing the works of his tutors and contemporaries, and, in many cases, serving as models for all posterity.

The seventh century before our era witnessed the bright twilight immediately preceding sunrise. Persons and events appeared in clearer outlines. Lycurgus (880) organized the Spartan, and Draco (624) and Solon (638 B. C.) formed the Athenian state. These famous lawgivers did not create social and political order out of chaos, as legend and hero-worship represent them; they simply organized society on the basis of the written and unwritten laws and customs and usages already existing and in full force, and with the full recognition of the struggle for power, rights, privileges and freedom, raging between the monarchial, aristocratic and democratic parties.

The progressive spirit of the young Hellenic nation endeavored at an early age to solve the great social and political problems which then made their appearance for the first time in the evolution of mankind. The Greeks began to strive early for the realization of their high social and political ideals, which would give to the individual a full share in the government, develop his faculties to the fullest extent, and thus secure to the state the highest aggregate of wealth, power and culture.

This was an entirely new movement, and indicated that the Greeks were ordained to lead humanity to a higher social and political level. The Orient never rose above the autocracy of a king. The Hellenes attempted to substitute the collective will, intelligence and interests of the masses for those of an absolute ruler and of a privileged class. The democratic principle which henceforth was to be the leaven, the vital, motive force in social and political life, was introduced by the Greeks. The rule of impersonal law, the will of the people, was substituted for that of the will of the monarch. Henceforth, democracy became a leading and permanent factor in the political evolution of man; the thermometer of the rise and fall of a nation's civilization.

Athens, and the Ionians generally, being of nearly pure Aryan stock, took the leading part in the movement for democratic rule; while Sparta and the Dorians, due to the strain of degenerate and unprogressive Pelasgic blood in their veins, favored the old, oriental, conservative government by autocratic royalty and privileged classes.

This ingrained, racial and organic contrast between the democratic Aryan Ionians, led by Athens, and the monarchic, oligarchic, semi-Aryan Dorians, marshalled by Sparta, formed the pivot around which Grecian history turned. Monarchy and oligarchy were victorious in the Doric states; and the democratic principle triumphed among the Ionians. The Ionians, however, under the hegemony of Athens, were the true representatives of Aryan or Hellenic genius in government, art, literature, philosophy and science.

The Orient became stationary and petrified at the stage of patriarchal and tribal rule. The Greeks made a tentative movement toward the higher level of nationalism. The attempts failed. The Hellenes never evolved a true, organically united nation. They instituted the Amphictionic Council, the Aeolian, Ionian, Peloponnesian, Theban and Achaean leagues or confederacies, and the periodical, national festivals, such as the Pythian games at Delhi, the

Olympian in Elis, the Nemean festival in Argolis, the Eleusian at Eleusis and the Isthmian games at Corinth, to foster the national idea; but the propaganda was never quite successful. The tribal instinct and organization remained dominant. Hellas became stationary politically, in the transition from the tribal to the national form of government; but she ascended to a higher level than the Asiatic nations.

Hellenic philosophy, poetry and art began an era of rapid development during the seventh century. The youthful spirit of Greece commenced to exhibit its vigor, originality and high qualities.

With Thales of Miletus (640 B. C.) opened that long procession of Hellenic philosophers, destined to rule the world's thought for many centuries. Thales, Diogenes of Apolonia, Anaximenes of Miletus (550 B. C.), Heraclitus of Ephesus (500 B. C.) and Anaximander of Miletus (610-546 B. C.) were the pioneers of philosophical speculation. Their philosophy is tinctured with Egyptian and Semitic ideas. They were Aeolians. Fusion with the inhabitants of aged Egypt and Phoenicia had accelerated their progress, and the first blossoms of Greek philosophy sprang up in Aeolia.

Homer (907 B. C.), Hesiod (800 B. C.) and their contemporaries, represented in literature the poetic and heroic childhood of Greece. It was an age of vivid, luxuriant and unrestrained imagination.

Intellectual activity was lulled to rest during the eighth and ninth centuries, B. C. It was the barren transition from childhood to youth, when the native genius was storing forces for greater efforts.

A new order of poets, the contemporaries of the early philosophers and lawgivers, now came to the front. Lyrics, elegies, songs of war, patriotism, love and conviviality, supplanted the sublime epic. Poetry grew less natural and spontaneous, and more learned, artistic and mature. The national soul had undergone a change. Reason began to overshadow fancy. Men saw things in the bright light of day instead of the rosy dawn. Sapho (600), Pindar (522-442 B. C.) and Anacreon were the poetic representatives of this epoch.

Young Hellas had submitted to the tutorship in art of Egypt, Babylon and the Pelasgians, anterior to this age. Simplicity and massiveness, therefore, were the characteristics of early Greek architecture. Now the Hellenes severed the leading strings and followed their own bent. The Hellenic artists reached maturity and emancipated themselves. Their metemorphosis from imitators to creators was swift. Only one temple, artistically important, was known before the sixth century, but in a few generations thereafter all the hills and valleys were adorned with magnificent public buildings, filled with superb paintings and statuary.

Two styles of architecture the Doric and Ionian, were evolved. The former with its massive, imposing, solemn grandeur, pointed to the admixture of Pelasgian blood; the latter, with its elegance, gracefulness, symmetry and refinement, was Aryan. The influence of Pelasgic blood is plainly apparent in all Doric art, religion, poetry and social and political institutions.

With accelerated pace the Greeks now advanced towards the meridian of their national existence. It was the season of efflorescence of Hellenic genius. An unparalleled intellectual activity pervaded all classes. Master minds, in every field of human endeavor, sprang up by the hundreds. Pathfinding, epochmaking thinkers rose by the score. A pyrotechnic display of Hellenic genius of uncommon splendor filled Greece with brilliant light and color, from the Persian wars (490 to 479 B. C), to the time of Alexander the Great (333 B. C.). Greece stood at or near its zenith, in the prime of manhood, during three centuries, or from about 500 to 200 B. C.; but its actual point of culmination must be placed at the beginning of the Peloponnesian war, 421 B. C. It evolved a civilization in this time, which, in regard to originality, force, scope, invention, creative power, brilliancy and symmetry, is peerless in the world's history.

Social and political progress kept pace with the general intellectual advance. Democracy gained ground steadily from Solon to Pericles (d. 429 B. C.). At the time of this famous statesman all classes, with the exception of slaves, participated in the government. Laws were made and executed by elected representatives of the people. The administration of justice was public and well regulated. The privileges of the nobility were curtailed and reduced to a minimum. Commerce was unrestricted. Free speech prevailed. Education was general and well calculated to produce intellectually, morally and physically strong men of great independence, originality and individuality. If the Hellenes had been trained to look upon Egyptian and Chaldean culture as a perfect model and as absolute in authority, they would never have achieved what they did in art, philosophy, science, statesmanship and war.

Only master minds of a robust individuality, subject to the moulding influences from all quarters, and free from the restraints of absolute authority, can produce masterpieces. A continuous breeze from one direction bends, warps and distorts the strongest oak; but the play of currents from all points of the compass secures symmetrical growth. Hellenic education promoted the harmonious and symmetrical development of the individual to a high degree.

This is true only of democratic Athens and her Ionian allies. Oligarchic and monarchic Sparta remained a military community. She produced good warriors and statesmen and nothing else. She contributed little or nothing to Greek culture. The barracks is no civilizing institution.

It is but natural that the educational methods and the social and political institutions of Athens and her Ionian confederates should breed such a large number of famous men in statesmanship, art, literature, oratory and science.

Themistocles (514 to 449), Miltiades (about 490), Aristides (490), Pericles (d. 429), Alcibiades (450 to 404), Epaminondas (414 to 362) and Pelopidas (about 371 B. C.) were the illustrious statesmen who guided Greece during this period.

Plygnothes (450), Zeuxis (425), Appelles (352 to 308), Polycletus (445), Pheidias (d. 432), and Praxiteles (364 B. C), elevated the arts of painting, sculpture and architecture to a high degree of perfection.

The drama, the highest type of poetic productions, was characteristic of this literary epoch. It belongs to a nation's age of maturity, where reason restrains imagination. Aeschylus (525-436), lofty, dignified and aristocratic; Sophocles (495-405), devout, individualistic and democratic; Euripides (480-406), liberal, broad and opposed to privileges; and Aristophanes (427-388 B. C.), witty, cynical and satirical, assailing extravagance, corruption, mobocracy, sophistry, cant and sham; mirrored the intellectual and moral condition of their contemporaries. Aeschylus represents his people as still ascending; Sophocles, as standing at the zenith; and Aristophanes, as having begun the descent.

Literature sets the milestones on man's up and down-grade journey. The grand epics of Homer mark the childhood's phase of Greece; the passionate, fervent, sensuous and sentimental lyrics and songs of Pindar and his contemporaries, belong to stormy, boisterous youth; and the drama and the works on science of Sophocles and his literary associates, are the characteristic features of manhood and maturity.

Oratory, a necessary and natural companion of free, democratic government, was cultivated to perfection. Isocrates (436-338), Aeschines (389-314), and Demosthenes (385-322 B. C.), were illustrious examples of Greek orators.

The Greeks raised history to the rank of a science. Instead of the uncritical, legendary, mythical, disconnected and anecdotal tales of the Orient, they introduced the rational, critical and philosophical treatment of men and events. Herodotus (484-408), the "father of history"; Thucydides (471-408), unrivalled for impartiality, brevity of style and descriptive power; and Xenophon (445-395 B. C.), excelling in charming narrative; were without peers among their contemporaries, and served their posterity as models.

The great philosophers belong to this period. They led no exclusive life of idle contemplation. They were men of affairs as well as of ideas. They shared in the hardships of military campaigns, pleaded the cause of their clients in the courts, debated measures in the public assemblies, harangued the crowd at the market places, participated in the civil administration and taught in schools, studios and laboratories. The strenuous, democratic life demanded men of this type.

A long procession of these philosophers passed across the stage. Pythagoras oi Samos (570-504), aristocratic, mystical and monotheistic; Xenophanes of Ionia, skeptic and pantheist; Aruxagores of Clazomene (about 450,, a believer in the eternity of the universe and government of chaos by intellect; Parmemides, (about 450), asserting that all observation of the senses is illusory; Zeno of Elea, in Italy (450) firm monotheist and skeptical of observed phenomena; Empedocles of Agrigentum, (410), with strong, democratic proclivities, and faith in metempsychosis, emanation from a universal soul, and anangement of matter in accord with inherent love and hate; Democritus of Abdera (b. 470), skeptic, believer in the rule of fate and promoter of the atomic theory; Socrates (469-400), with aristocratic tendencies, accurate in definitions, and teaching that virtue is of prime necessity to man's well being; Aristippus of Cyrene (b. 424), advocate of pleasure; Antisthenes (440-370), founder of the cynic school; Diogenes of Synope (412-323), teaching austerity, contempt of wealth and abstinence from pleasure; Plato (429-347), believing in one god as the supreme intelligence, and in the organization of matter in accord with original ideas and types; Pyrrho (about 330), founder of the skeptic school; Epicurus (342), denying that the truth can be learned, recommending the enjoyment of pleasure and the acceptance of the world as it is with resignation; Aristotle (384-322 B.C.), inaugurating true scientific investigation; these were the eminent leaders of Hellenic speculative thought.

The course of the twin sisters, poetry and philosophy, from Homer and Thales to Aristophanes and Aristotle, is well marked through the stages of childhood, youth, manhood and old age of Greece. Both, poetry and speculative philosophy, are the product of the imagination rather than of reason, and belong to a nation's youth. Poetry is philosophy in rhyme; and philosophy is poetry in prose. The early philosophers of Greece, like the early poets, were endowed chiefly with an exuberant fancy. Reason gained the ascendency with Socrates, Plato and their contemporaries, and Aristotle was really more a scientist than a philosopher. The cynic, skeptic and stoic schools indicate the intellectual decline of Hellas. A consciousness of waning power, and a depressing pessimism fell upon Greek speculative thought after Plato. A horde of imitators, compilers and commentators followed the bold, original thinkers of the classical period. A deterioration in philosophical speculation is apparent from generation to generation.

The tribal cults of Greece formed a conglomerate in which ancient myths, legends and fables were imbedded. Aryan and Pelasgic conceptions of spirits, demons, demi-gods and gods, in all stages of development, originating in various localities and at different times, were finally deposited in a vast stratum of religious thought.

The Hellenic deities rose and fell with their worshipers. The genesis of the gods is everywhere the same. They were originally the tutelary deities of persons, families and clans. The cults of certain divinities rose into prominence in proportion as the clans or tribes to which they belonged attained wealth, power and influence. Zeus was originally the local tutelary deity of Dodona and Crete, Hera of Argos and Samos, Athene of Attica, Apollo of Delphi, Aphrodite of Cyprus and Cythera, Hermes of Samothrace, etc. Political organizations and religious conceptions were in a constant flux. Tribes and gods changed rank and position continuously.

No tribe secured permanent and unquestioned supremacy and, consequently, no national religion could arise. When Athens attained to intellectual leadership, her myths, legends and gods came into prominence, but the cult of Pallas-Athene remained local. The Greek mind was individualistic, tribal and centrifugal, and was averse to centralization. Every man, every family, every class, worshiped its own tutelary deity. The autocratic gods of the Orient were impossible in Hellas. Hellenic society was permeated by the democratic principle of equality, and the divine court on Mount Olympus was modelled after this, and impregnated with democratic ideas. Zeus was rather the presiding officer at a meeting of peers than a despotic ruler. And as the Greeks obeyed the impersonal law, so their gods were subject to a mysterious, impersonal fate. The government of the world by universal, eternal and inexorable law to which even the gods had to submit, dawned first upon the Hellenic mind.

Greece was without an organized priesthood to establish a dogma and regulate a cult. Poets, artists and philosophers, rather than priests, gave expression to the religious conceptions and sentiments of the people.

The Hellenic religion was the most cheerful of all. The Asiatics approached their gods with the fear and awe of slaves; the Greeks theirs with love and confidence as friends. Theirs was essentially a religion for freemen, and it harmonized intimately with the spirit, character, and institutions of the people. Their deities were no "strange gods" forced upon them by foreign conquerors and missionaries. They were Hellenic and had sprung from the hearts and minds of the people. Even the old Pelasgic deities, Kronus, Zeus, Hera, Poseidon and Haephestus were Hellenized, and hid their grim and sombre oriental forms and features under the folds of cheerful and graceful Grecian drapery.

Ethics kept pace with the advance of Hellenic civilization. It kept aloof from religion in the infancy of the nation. No Greek promulgated decrees and codes of laws with an authoritative "Thus sayeth the Lord." Ethics was exclusively a secular affair in Hellas. It was developed at the family hearth, in the shop, the market, the legislative hall, the court and the study of the poet, and philosopher. And as Greek civilization far surpassed that of any of their contemporaries, so was their system of ethics superior in refinement, humanity and justice.

Hellas stood at its zenith in the age of Pericles, Sophocles and Socrates. Then the decline began. The downward step was hastened by the complete defeat of Athens, the champion of democracy, progress and culture, by Sparta, the conservative representative of militarism, oligarchy and monarchy. The great luminaries of art, literature, philosophy, statesmanship and science, were extinguished one after another, and left the land in a dismal twilight. A race of dwarfish epigoni entered the arena where giants trod so recently. Originality, invention and creative force, the true tests of genuine culture, disappeared. Poets, artists and philosophers were content to act as the imitators, compilers and commentators of their great forebears. The waning of the public spirit, the decay of public and private virtue, the weakening of intellectual strength, the spread of cynic and pessimistic views of life, the lack of patriotism, the centralization of wealth and power in the hands of the few, the spread of corruption, luxury, profligacy, effeminacy and pessimism, and the decadence of democracy, pointed to the fact that Hellas was rapidly and irretrievably sinking into the marasmus and decrepitude of old age. Epaminondas, Pelopidas and Demosthenes endeavored in vain to check the downward course. Degeneracy, due to advancing old age, continued unabated. The state fell an easy victim to the assault of the Macedonians, and shortly after became a protectorate and a province of Rome. Greece had ceased to exist as an independent nation.

Hellas was dead politically, but the Hellenes still lived, and by their genius, their prestige and their civilization continued to rule the world for centuries after Aristotle. The sage of the Aegean became the tutor of humanity. Greek speech, Greek culture and Greek taste were in vogue throughout the eastern basin of the Mediterranean.

Once more the light of Greek civilization flashed up. Once more, this time at Alexandria and Antioch Hellenic genius gathered up its remaining intellectual and moral forces, to regain its former prestige. The Alexandrian revival was but a rich aftermath of Greek culture. A bright array of authors and scientists made the Egyptian metropolis luminous; but the rays it shed were not the pure, white light, radiating from Athens in its classic age. The nations of the East, Egyptians, Chaldeans, Hindus, Persians, Jews, Syrians, Phoenicians, Greeks and Romans were all aging, all in a moribund condition. Representatives of all of them met at Alexandria. The friction ensuing between these heterogeneous elements caused intellectual activity, heat and flame, but the light emanating, while essentially Greek, was strongly colored by the mysticism and the superstitions of the decaying and disintegrating Orient.

But even in their dissolution the Hellenic people were destined to achieve something which was to outlive their magnificent temples, sculptures, paintings and philosophic systems. They became the nurse, guardian and tutor of the infant religion of Galilee. They transformed the Semitic infant into an Aryan, in order to conquer the Aryan world. The degenerate descendants of Socrates, Plato and Aristotle, breathed their souls into the young infant. The church fathers, of Greek extraction, formulated creed and doctrines of young Christianity, and made it Hellenic, or at least semi-Hellenic, and acceptable to Aryan minds. Grecian philosophy moulded the Christian dogma, and without this change, the new cult would have perished in obscurity, like the other Semitic cults of the time.

That was the last great effort of the expiring nation. Slavs, Arabs, Turks and various hordes from Asia and eastern Europe overran the land, and absorbed and assimilated what was left of the Greeks. A new nation, fairly homogeneous, sprang up from the amalgamation, but it is not Hellenic in character.

All the genuine Greek colonies rose, flourished, declined and perished simultaneously with the great Hellenic states on the Aegean Sea, of which they were off-shoots.

The immutable laws of nature which govern the rise and fall of nations, are beautifully illustrated in the history of the Greeks. A normal development through all the phases of life is exhibited in the biography of the Hellenic nations. Theseus, Heracles and the Argonauts, represented the early, Homer and Hesiod, the later infancy. With Pindar, Anacreon, Solon and Thales, the nation passed from childhood into youth. Pericles, Sophocles Pheidias, Socrates and Thucydides, were representatives of its prime of manhood. With Plato and Aristotle came the unavoidable decline. The venerable sage of the Aegean, who had laid down the laws of art, letters, science, philosophy and government for mankind, and who had achieved more for the advancement of the human race than all the other nations of antiquity, passed into dotage, but, in his hour of death, was still able to shape the course of human thought for centuries to come.

12. The Romans.

The main body of the Aryan invaders of south-eastern Europe had secured lodgement on the shores and islands of the Aegean Sea, and had there laid the foundations of the Ionian, Dorian and Aeolian states.

The vanguard pushed on to southern Italy, and Sicily. It conquered and subjugated the natives, and organized an Aryan, feudal aristocracy, but was eventually absorbed and assimilated by the numerically much stronger aborigines.

The Aryans who conquered Greece and Rome were of the same ethnic stock. The affinity of speech, the similarity of thought and customs, the uninterrupted, intimate relations existing between them, and the almost simultaneous passage of both through the successive phases of childhood, youth, manhood and old age, point to a near kinship between Hellenes and Romans.

The Greeks, particularly the Ionians, remained Aryans of pure blood for a long time; but their cousins, who conquered and colonized Italy and Sicily, sacrificed their racial character early to a great extent, and were finally completely swallowed up by the mass of the aborigines. The contrast between Greek and Roman civilization is due to this fusion. Greek culture was always essentially Aryan, but many of the characteristic features of Roman social, political and religious life betray the strong infusion of aboriginal blood. The Aryan conquerors of Italy forced their language, form of government and some of their deities on the natives; but, in turn, adopted a large part of the latter's laws, customs, art and social and religious institutions.

The aborigines belonged to the Pelasgic, Turanian or Etruscan race; the race that had erected tumuli, cromlechs and megalithic structures all over southern Europe; had made Etruria a center of culture of no mean order; and which, probably, had developed a high civilization on the Nile and the Euphrates. They were of a swarthy complexion and low stature, and were representatives of the infancy or childhood's phase in the life of humanity.

This race had passed through the stages of infancy and youth with its exuberant fancy, exultant vigor and daring originality; of its manhood of progress, creative force, expansion and power; and was sinking into the physical, mental and moral weakness and unprogressiveness of old age, when the Aryan invaders made their appearance.

The two races, unequal in number, character and age, settled down together and, in the course of some centuries formed a new, homogeneous nation, which, in physical aspect, and in its intellectual and moral traits of character, manifested Pelasgic or Etruscan extraction rather than Aryan. The Roman with his dark complexion, medium height, well-knit frame, aquiline nose, saturnine brow, steadfast, resolute, self-confident, of a frugal and practical nature, and with his lack of originality, invention and idealism, was evidently more an Etruscan or Pelasgian than an Aryan.

The conquering Aryans rejuvenated the aboriginal aging race. They furnished the leaven, the motive force, the spirit of progress to the civilization which both races were to evolve. The natives acted only as a strong modifying and restraining force.

The Romans, for this reason, never rose above the rank of imitators in art, literature, philosophy and religion. They were devoid of inventive and creative force, except in war, politics and law. The rejuvenated native race began another national existence. It passed rapidly through the phases of infancy and childhood, and, really, commenced life at the stage of later youth, near maturity. It is for this reason that Rome brought forth no Argonauts, no Homer, Hesiod, Trojan heroes, Thales or Anaximander. It had no heroic and poetic childhood.

The infancy of the new Latin people is lost in the obscurity of prehistoric times. Its childhood covers the early part of the last millennium before Christ, and is enwrapped in a cloud of myths, legends, fables and traditions, through which the vague forms and deeds of gods, demi-gods and heroes may be discerned. The tribal organization still prevailed. Dialects, cults, mythologies and rulers, were as numerous as tribes. Religion was patriarchal and tribal. Every individual, family, clan or tribe possessed its tutelary deity. Penates, lares, lemures and larvae, the household gods and the souls of ancestors, clung to the old family hearth, and were adored, worshiped and prayed and sacrificed to by the head of the family, acting as priest. A host of superhuman beings, spirits, demons and gods, dwelt in all the striking objects and phenomena of nature. Omens, signs, auguries and oracles were relied upon to learn the wish and purpose of the deities.

In old Italy, as elsewhere, the tutelary deities of prominent individuals, families, clans and tribes, were exalted to positions of high rank, dignity and eminence; the authority and power of a god depended on the number, intellectual force, wealth and political standing of his worshipers and adherents. The great gods of the Greeks were imported, adopted and naturalized, at an early date. They came with great prestige and soon took first rank. They were worshiped with magnificent ceremonies in splendid temples, but, at the same time, the ancient native deities were regaled by sacrifices at the family altar. There was no regular, organized, zealous priesthood, no intolerance and no religious strife, in ancient Rome.

The Aryan conquest created two social and political classes. The conquerors divided the land among themselves and their retainers, and reduced the subjugated natives to the conditions of serfs, who could enjoy no freedom, no real estate, and only a few civil rights. A long civil conflict ensued. The disfranchised people struggled incessantly for the restoration of their rights; and the landed, hereditary, feudal aristocracy tenaciously combatted the popular movement.

Gradually, however, the two classes, originally divided on ethnic lines, fused and became more homogeneous, and the governing class lost its distinctive racial character. Homogeneity was an accomplished fact in the sixth century, B. C., and the haughty nobility which owned nearly all the land and rilled nearly all the high offices of the state, and the landless, oppressed and disfranchised plebeians, were now practically of one race. The old race antipathies, in which the institution of caste or classes was rooted, had vanished forever.

Authentic Latin history begins with the sixth century. The mist of myth and legend lifted. The earlier kings are legendary; but Lucius, Tarquinus, Priscus and Servius, step forth into the twilight of history.

The city of Rome rose into prominence and took the lead among the many tribal capitals of the peninsula. The geographical position, the fertility of the soil, and, probably, a happy combination of Aryan and Etruscan elements, secured a confluence of intelligence, vigor, energy, courage, wealth and power, at the capital on the Tiber.

Roman history, from the sixth to the first century, B. C., from the abolition of kingship to the civil wars of Marius and Sulla, presents scarcely anything but an endless chronicle of conquests abroad, and interminable strife between patricians and plebeians at home. War, politics and legislation monopolized public attention. A sound, sturdy democracy was the main factor which gave to Rome its preponderant position on the peninsula. The constant and invariably successful contest of the commons for equal rights and against the privileges and prerogatives of the nobility, was the chief cause of Roman ascendancy. All the national intellect, talent, genius and energy was diverted into the channel of politics. The courts, the halls of legislation and the popular assemblies formed the arena for the training of the Latin youths.

There the great statesmen, generals and jurists, developed their powers. Upon the whole, Rome was progressive, prosperous and victorious, when democracy was triumphant; but trade languished, industry was paralyzed, public life became stagnant and corrupt, and the disheartened, mutinous legions were routed, when the arrogant, unprogressive and selfish aristocrats took the reins of the government in their hands.

The growth of the Roman people from childhood to youth, and from youth to manhood, can best be traced by observing the evolution of their democracy. The abolition of kingship, the plebeian strikes, the repeal of the drastic debtor laws, the codification of the customs, usages and the unwritten law of the land, the recognition of the general assembly as the supreme legislative power, the revocation of the prohibition of marriages between patricians and plebeians, the enfranchisement of the lower and middle classes and the provincials, and the eligibility of the commons to all the high offices of the commonwealth, mark the strides by which the Romans ascended to the apex of power. Democracy unfetters the best qualities of the citizen. The aggregate intellectual and physical work performed, both quantitatively and qualitatively, is proportionate to the freedom enjoyed by a people.

Rome would have achieved more in art, literature and science, and sustained herself longer in the prime of manhood, if in her intellectual and economic progress she had not been handicapped by slavery. The disintegrating and corrupting effect of this institution became specially noticeable immediately after the Punic wars. The number of slaves held increased rapidly after that age. Captives of war were brought to Rome in such numbers, and there sold so cheap, that free labor was virtually driven out of existence. The sturdy, independent, virtuous, middle class, the seat of the progressive spirit and national regeneration, vanished. The large estates, managed and worked by slaves, absorbed the small farms. Merchants, mechanics, laborers and even professional men were reduced to clients and dependents of the wealthy nobles. The unequal distribution of the rapidly increasing national wealth generated luxury, extravagance, vice and corruption in the upper strata of society, and created a brutalized, idle, vicious, unpatriotic and unprincipled proletariat at the other extreme. The obsequiousness of the lackey supplanted the dignified pride of the Roman yeoman and citizen. Socially and politically the Romans stood at the zenith during the Punic wars. They possessed the plain and simple virtues, industry, frugality, pride, courage, perseverance, fortitude, energy, veracity and honesty, upon which national greatness rests, to a high degree. A premature decline, due to the vices engendered and fostered by slavery and aristocratic rule, set in at the close of the Punic wars. Democracy gradually lost its hold on the populace. The nobility grew more reckless, ambitious, unprincipled and profligate. A mighty stream of stolen wealth flowed incessantly from the 'exploited provinces to the capital on the Tiber. Profligacy, servility and sensual pleasures sapped the vitality of the people. Cato (195), the Gracchi (134-122 B. C), Marius and Caesar, strove in vain to stem the downward course. Civil wars, murder, proscription, confiscation and brigandage, endangered the constitution, devastated the land and decimated the populace. Unable to uphold the honor and integrity of the republic against the assaults of a selfish, unpatriotic and corrupt nobility, the enervated Roman democracy endowed Caesar, its champion, with imperial power. Democracy, as no longer fit to rule, abdicated, and imperialism, or Caesarism, its logical successor, inherited its power.

The social and political decline of Rome began at the end of the Punic war; but in art, literature and science she crossed her meridian during the last century before the birth of Christ. The early centuries, the age of childhood and youth, had brought forth nothing but warriors, statesmen and jurists. No poets, philosophers, artists or scientists of merit appeared until the middle of the third century before our era. They increased slowly in number and brilliancy from the Punic wars to the classic age of Virgil and Caesar, when they began to diminish in number, talent and genius; and the second, third and fourth centuries A. D. saw only a few mediocre stragglers and camp-followers.

In an ascending line we find Livius Andronicus (250), the father of Latin epics and dramas; Plautus (254-184), the comic poet; Ennius (240-190), the dramatist and satirist; Terentius (195-159), the comic poet; Lucian (about 150), the classic humorist; Varro (116-28), the scientist; Cicero (106-43), the orator; Caesar (100-44), the historian; Lucretius (99-55), the philosophical and didactic poet; Catullus (b. 87), the lyric poet; Sallust (86-34), the noted historian; Virgil (70-19), the illustrious poet; Horatius (65-8), the renowned lyric and satirist; Livius (61 B. C. to 19 A. D.), the famous historian; and thence on a descending line, Ovid (43 B. C. to 18 A. D.), the poet; Seneca (3 B. C.-65 A. D.), the poet, philosopher and scientist; Lucanus (38-65 A. D.), the eminent poet; Pliny, the Elder (d. 79), and Pliny, the Younger (about 100), both famous scientists; Tacitus (about 80), the illustrious historian; and Juvenal (50-120 A. D.), the popular satirist.

This nearly exhausts the list of men eminent in letters and science. During the first centuries of our era there were also some famous men who, as fathers of the church, exerted a strong influence on Christianity, then in the process of formation.

From Livius Andronicus (250 B. C), to Juvenal (120 A. D.), the classical era of Rome, we note a marked change in the personnel of the eminent procession as it files by. The poets, the men of imagination, the representatives of youth, were in the van; the scientists and historians, the men in whom reason predominates, the representatives of manhood, appear when the nation, with Caesar and Livius, reached its point of culmination. They were followed by mediocre imitators and commentators, the representatives of decadence and old age.

Few of the Roman poets, scientists and philosophers rose above mediocrity. By the side of the Hellenic giants of thought the Romans appear dwarfish.

They were wanting in originality, invention and creative power in all except in war, law and government. They were the servile imitators of Greece in art, literature, science, philosophy and religion. They were men of action rather than of thought. With Virgil, Cicero and Caesar, Rome crossed the meridian of her national life. That was her classical age; her prime of manhood.

The Romans created a world-empire, but no true nation. They never rose above the tribal state. The great republic and later, the empire, was no organic whole, but a congeries of heterogeneous tribes and nations, welded together mechanically by the statecraft, wealth and military skill of Rome, but not organically united by the ties of a common country, language, religion, customs and traditions. The Roman government remained to the last essentially a government of a city or a tribe. Roman citizenship really meant citizenship of the capital.

The general decline of Rome began with Augustus. The downward course was accelerated by a number of weak, corrupt, brutal and degenerate emperors during the first century. The people were deteriorating physically, intellectually and morally. Luxury, profligacy and vice sapped the nation's vitality. In vain did a few able and virtuous emperors endeavor to stem the rising tide of corruption and degeneracy. Even Christianity, the new religion, could not regenerate the people nor arrest the downward course, but participated in the universal decadence. Old age was approaching.

But in spite of a succession of imbecile, weak and despicable emperors; in spite of the decay of patriotism, public spirit, physical, mental and moral vigor; in spite of interminable civil wars between ambitious generals and Caesars, the mighty political fabric survived all external and internal dangers and held together for six centuries after the descent had commenced. The empire was but a hollow shell and would have collapsed under the assault of a powerful adversary; but no such foe existed. The then known civilized world Rome, Spain, Gaul, Illyria,' Greece, Egypt, Babylon, Persia, India and the Semitic countries of Asia Minor was in a state of disintegration and decomposition. All the nations around the Mediterranean were rapidly drifting into the decrepitude of old age. The hoary sage of the Tiber was surrounded by imbecile octogenarians; he ruled only by tradition and prestige. But portentous clouds were gathering on the northern horizon. A young, growing, progressive and vigorous people pressed with ever redoubling force against the fortified frontiers of the Rhine and the Danube. Generation after generation, from Marius to Theodosius, assailed the long line, bristling with palisades, castles and forts. At first the well-equipped and well-disciplined legions resisted the onslaught of the barbarians, but, with every century, the power of resistance of aging Rome became more and more exhausted, and the Teutonic race grew more daring, stronger and confident with every decade.

And the day came when Rome's arms, palsied with age, dropped sword and shield before the irresistible assault of the young, aggressive and expansive race. Burgundians, Suevi, Vandals, Alemanni and Franks, swept across the northern boundary in the early part of the fifth century and crushed the empire. The Burgundians and Alemanni took possession of eastern Gaul; the Franks extended their boundary to the Seine and the Loire; the Suevi founded a kingdom on the Iberian Peninsula, and the Vandals conquered the Roman provinces of northern Africa.

Other German tribes made an almost simultaneous attack on the empire from the northeast. The Visigoths crossed the Danube, invaded Italy, sacked Rome, raided southern Gaul and Spain, and there founded a powerful kingdom. Odoacer, with a mob of German mercenaries, destroyed the western empire, and on its ruins erected an ephemeral German kingdom in 476, A. D. The Ostrogoths, under Theoderic, the Great, defeated Odoacer in 493 A. D., and established a Gothic kingdom in Italy; Magnificent, proud and mighty Rome was no more. The empire crumbled to pieces under the blows of northern barbarians. Portugal, Spain, Gaul, Helvetia, Rhaetia, Noricum, Pannona, Italy, North Africa and the British Island, passed under the rule of the German conquerors. The proud, refined, cultured, effeminate and stagnant Latins became the subjects and, at the same time, the tutors of the rude and uncivilized, but young, energetic and progressive conquerors.

The warriors and colonists of the juvenile, virile and rising race were destined to rejuvenate the aged and degenerate Latin people. Out of the fusion of the two races, four new, homogeneous and progressive nations were to rise.

Rome suffered premature death on the threshold of national dotage. Without this conquest she might have lived through many centuries of decadence and short-lived revivals.

The Etruscans of prehistoric times had evolved a comparatively high civilization in Italy. In their old age and decline they were conquered by the younger, more progressive, but less civilized Aryans. The two races fused; the Etruscan was rejuvenated, and out of the fusion sprang a new, young, progressive and vigorous race the Roman people. This nation passed through the phases of childhood and youth during the political struggles between the nobles and the plebeians; stood at its zenith when democracy was triumphant, from Cato to Caesar, and when Virgil composed his epic, Livius wrote his history, Cicero delivered his orations and Caesar conquered a world; and, aided by wealth, luxury and extravagance, it passed into the rapid decline towards old age, after Augustus. When grown old and infirm, it, in its turn, was conquered, subjugated and rejuvenated by a younger people. Out of the amalgamation of the youthful Gothic and Langobard peoples with the aged and aging Roman sprang the modern Italian nation.

Rome had accomplished the task assigned to her, and played her important and interesting role in the drama of the human race. She did not achieve much in art, literature, science and philosophy; in these fields she copied after the superior genius of Hellas. But in war, law and constructive statesmanship, she was great, inventive and creative. The campaigns of her generals are yet studied by ambitious soldiers; her code of laws is still regarded as an inexhaustible fountain of justice and equity, by many nations; the development and decline of her civil government is studied with profound interest by aspiring statesmen; and her imperial government, even in its decay, served as a pattern for the organization of the Christian Church. Under normal and more favorable conditions she might have survived for centuries, but old age would have prevented her from rendering further service to humanity.

12. The Arabs.

Death and decomposition of nations was the almost universal rule around the Mediterranean when Rome fell. The stirring life with which Egyptians, Chaldeans, Assyrians, Persians, Semites, Greeks and Romans had successively filled that region for upward of three thousand years, had given way to the impotency of old age. Nations sat like hopeless sages on the ruins of the masterpieces of their youth and manhood. No man was able to prescribe an elixir to regenerate the world socially, politically, intellectually and morally. Even the Christian faith, which had become the state religion of Rome in the fourth century, and from which a general renaissance was expected, was unable to revivify the aging people. Deterioration continued unabated under Christian bishops and popes as well as under heathen governors and emperors. A change in deities and cults did not stop the general stagnation and retrogression.

Between the demise of the Graeco-Latin civilization, in the sixth century, and the thirteenth century, when a new civilization of the Teutonic people approached maturity, an interregnum of about seven hundred years, intervened. Aryan culture was without a standard bearer or champion during this long period. The Greeks and Romans had perished from the effect of old age, and the German nation, their heir apparent, was still a mere child. No Aryan people, full of the vigor of youth or manhood, to carry on the work, was in sight. The epoch between the cataclysm of the ancient Graeco-Roman civilization and the rise of the modern Teutonic is properly called the Middle Age.

Into this wide gap stepped the Semitic Arab, to form a connecting link between two Aryan civilizations. The violent storm of Teutonic migrations had swept away nearly every vestige of classic culture west of the Adriatic. But some germs of Hellenic civilization found their way to western Europe along a circuitous route via Damascus, Alexandria, Cairo and Cordova.

The Arabs were Semites of pure type. It is quite probable that, in early prehistoric times, a confluence of many heterogeneous ethnic elements, from Asia and Africa, took place on the Semitic peninsula. Complexion, facial outlines, curled hair, proper names, language, tradition, social institutions, racial affinity and the ancient civilization of Yemen, point to an early and extensive intercourse between Arabia and Africa, and a blending of the races. But, in the course of thousands of years, a fair degree of homogeneity was attained, and a new race appeared.

The Arabs, like all Semites, were representatives of humanity's childhood phase. Their agglutinative speech, patriarchal institutions, nomadic habits, tribal proclivities, their literature composed of songs and anecdotal narratives, and their religion, consisting of a shamanistic worship of a multitude of personal, familiar and tribal divinities, place them among the primitive races. The Semitic race stood at or near its zenith when Nineveh, Tyre, Sidon, Carthage, Damascus and Jerusalem flourished, or from about 2000 to 700 B. C. The Arab civilization was a Semitic aftermath; a belated crocus, blooming in June.

The early history of the Arabs is dark and obscure. They remained isolated for a long time, and were rarely in touch with their cultivated neighbors. Their progress was extremely slow. Their social and political institutions were pre-eminently patriarchal and tribal. National ties did not exist. Inter-tribal feuds prevailed. Popular poets sang in a crude manner of war, love, adventures, horses, nomadic and pastoral life. Each family, clan or tribe, worshiped its tutelary deity with shamanistic rites. The tribal spirit predominated and prevented political and religious centralization. Only Mecca, the Kaabah and the tribe dwelling there, enjoyed a peculiar prestige over other sacred places and tribes. Great fairs at Mecca, and pilgrimages to the Kaabah, united the Arabs to some extent. Ilah, the local Meccan deity, outranked all other tribal gods, and his cult was almost national.

A new, strong and progressive life began to pulsate through Arab society during the last centuries immediately preceding the Hegira. Poets became more abundant and began to sing of grander themes in an improved style. The old deities and old cults became distasteful and unsatisfactory. The folk-soul grew expansive and sought to widen the narrow limits of thought and action. The people were in a ferment. They were in a state of transition. They were preparing to leave behind them the long era of passive infancy and childhood, and to enter the phase of active, turbulent, passionate youth.

Then Mohammed appeared, and the age was ripe for him. He was born in 570 A. D., and when he died in 632 A. D., this zealous visionary had given a powerful impulse to a religious and political movement, which was to triumph in large parts of three continents. It is still a powerful factor in the affairs of the world.

Islam, the new religion, contains little that is original. It shines with reflected light. It is essentially Semitic, being an evolution of an Arab tribal deity and cult, but it is also a compound of parts of all the religions then known to the prophet. Mohammed was an eclectic, and what he borrowed he fused and blended with native beliefs, conceptions, tenets and rites, into a fairly consistent system.

The god of Islam is an absolute, autocratic ruler, such as the Semites were used to on earth. His will is irrevocable law, which makes his worshipers fatalists. His favorite abode was the mysterious Kaabah at Mecca. He sprang naturally from the mind, character and social conditions of the Arabs. He was a new edition of the ancient Semitic gods Chemosh, Baal, Astaroth, Moloch, Yahweh and others. He was a magnified and idealized Bedouin sheikh.

Islam is no monotheistic religion. A host of angels, archangels, devils, demons and saints, all endowed with divine powers, aid Allah in the government of the world. In pagan religions these imaginary beings are classed as divinities, but not so in the so-called monotheistic religions.

As man is, so are his gods. The Orient, and especially the Semitic tribes, knew only of a despotic ruler, wrapped in solitude, majesty and mystery, and -separated by a wide interval from his ministers, attendants and subjects. The Oriental's conception of the government of the universe is an enlarged copy of their terrestrial, political condition. The Moslem's heaven is the picture of an enchanting oasis which the fata morgana of the desert casts against the azure vault of heaven.

Patriotism, race instinct and religious fervor were fused into one all-pervading sentiment by the prophet. State and church were made one and inseparable. The Arab had not yet emerged from that primitive phase, when ruler, judge and priest were still combined in one person.

The religion of the Prophet spread with marvellous rapidity. His able successors, especially the Califs Omar (634-644), Othman (644-655), and El Walid (705-715 A. D.), conquered Persia, Armenia, Mesopotamia, Asia Minor, Egypt and northern Africa; and carried the triumphant crescent into India, Turkestan and Spain. It was a phenomenal success.

As the agave of the desert, the Bedouin's emblem, continues in a quiescent state for years, and then, all of a sudden, shoots forth a tall stem with a panicle of beautiful flowers, and perishes, so the Arab people lay inert and dormant for centuries, and then burst forth precipitately and violently, to fill the world with their fame as prophets, conquerors, rulers, poets and scientists, and subsided as quickly after a brief age of glory.

The Arabs undoubtedly possessed an unusual aptitude for war and government, but their extraordinary career was largely due to the favor of unusual circumstances. They were a youthful, optimistic, enthusiastic and energetic people, and they encountered nations in their dotage, which collapsed at the first blow. And then, from the Atlantic to Central Asia, through northern Africa and southwestern Asia, they met with tribes and nations akin to them. Blood will always tell. The Arab's ideas, ideals and aspirations were readily accepted by their Semitic, Hamitic and Turanian kindred. But, as a rule, the Islamitic conquest halted at the boundary of the Aryan race, and when the impetus of the assault had carried the Arab across the ethnic border, he soon began to recede. Race and religion are conterminous.

The Arab's whole mind, talent and energy were concentrated on war and conquest during the first century after the Prophet's death. All other intellectual labor was neglected.

The eighth century of the Christian era witnessed the birth of Arab civilization; the eleventh and twelfth saw its culmination; and the thirteenth the beginning of the decline.

And, strange to observe, Arab civilization never flourished in Arabia proper. Not on the Semitic peninsula, but at the periphery of the Islamitic world, at Basra, Kufa and Bagdad in the East, and at Sevilla and Cordova in the West, rose those great centers of Moslem poetry, art, learning and political power. Neither Mecca nor Medina became a focus of culture.

An Arab civilization, indigenous to the soil and of a distinctive national or racial character, was never evolved. What is called Arab culture is the joint product of the conquering Arabs and their subjects. The peculiar mission of this youthful and vigorous people was to fuse with and to rejuvenate aged and decadent nations. Its fresh young blood was to revivify the deteriorated Persians at Bagdad; the sluggish Syrians at Damascus; the fossilized Egyptians at Cairo; and the degenerate Iberians and Goths at Cordova.

Arab civilization ran in two separate and distinct channels. One was Perso-Arabic and the other Gothic-Arabic in character, Bagdad and Cordova became the great centers of light, life and intellectual activity. Damascus, Cairo, Basra and Kufa, were only of secondary importance.

The Arab conquerors at first formed a leading and governing class in the subjugated countries. They were prohibited from the acquisition of land, and subsisted on taxes and contributions. They were soldiers who garrisoned the fortresses, and statesmen and politicians who filled all the civil offices.

Consequently, as Arabia contained only about five millions of inhabitants, and as the conquered territory was of enormous extent, the peninsula was drained of its best blood, and yet only a thin crust of warriors and administrative officers covered the annexed provinces. The Arabs were in a decisive minority in all the conquered territory, but they constituted the dominant, active class, and gave form and color to the intellectual life at Bagdad, Cordova, Granada and Damascus. Their bold, aggressive and progressive juvenile spirit formed the leaven and ferment in the inert mass of humanity which at that time filled Mesopotamia, Asia Minor, northern Africa and the Iberian peninsula.

These class distinctions, however, were only transitory. Conquerors and conquered soon merged. The numerically weak Arabs were soon absorbed and assimilated by the mass of the natives.

Arab blood regenerated the aged populations of Iran and of the valleys of the Euphrates and Tigris, and gave them a new lease of life. Basra, Kufa and Bagdad loomed up as foci of light and intellectual activity. But the Arab civilization of the East was strongly tinctured by Iranian ideas and ideals. The Persians accepted Islam only in a modified form. The schism between the orthodox Semitic Sunnites and the heterodox Iranian Shiites can be traced to ethnical causes. Ideas and ideals, on the march, be they social, political, artistic or religious, always respect ethnic boundaries.

The Persian nation, although aged and degenerate, stood on a higher level of development than the robust, energetic and juvenile Arab. The Arab was still rooted in the primitive patriarchism or tribalism; but the Persian had risen, tentatively at least, to nationalism and kingship. The Persian mind was prone to mysticism and speculation; the Arab thought was simple, clear and practical.

Fusion of the two races was fairly complete in the eighth century. A new homogeneous people had arisen. Its intellectual life was essentially Arabic, modified by Iranian influence.

The brilliant era of Perso-Arabian civilization began with Hisham (724-743 A. D.). Magnificent mosques were erected in a new style of architecture, originally Byzantine, but reformed to suit Arab taste and ideals. Men of talent and genius began to occupy themselves with commentaries on the Koran, theological disputes, collection of legends and traditions; with law, history and geography.

This illustrious epoch culminated during the reigns of the Califs Mansur (754-775), Harun al Rashid (786809), and Maamun (813-833 A. D.).

Prosperity prevailed in the land throughout the reigns of these famous Califs. Education and intellectual life were fostered, schools and libraries were established, Greek literature and science were introduced, Hindu poetry and tales were translated, the old folk-songs gave way before more refined and artistic verse, and much meritorious work in all the fields of human endeavor rose to the surface. A long line of brilliant poets, artists, savants, theologians and historians illuminated Bagdad and the Moslem Orient during the eighth, ninth and tenth centuries.

Arab influence had spent its force in Iran by the middle of the tenth century. The Iranian element had absorbed and assimilated the Arabian. The two races changed positions. The Iranian character was in the ascendant and the Semitic on the wane. Firdusi (940-1020 A. D.), the greatest and most representative Persian poet, was Iranian or Aryan in sentiment, boldness of conception, mode of thought and manner of expression.

Then came the inevitable decline. The descent was as rapid as the ascent had been. The new Perso-Arabic nation had passed through the phase of youth and manhood into old age within five centuries. The revival had been of short duration. Stagnation, fossilization, impotency, apathy and pessimism again assumed permanent control of Iran. The Arab had only temporarily suspended the downward course to the decrepitude of old age. Iran sank deeper and deeper into its dotage.

The Arab course of life in the West was analogous to that in the East. The Iberians and Goths of Spain were in a condition of complete degeneracy, when Tarik crossed the Strait of Gibraltar in 711 A. D. and overthrew the deteriorated Gothic chivalry in the sanguinary battle of Xeres de la Frontera.

The Goths of Spain had lost their wonted warlike spirit. Two centuries of the possession of suddenly acquired wealth, of unrestrained power, and of intimate contact with an effete and luxurious people, had transformed the brave, sturdy and hardy Gothic chiefs into a pleasure-loving, corrupt and effeminate feudal nobility. A narrow-minded, ambitious, arrogant and ignorant priesthood ruled kings and lords; and the common people Iberians, Latins and Goths, were reduced to poverty and servitude.

The much-oppressed classes looked upon the invaders as their liberators. The democratic spirit of social and political equality, which pervaded Islam, and animated its defenders, secured a ready submission of the persecuted and downtrodden.

The Moslem overran Spain, with the exception of the Basque provinces, and southwestern Gaul, in a very few years. An Arab government was instituted, and Arab garrisons were distributed throughout the land. The conquerors collected the revenues and ran the administration. Many Gothic lords, in order to hold their estates, acquiesced in the new order of things. The tolerant Arabs permitted the common people to think, speak, believe and act with much more freedom than they had been accustomed to under Gothic knight or Latin prelate.

A medley of very heterogeneous elements filled the peninsula. Arab soldiers and administrative officers, Berber warriors and colonists, Moorish marabuts, Gothic nobles and their retainers, Latin priests and savants, and underneath all, the thick substratum of native serfs, met in beautiful Spain, all, willingly or unwillingly, working for fusion and homogeneity.

Islam made rapid and extensive inroads into Spanish society. It came with the prestige of unparalleled success; it represented a higher civilization than the Christians of the Occident could boast; and it offered greater liberty and better material advantages than either Gothic princes or Roman bishops had granted. Vast masses turned Moslem. Islam was very popular in Spain immediately after the conquest. Even the Christians, who adhered to their faith, adopted the language, laws, customs and modes of thought of the Arabs. If the Arabs had provided for a strong and continuous immigration from Arabia and the Islamitic Orient, the Koran would never have been dislodged from the land beyond the Pyrenees.

The fusion of these various elements created much friction and intellectual activity. A new and young people sprang from the amalgamation, to enter upon a short but glorious life. The aged Iberian and Latin race was rejuvenated by the infusion of young Arab blood. The civilization which shed such a brilliant light on Spain from the eighth to the fifteenth century, was the joint product of Arabs, Goths, Iberians and Latins; of Moslem, Christians and Jews. But it was inaugurated and fostered by Arab emirs, sustained and directed by Arab scholars, and bore the impress of Arab genius.

The illustrious era of uncommon intellectual activity in Arabic Spain began with Abderahman, emir of Cordova (755-788 A. D.). The Arab civilization advanced with rapid strides, from generation to generation, until it reached the point of highest culmination during the reigns of Abdirahman III (929-961), El Hakam II (961-976), and Hisham II (976-1013 A. D.).

Arab poets, philosophers, historians and scientists adorned this age. The poets Said Ibn Deshudi, Jackja Ibn Hackam, Achmed Ibn Abd-Rabbih, and Said Ibn Mundir, the historians Mohammed Ibn Omar, Achmed Er Rasi, and his son Issa, and the philosopher Ibn Massara, were ornaments of their time. Greek authors were translated; mathematics, geography, history and medicine, received the fullest attention; commerce and industry were patronized; education was promoted to an extent that almost every person in Andalusia could read and write; and Cordova, the residence of the emirs, with its palaces and libraries, and its university attended by thousands of students, became the most celebrated seat of learning of that age.

Decline set in immediately after Hisham II and the great minister Almansor. The Arab element, not being reinforced by a strong immigration from home, weakened gradually; the numerically stronger, but intellectually and morally weaker Berber wrung the scepter from the nobler Arab; and the Gothic Christians of the northern kingdoms, having recovered their old time virtue, vigor and courage in the school of adversity, began aggressive operations against the Moslem.

A brief revival, at the close of the twelfth century, interrupted the downward course. Ibn Tofeil, Ibn Roshd (Averroes), Maimonides, Ibn Soehr, Ibn Dshobeir and others, made that generation illustrious. Order was restored and the Moslems were once more united (1230 A. D.). But they could not withstand the unceasing, vigorous assaults of the now hopeful and aggressive Christians. City after city, province after province, was snatched from the nerveless grasp of the aging Arab race, until only the emirate of Granada remained under the control of Islam.

This rich and charming province was the last asylum of the Arabs in Spain. Here all the Moslem fugitives from the other provinces found a temporary refuge. Here they made their last, desperate stand and defended it against the superior forces of the Christians for two and a half centuries.

Once more the light of Arab civilization flashed up. The magnificent Alhambra was built. Ibn Chaldoun (1332-1408 A. D.), and Ibn Chatib, renowned poeti and historians, the evening stars of Islamitic Spain, approached the horizon. Then came Ferdinand, and Isabella, the Catholic, and Boabdil, the unfortunate, and Arabian culture of the West vanished in gloomy night.

In the course of about a thousand years the Arab people passed through the phases of youth and manhood into old age. If they had not suffered a premature death in the West at the hands of the Christian Spaniards, and in the East by the invasions of fierce Tartars and Mongols, they might have continued for many centuries on the downward slope of life to the imbecility and petrifaction of extreme old age. But their career was cut short in the provinces where they had evolved a high civilization. This civilization shone mainly in borrowed or reflected light. It is not noted for much originality, invention or creative power. The Arab's religious conceptions were largely taken from Judaism, Christianity, Zoroastrianism and Hinduism; his science was imported from Hellas; and his literature remained stationary at the stage of the song, the epigrammatic proverb and the anecdotal tale; rarely climbing to the higher level of the epic and the drama. His most meritorious achievement is the preservation and transmission of Greek culture.

Two civilizations, each quite distinct from the other, the one mainly Semitic, the other chiefly Aryan, were evolved on the Iberian peninsula, and advanced on parallel lines for centuries, until that of the Arabs was ended abruptly by Ferdinand and Isabella. Of the Gothic or true Spanish culture we shall treat in a subsequent chapter.

The Arabs of their native peninsula never created a civilization of any significance. But there, too, the decay of old age became manifest simultaneously with that of Bagdad, Cordova and Granada. They have been on the descent ever since. Arabia is in a state of petrifaction. But there is a good prospect that this race will some day be rejuvenated by a fusion with young, vigorous, progressive and rising people from Africa.

America, so far, has received but few immigrants from Arabia. But news of our splendid opportunities for every man has at last penetrated to the inhabitants of Asia Minor, and even to the Bedouin of the desert. A tiny but swelling streamlet of these denizens of Semitic Asia has found its way to our shores; and if we do not close our gates in time, this undesirable and improgressive element may become a factor for evil in the formation of our nation.

13. The Teutons.

The Romans and Greeks yet held the front and center of the world's stage, when suddenly, in the year 115 B. C, with clangor of arms, blowing of horns and wild war shouts, a new race entered upon the stage and made its impressive debut.

The Cimbri and Teutons, veritable nations in arms, swept across the northern border of the Latin republic and destroyed several consular armies. Rome was panic-stricken. Veteran legions, commanded by the ablest generals, were hastened to the front. Superior Roman equipment, discipline and generalship overcame rude, savage force and courage, and the invading host was annihilated. Rome triumphed, but not for long. Forty years subsequently Caesar met the same people in serious combat, and again defeated them; but in A. D. 9 Arminius or Hermann, a German chieftain, destroyed the almost invincible legions under Varus, in the defiles of the Teutoburg Forest. The Roman advance northward was checked permanently. The legions halted at the boundary of the Rhine and the Danube. After much desultory fighting along this border, during the next four centuries, the German tribes rushed irresistibly across the long frontier and demolished the Latin empire.

The Graeco-Latin actors stepped back, the Teutons advanced to the front of the stage, and, with the exception of the interesting Arab interlude, monopolized and held the world's attention down to the present.

These fierce invaders, who shook Rome to its foundation even when it stood at its zenith, and in whom the Latins instinctively recognized their most formidable adversaries, were Aryans of pure type. Their tall forms, blonde hair, blue eyes and fair complexion, assigned them a unique place among the races on earth.

The cradle of this race stood on the shores of the Baltic and German Ocean.

To designate this race as Aryan or Teutonic is practically the same, By both terms we mean the same thing. Hindus, Iranians, Armenians, Greeks, Romans, Neo-Latins, Germans, Anglo-Saxons, and, partly, Celts and Slavs, had a common origin. Languages, myths, traditions, social institutions, physical, mental and moral traits, common to all, betray kinship and racial affinity. Contrasts between the different branches are due to long separation and merger with other races. At intervals, in prehistoric and historic ages, Aryan offshoots were transplanted to other regions. This was the case with Goths, Burgundians, Suevi, Vandals, Alemanni, Franks, Langobards and Anglo-Saxons, in historic times, and we may safely assume that Hindus, Iranians, Hellenes and Latins experienced a similar fate in prehistoric ages.

These successive migrations formed different groups. We can readily distinguish a Hindu-Iranian, a Graeco-Latin, a Neo-Latin and a Teutonic or Germanic subdivision of the Aryan race. The terms, "Teutonic" and "Germanic" are confusing. By either we mean to designate the group which includes Germans, Anglo-Saxons, Scandinavians and Dutch; but "Germanic" is limited by many writers to the Germans only. I have chosen, therefore, the term "Teutonic" instead of "Germanic" in this work.

For the purposes of this book I have divided the Aryan race into the following groups or subdivisions:

1. Indo-Iranian group
2. Graeco-Roman group
3. Neo-Latin group, including Italians, Spaniards, Portuguese and French.
4. Teutonic group, consisting of Anglo-Saxons, Germans, Scandinavians and Dutch.
5. Slavic group, comprising western Russians, western and southern Slavs.
6. Celts of Ireland, Wales, Scotland and Bretagne.

The Neo-Latin group might also be called the semi-Teutonic, as it sprang from the infusion of young Teutonic blood into the veins of the Latin race. The Gothic, Vandal, Suevic, Alemannic, Burgundian and Prankish invaders gave new life to the aged Latin race, and in conjunction with it formed the new nations of the group.

The life of nations, as that of the celestial bodies, in its duration, is in proportion to the mass. The smaller planets and satellites pass through all the phases of life or existence at a much quicker tempo than the larger central bodies. So it was with the different nations of the Aryan race. Hindus, Iranians, Greeks, Romans and Neo-Latins, being comparatively small bodies, passed through all the stages of national life faster than the greater central mass, from which they were successively detached. Their pace of development was also accelerated by fusion with aged ethnic elements.

Of the early infancy of the Teutonic race we know very little. It had already made considerable progress when it first appeared. Its speech had outgrown the phase of monosyllabic and agglutinative languages; the clan and tribe were the predominant social and political units; and the tribal deities had already attained a certain hegemony over the tutelary gods of individuals and families.

The ancient Teutons, fifteen hundred years or more before the beginning of the Christian era, worked in bronze and iron, carried on agriculture and stock raising, spun and wove, had invented the runic writing, and in popular songs celebrated the adventures of gods and heroes.

An ethnographical survey of Europe at that time would have given the following result: In the northwest, on the shores of the Baltic and the North Sea, dwelt the tall and fair race of the Teutons. In the south, along the coast of the Mediterranean, resided the Iberians, Ligurians, Etruscans, Pelasgians and Illyrians, probably all kindred people, who had created a civilization of their own, but had entered upon the decline. They were a swarthy race, of short stature and more highly civilized than the more backward Teutons. The steppes and woods of eastern Europe were filled with Mongols and Tartars, who, as a race, had crossed their meridian before that time, and who stood and remained on a low level of culture.

A wide zone, occupied by mongrel tribes, separated the blond Teuton of the North from the dark-skinned native of the South. The Celtic race was in the process of formation in this territory. If left to a normal evolution, the natural fusion of the border clans and tribes would have resulted in a great Celtic race, extending through central Europe, from Ireland to the Balkan. When the gigantic, untutored and savage Teuton came in contact with his small, swarthy neighbors of superior education and culture, he adopted the latter's language, myths, legends, religion and manners. The Mediterranean race became the tutor of the Teuton. All the ancient Teutonic epics, myths and legends, speak of the struggles between the rude, gigantic and ignorant Teutons, on the one side, and the dark, dwarfish, intellectual, intelligent, skillful, mining, metal-working race to the south of them, on the other.

It is quite probable that in prehistoric times the pressure of this superior race upon the Teutons caused the early migrations of Hindus, Iranians, Greeks and Romans to the eastward.

The Celtic people never attained homogeneity. Ancient Greek and Latin authors speak of tall and fair, and of short and swarthy Celts. The race was annihilated and suffered a premature death, in the wars between the Latins and the Teutons.

The condition in the East was analogous. There, too, a broad belt was inhabited by the clans and tribes of mixed Teutonic and Mongol ancestry. These in the course of time formed the great Slavic race. The old German epics also speak of the fierce combats between the fair Teutons and the dull, uncouth and gigantic natives of the East.

The borders naturally vibrated to and fro, but Rhine, Danube and Vistula, may be regarded as the fairly permanent southern and eastern boundaries of the Teutonic race, two thousand years ago.

The political and religious evolution of the Teutons had reached the tribal stage, verging towards the national. Clans and tribes rose, flourished and perished, and with them their tutelary deities.

The Teutonic race was in its infancy at the time of Caesar. Its fertile, vivid and luxuriant imagination, its grand epics, its fanciful myths, its picturesque speech, its proneness to symbols, its propensity for war and games, its predisposition to exaggeration, its impulsiveness, its fickleness, its love of adventure and its lack of dignity, self-control and perseverance, indicate that it was still in the phase of early childhood.

The Teutons received their first impulse on the road of progress from their dwarfish, swarthy, southern neighbors. The later contact with the civilized Romans caused a more rapid development.

Caesar and his immediate successors established Latin colonies north of the Rhine. A hundred thousand legionaries, accompanied by their families, by their sutlers, mechanics, contractors and laborers, and by traders and colonists, guarded the boundary of the Rhine and the Danube. Roman merchants introduced Latin goods and ideas in the interior of Germany. Centers of commerce, industry, wealth and intellectual life grew up around the Roman camps. German youths enlisted in the legions, or found employment in the homes, shops and plantations of the Romans, and acquired the manners and culture of their masters. There was a continuous and extensive intermingling of German, Latin and Celtic elements in the border lands during the first five centuries after Caesar; and the effect of this amalgamation crops out continuously in the subsequent political and religious history of Germany.

A radical internal change occurred at that period. It was a transition from the phase of childhood to that of early youth; from tribal to national conditions. The political and religious trend was toward centralization into larger organizations. Clan united with clan, tribe coalesced with tribe into larger confederacies under powerful chieftains. Incipient, genuine kingship appeared. Caesar and Tacitus speak only of tribes and chiefs, but hereditary kings and ephemeral kingdoms are mentioned already in the fourth and fifth centuries.

The local and tribal myths, legends and fables of gods and deified heroes coalesced also into more systematic mythologies of larger scope. Some tribal deities rose in popularity and importance, and others sank into insignificance, or were entirely eliminated from the Teutonic pantheon, in accord with the fate of their worshipers, Wotan, Frigga, Freya, Froh, Thor, Balder, Braga, Loki, Iduna, Heimdal and Widar, originally nothing but local divinities and tutelary gods of families, clans and tribes, grew to be the gods of leagues and larger provinces. Ancient places of worship, particularly awe-inspiring, such as the thunder-riven, fog-encompassed brow of the Brocken, or the dark, solemn groves of the rocky island of Ruegen, became centers of cults of almost national scope and celebrity.

Our knowledge of ancient Teutonic mythology is but fragmentary. We have only the ancient epics as a source of information, and these are merely local and tribal, and do not furnish us with a picture of the religious conceptions, rites and practices of the whole race. They are merely conglomerates, in which lie imbedded the myths, legends and sagas, of many ages and various localities. As the genesis and evolution of the deities runs parallel to the social and political development of man, clans and tribes, under normal conditions of growth, would have coalesced into an organically united nation with a national head, and out of the struggle for supremacy and existence between the familiar and tribal gods, Wotan, Thor, Balder or some other leading divinity would have risen as the supreme national god, with the host of fairies, elves, Valkyries, kobolds and others, attending his court as vassals, messengers and servants. And all these strictly anthropomorphic deities would have been idealized Teutons. They would have thought, felt and acted like the men who created them.

The horizon of the local bards also widened. They collected the scattered songs, celebrating the heroic deeds of local gods, demi-gods and heroes, and transformed them into grand national epics. The epics of Gudrun, Beowulf, the Eclda, and others, which promised grander achievements under normal development, originated in this age.

The Teutonic race at this time passed from childhood into youth. Under continued normal conditions it would soon have evolved a national kingship, a national religion and cult with Wotan or some other tribal god as the supreme deity, and a national literature beginning with a number of epics, grand in thought, form and expression.

Then came a cataclysm which suspended and stunted growth for centuries. A terrific tornado, uprooting everything in its path, swept down from the plains of Asia, struck the German frontier, hurled the eastern tribes to the Euxine and the Mediterranean, and forced the western tribes across the North Sea to the British isles. Everything was in turmoil and commotion from the Vistula to the Rhine and from the Baltic to the Alps.

The cause of this great migration of whole tribes or nations is as yet unknown. It was not voluntary. It is against all reason and experience to suppose that the strong tribes of the Goths, Burgundians, Vandals, Suevi, Langobards and others, should voluntarily and in a reckless and adventurous spirit leave their cherished homes on the Oder and the Vistula, and fight their way through a hostile territory in search for another place of settlement.

The real cause must be sought for in events of the Far East. We know from Chinese chronicles that during the last two centuries before our era, a severe contest raged between the Celestial Empire and the savage, nomadic Mongol horde of the Hiung-nu or Huns. These Hiung-nu, after suffering disastrous defeat, were driven to the west. Carrying everything with them, the Huns pressed on to the Caspian, to the Volga, to the Theiss and eventually to the Rhine and the Loire. A general westward movement, gathering force and momentum with every step, was inaugurated. The impulse was communicated from tribe to tribe, and from nation to nation. The first gust of the cyclone struck the German tribes of the Vistula and Oder. They gave way before the irresistible impact and, as the western tribes could not yield, were driven southward towards the Euxine, the Danube and the Rhine. The territory vacated by the Goths, Vandals, Suevi, Burgundians and Langobards was occupied by the victorious Mongols, Tartars and Slavs.

An entirely new order of things prevailed in Europe when the storm of the Migrations had subsided. Europe had been radically revolutionized geographically and ethnographically. The Asiatic invaders had pushed their frontiers into the heart of Germany and up the Danube to the vicinity of Vienna; the Roman empire was annihilated and with it classical culture; and among the ruins, youthful, vigorous and progressive Teutonic tribes were laying the foundations of new empires, and a new civilization which was to bear the stamp of Teutonic genius.

True, the Franks, Burgundians, Goths, Suevi, Alemanni, Heruli, Gepidae and Langobards were gradually absorbed and assimilated by the numerically stronger subdued people; true, they lost their national and racial identity and, in a modified form, adopted the language, religion, customs and manners of the conquered; but they rejuvenated the aged Latin race. That race had sunk into dotage and was incapable of regeneration and reform through its own exertions. The infusion of young, strong and progressive Teutonic blood revivified and reinvigorated the decomposing, moribund organism. Out of the fusion of the youthful Teutonic element with the aged Latin, Celtic and Iberian, rose the new, young, vigorous and progressive nations of Italy, France and Spain.

The civilization which these new nations created on the Tiber, the Seine and the Ebro was essentially Teutonic in spirit, form and character. The Teutonic invaders furnished the leaven, the active, creative and positive force, and the progressive spirit, for the new-born political organisms of the South. The passive and decadent Latins, Celts and Iberians could only serve as modifying factors in the formation of national types and character. Indeed, the elite of intelligence and of society in these countries was typically Teutonic for a long time after the Migrations.

Bearing in mind these facts, we may say that all the nations of western, southern and northern Europe Italians, French, Spanish, Portuguese, British,

Dutch, Germans and Scandinavians have a common origin, and also a common history anterior to the great Migrations.

The strongly manifest affinity and family resemblance between the intellectual and moral achievements of the Teutons of the North and the semi-Teutons of the South is due to the fact of actual blood relation. All the great intellectual and moral movements of Europe since the Migrations, the adoption of Christianity, feudalism, kingship, epic poetry, scholasticism, municipal democracy, crusades, knighthood, the poetry of chivalry, religious art, monachism, decay of chivalry, rise of money power in the cities, humanism, renaissance, reformation, baroque, puritanism, rococo, republicanism, classicism, romanticism, materialism, realism and decadence affected them all almost simultaneously and in a similar manner.

Modern European civilization is the joint product of the Italians, French, Spaniards, Britons, Germans, Dutch and Scandinavians. None of these nations is historically isolated. Each is an integral part of a whole. All of them spent their infancy together at the old Teutonic home on the Baltic and the German Ocean. Each one of them began a separate and independent life immediately after the great Migrations. All of them passed through the phase of childhood, youth and manhood almost synchronously; and the work of their poets, artists, philosophers, statesmen, theologians and scientists, proclaim race affinity.

14. The Italians.

The Teutonic blood which, to a greater or less extent, courses through the veins of all European nations, unites them organically. They, with their colonies, form a distinct and separate group.

But we cannot select any one of them as a representative of all. For, notwithstanding the strong racial traits common to all, the climate, environment and a great variety in the kind and degree of admixture of other ethnic elements, wrought a notable differentiation in type and character.

The rapidity of development of these different nations was proportionate to the mass and to the amount of aged ethnic material absorbed and assimilated by the Teutons at home or abroad.

The substratum of the population of Italy, Spain and France is Latin, Iberian and Celtic. The Teutonic blood acted mainly as a leavening or revivifying principle. The evolution of the national life of the Italians, Spaniards, and French was hastened by the amalgamation of youthful Teutonic with aged Celtic-Latin-Iberian elements. The neo-Latin nations, for this reason, passed through the phases of childhood and youth, and reached manhood and decline some generations or centuries earlier than the Teutons of purer descent.

Like a row of brothers advancing to maturity one after the other, so did the Italians, Spaniards, French, Anglo-Saxons and Germans successively reach the zenith of their national lives.

The neo-Latin nations, having absorbed and assimilated a large percentage of the old Latin, Celtic and Iberian element, advanced with accelerated speed and became the leaders and guides in the European family of nations. They were the older brothers and sisters.

Italy formed the vanguard.

We have seen the old Roman Empire collapse under the assault of Odoacer in 476 A. D. He founded an ephemeral German kingdom on the ruins of the empire, Theoderic the Great demolished this kingdom thirteen years later, and in its stead formed an Ostrogothic kingdom. He was a wise, energetic and humane ruler. Roman law, administration and customs were retained. The officers of the army were Goths, but Romans retained all the higher places in the judiciary and in the civil administration. The proud but rude and ignorant conquerors submitted willingly to the superior intelligence and refinement of the effeminate and decadent but cultured natives.

The Gothic kingdom was of short duration. The Eastern Empire, with its capital at Constantinople, experienced a brief revival at that time, during the reign of Justinian. His famous generals, Belisarius and Narses, vanquished the Goths, and exarchs were sent to govern Italy.

The Gothic revival was brief. Decline and decadence soon set in again. The Langobards or Lombards, a German tribe or nation, originally from the lower Elbe, invaded Italy in 568 A. D., conquered the north and center of the peninsula, drove out the exarchs, and established a Teutonic kingdom on a more enduring base than either Heruli or Goths had been able to accomplish.

The Langobards divided the land in accordance with the then prevalent feudal system, creating a feudal, Teutonic nobility and a class of disfranchised serfs. The cities were deprived of their ancient rights and privileges. The old Roman constitution was blended with the principles of Teutonic feudalism. The classic Latin deteriorated into a vulgar, rustic dialect; culture was on the wane; the heretical invaders adopted the orthodox faith; and slowly yielded to the more numerous, more intelligent, refined and accomplished natives in speech, religion, mode of thought and manner of living.

The change wrought was radical. Old Rome had disappeared forever. Its social and political decline had really begun at the time of the Gracchi, when democracy was struck down; but the decadence became general and more pronounced immediately after Caesar and Augustus. Rome saw before it only the impotency and decrepitude of old age and final extinction. Then came the juvenile Heruli, Goths and Langobards and rejuvenated the aged native people. Out of this fusion of young and old ethnic elements sprang a new nation, which, in obedience to the law of the parallelogram of forces, was neither young nor old, neither Teutonic nor Latin in type or character, but a combination of both.

The fusion of the two people took its natural and normal course, and a new, homogeneous nation arose in the course of the first five centuries after the invasion by the Germans. This new nation did not begin its life at the stage of childhood but of youth. Due to the admixture of old Latin with young Teutonic blood in its arteries, it passed with quickened pace through the stage of infancy. In consequence, it would cross its meridian a century or more in advance of the German nation.

We know very little of the relative value of the various factors that entered into the formation of the new Italian nation. The country was very populous under the first emperors, but incessant external and internal wars, deportations, emigrations, colonization of provinces, wholesale executions, famines, epidemics, luxury, extravagance, vice and corruption, had decimated the population repeatedly.

Of the numerical strength of the Heruli, Goths and Langobards, we know scarcely anything beyond the facts, that they were powerful enough to destroy the empire; that Theoderic could mobilize an army of 200,000 warriors, and that the Langobards appropriated one-third of the land for their own use.

The Latins outnumbered the Teutons greatly and furnished the substratum of the new nation. The Teutons formed the military and ruling class, and supplied the active, vital, moral and intellectual force in the formation of the new national life and character, and in the evolution of a new civilization on the banks of the Tiber, the Arno and the Po. The inert, passive mass of the Latins could only act as a modifying influence.

The Teutonic invaders settled mainly in the northern provinces. The percentage of young, virile Teutonic blood diminished steadily from the Alps southward. The Teutonic element preponderated in the valley of the Po, and even gave that region a German name. A strain of Teutonic blood is scarcely perceptible in the southern provinces of Campania, Apulia and Calabria.

This unequal distribution of the Teutonic element was a determining influence in Italian history. In the north, where the Teutonic element was strong, progress and intellectual activity prevailed; in the south, where it was weak, stagnation and retrogression was the rule. The new life of the nation was essentially Teutonic. A great majority of the men who made Italy famous, from Lan franc to Marconi, came from the regions where Goths, Langobards and Heruli had settled in large numbers. The elite of society and intelligence was typically Teutonic for centuries after the conquest; and the features of madonnas, angels, saints, heroes and heroines, the embodied ideals of painters and sculptors, bore, as a rule, the true stamp of the Teutonic race.

The period between the Lombard conquest in the year 568 A. D. and the close of the tenth century was the formative age of the new Italian nation was the phase of childhood, and is wrapped in darkness. Through the dim twilight we discern nothing but a seething, boiling, fermenting mass of humanity; nothing but internecine strifes, friction, anarchy, disorder, riot, turmoil and devastation the concomitants of fusion and the companions of a nation's childhood.

A nascent, homogeneous Italian nation emerged from this chaos in the tenth century. Fusion was nearly complete; order was to some extent restored; the turbulent, bellicose, feudal chieftains quieted down; democratic cities grew in importance, and gradually became the nuclei of culture, wealth and power. Unfortunately for the normal development of the nation, at the very time of its first awakening to the consciousness of youthful vigor, courage and aspirations, the German emperor Otho I crossed the Alps and made Italy a German dependency.

Then ensued the long, picturesque, triangular struggle for supremacy between the German emperors, the popes and the powerful city-republics. It was the adolescence, the romantic and heroic age, the phase of early youth of the Italian nation. It brought forth Lanfranc, Hildebrand, Peter Lombardus, Anselm, Francis d'Assisi, Aquinas and Innocent III all great churchmen, scholastics and statesmen.

This era witnessed the wild, insane enthusiasm of the crusades; the inauguration of scholasticism, a sort of juvenile sport of theologians; the rise of romantic chivalry; the birth of a new art; the beginning of a new literature in the lyric songs of the troubadours, and the phenomenal growth of the city-republics, Venice, Milan, Genoa, Pisa, Florence, Naples and others. This heroic age found its Homer in Dante.

The general unrest, the incessant fermentation, the exuberant fancy of poets, artists and scholastics, the religious fervor and enthusiasm, the rapid alternations of folly with sound judgment, of grand outbursts of genius with complete mental prostration, and of daring enterprise with helpless despondency, the vacillation in friendship and enmity, the curiosity, the inquisitiveness, the uncommon desire to acquire knowledge, and the universal fondness of the heroic, the symbolic, the gay, the bright and picturesque in state and church, in language, dress, manners, literature, art, rites and ceremonials, designate this era as the phase of early youth in the life of the Italian nation.

Dante (1194-1251), Petrarch (1304-1374), Boccaccio (1313-1375), and Cola di Rienzi (b. 1313 A. D.), were the true representatives of their nation's youth.

A short pause of inactivity and recreation succeeded the strenuous and exciting life of youth. Princes, nobles and cities needed rest after the exhausting feuds. Pestilence and famine decimated the people. Scholastic learning grew weak, nerveless and unpopular. The grand epics of the classics dwindled to the mediocre sonnets, canzonets and anecdotal tales of pigmean epigoni.

The decadence was only apparent and ephemeral. It was an era of transition from youth to early manhood. Talent and genius sought other channels of activity than epic poetry, romantic knighthood, religious crazes and speculative scholasticism. Cool, calculating reason began to push aside the wild enthusiasm and vivid imagination of youth. The center of gravity of intellectual life shifted from the feudal castle to the city hall and the market place. Money became a great factor. Opulent merchant princes and plebeian leaders superseded the poets, theologians and feudal lords of the preceding age. The democratic principle gained ground. The intellectual life of the nation began to be concentrated in the city-republics.

It was a preparatory era; an era for the collecting, husbanding and disciplining of forces for coming events. There was a dearth of great poets, artists, scholars and statesmen, in Italy, from 1350 to 1450 A. D.; but the national intellect was not idle. Great men, as a rule, are the fruitage of the quiet, silent, unostentatious labor of the preceding generations. One generation sows, and the next harvests. The "golden age" of the 16th century would have been impossible in Italy, without the storage and training of the physical, intellectual and moral forces of the preceding century.

Italy produced masterpieces in art, poetry and scholastic learning, during the Middle Ages, but its political development was stunted. It did not rise above the tribal stage. Every attempt to create a nation failed. A proud, independent, jealous and unyielding spirit ruled in palace, castle and city hall. No ducal or royal dynasty was able to gain the ascendancy over all, and form a nation. The centrifugal forces were greater than the centripetal. Venice, Genoa, Milan, Florence, Naples, Rome and other cities represented so many ganglia, but the organism lacked an all-controlling nerve center. Nationalism did not germinate in that period, and patriotism confined itself to city and castle.

The epoch of transition, rest and preparation ended about the middle of the fifteenth century. The glorious age of Italian manhood dawned. Heralded by the humanists, the restorers of classical learning, and the discoverers of unknown lands, a long and illustrious procession of great poets, artists, thinkers, scientists and composers began to file across the stage of Italian history.

The classical era of Italy, the era when that country stood at its zenith, was ushered in by the authors Bellini (1422-1512), Boiardo (1430-1494), and Pulci (1431-1487), and the reformer Savonarola (14521498); it culminated in the writer Machiavelli (14691527), the artist Michelangelo (1474-1565), the poet Ariosto (1474-1533), the painters Titian (1477-1576), Raphael (1484-1520), and Corregio (1492-1534), the architect Palladio (1518-1580), the poet Tasso (15441595), and the scholars Bruno (1550-1600), Sarpi 1552-1623), and Galileo (1564-1642); and it terminated with Marini (1569-1625), Guido Reni (15751642), Davilo (1576-1631), Domenichino (1581-1641), Toricelli (1608-1679), Cassini (1625-1712), and Malpighi (1628-1694).

The age when Michaelangelo, Titian, Raphael, Corregio and Palladio painted, carved and built; when Ariosto and Tasso composed; and when Bruno and Galileo thought and investigated, was the age when the Italian people crossed their meridian.

A change in the personnel of the procession, due to the advance in the nation's age, is quite apparent. The van is led by the poets and artists full of vivid, exuberant imagination and great creative and inventive genius. They represent early manhood. The men of science, of reason, of original thought and of daring research the representatives of manhood's prime, follow. Decadent artists and authors bring up the rear.

The men of talent and genius, barred from active participation in affairs of church and state, were confined to the narrowed arena of art, literature and science, where they achieved unequalled success.

In her Waldenses and in Savonarola Italy sent her precursors of church reform into the field, but when the Reformation came, she remained indifferent to the great revolutionary movement of the North. She produced no Luther, Zwingli, Calvin or Knox; but she gave to the world Michaelangelo, Raphael, Ariosto, Tasso, Bruno and Galileo.

The Italians were the pioneers of modern European civilization. Their scholastics and epic poets led the way. They were the standard bearers of humanism and the renaissance, and they fostered the study of the classics.

The nation was aging rapidly and prematurely during the seventeenth and eighteenth centuries. Art and literature degenerated, and little was accomplished in science. Age was approaching fast, and neither church nor state permitted bold, original investigation and the free, daring word.

A revival took place at the close of the eighteenth and during the early decades of the nineteenth centuries. Italy was galvanized into the appearance of life by contact with French classicism and the French Revolution. Galvani (1737-1798), and Volta (17451826), were original thinkers and investigators; and Alfieri (1749-1803), the evening star of Italian poetry, announced the approaching darkness.

The normal development of social and political Italy was hindered by external and internal foes, from the beginning. Church and empire battled for supremacy during the Medieval Age, and the city-republics were never able to achieve victory for the democratic and national principle. Matters grew worse after the sixteenth century. Foreign armies made the peninsula a common battle-ground, and alien princes played football with Italian provinces. From Charles V. to Victor Emmanuel, Italy experienced nothing but disgrace and humiliation, politically. The once powerful city-republics, the patrons of letters, art and learning, crumbled into ruins; democracy found no refuge; the church crushed out all independent spirit and free inquiry; commerce, industry and wealth took wings and fled to other lands; and education was at a low ebb.

The French Revolution roused the aged Italian nation to renewed, spasmodic activity. A democratic wave swept over the peninsula. The people sympathized with the revolutionary movement on the banks of the Seine, and hailed Napoleon as their deliverer. The Austrian armies were brushed away. The Cisalpine, Ligurian, Roman and Parthenopean republics were organized. Intellectual life was regenerated under French impulses and auspices. Constitutions after the French model were adopted, feudalism was abolished, the code Napoleon was introduced, equality of taxation and general eligibility to office were established, convents were suppressed, education was promoted, and art, science and literature, were fostered.

The old order of things, however, was restored after the fall of Napoleon. The iron heel of despotism trampled all the young hopes, aspirations and resolutions, into the mire. Wholesale incarcerations and executions accompanied the suppression of the revolt of 1820; Austrian regiments crushed the uprising of 1830 in the bud; and the revolutionary movement of 1848 suffered disastrous defeat.

Soon after that the tide turned in favor of Italian unity, independence and freedom. The battles of Magenta and Solferino added Lombardy, Parma, Modena and Tuscany to Sardinia, which had been permitted to retain a semblance of autonomy and independence. Austria ceded Venice after the battle of Sadowa. The victories of Metz and Sedan transferred the Papal States to the Italian crown and made Rome the national capital.

For the first time in its history did a united and independent Italy step forth and take its place among the nations of the earth. The national principle had finally triumphed over the tribal. It came too late. The political achievements of the nineteenth century should have occurred in the sixteenth, when the nation rejoiced in the full vigor of manhood. Now, political union and independence was the gift of foreign princes, soldiers and statesmen, to a feeble sage.

It is a pathetic sight to see Italy endeavoring to keep pace with her younger and more progressive and vigorous neighbors. She has formed a liberal, constitutional government, and fosters agriculture, industry, commerce, art, letters, science and education. But the new civilization on the Tiber and the Po is an exotic. It is an imitation of foreign models. It has not sprung spontaneously from the hearts and brains of the masses.

Originality, inventive and creative genius have disappeared from Italy some time since. She is no more self-luminous, and only glows in the flame of foreign nations. The symptoms of the approach of sterile, stagnant and unprogressive old age are manifest everywhere, and cannot be disguised.

However, owing to the liberal infusion of Gothic and Langobard blood, over a thousand years ago, the population of the northern provinces exhibit some signs of life and progress; but in the southern provinces and in Sicily, which received no such admixture, all is stagnant, unprogressive and fossilized. Italy is approaching her dotage.

Was it due to its wonderful climate, its enchanting landscape, to its splendid geographical position, to its fertile soil, or to its recurrent happy mixture of ethnic elements? it is certainly remarkable that 'this little peninsula of Italy should have exerted such a tremendous and dominant influence on the affairs of this world for upward of three thousand years. The people of that little peninsula evolved the notable Etruscan civilization before the Latins landed on the banks of the Tiber; their senators, consuls and Caesars subsequently ruled the then known world for centuries; they moulded and shaped the organization of the Christian church through the genius of their church-fathers; their artists, poets, scientists and humanists led in the great revival of the fifteenth and sixteenth centuries; their priests, cardinals and popes dominated absolutely over Christendom for upward of a thousand years; and even today, although they suffer from the decrepitude of old age, and although the ecclesiastical power has been much curtailed during the last four centuries, hundreds of millions of men and women, of all races, colors, tongues and countries, bow voluntarily, reverently and submissively to the decrees of their prelates. No other country, in the same length of time, and in proportion to population, has produced as many master-minds as Italy. Her sway over the minds of men, through her statesmen, jurists, scholars, churchmen, artists and poets, from Romulus down to Marconi, was almost universal. Now, that glory is all of the past, or is passing. The vigor of youth and the creative force of manhood is gone. Prestige only, and the mental inertia of the masses, sustain the tottering frame of the sage of the Tiber. Italy has had her day, no rejuvenation is in sight, and her sun is setting on her fair valleys, picturesque mountains, charming shores and stately ruins.

15. The Spaniards.

The Spanish nation is composed of many very heterogeneous ethnic elements, now fused to a fair degree of homogeneity. Three successive waves of primitive civilization swept over the peninsula in prehistoric times. The men of the Palaeolithic, Neolithic and bronze ages followed each other, and the civilization evolved by each race surpassed that of the preceding. The race of the bronze age had passed through its phases of youth and manhood and sunk into the decline of old age, at the dawn of history.

Then the Celts of Gaul invaded and conquered the Iberian Peninsula. The two people mingled and formed a new, fairly homogeneous nation, called the Celt-Iberians. The natives of the inaccessible mountain regions of the North resisted amalgamation and absorption, and fragments and remnants of that race have been preserved in the Basques.

The Basques still speak a primitive, undeveloped language, which is related to the Turanian dialects of Central Asia. They are ultra-conservative and adhere to their language, customs and manners with great tenacity. They follow their leaders with unquestioning loyalty, and cleave to their primitive patriarchal and tribal institutions. It is a race that belongs to the childhood days of humanity, and has been in its dotage ever since the twilight of history. It is a fragment of hard, primitive rock imbedded in the ethnic conglomerate of the peninsula.

Moors and Berbers crossed the Strait of Gibraltar and colonized the southern provinces; Semitic Carthaginians invaded the country from the east; and after them came the Roman legions with camp-followers, officers of the administration, merchants and colonists. Spain was a Roman province as early as 205 B. C. The Basque provinces, however, defended their independence stubbornly until the reign of Augustus. The Spanish people of that time could enumerate the men of the Palaeolithic, Neolithic and bronze ages, Celts, Iberians, Berbers, Moors, Semites and Romans, among their ancestors.

In 29 B. C. Spain was divided into three provinces governed by Roman officers, customs, laws and religion. Revolts ceased, and the country enjoyed prosperity and uninterrupted peace during the next four centuries. Agriculture, mining, industry, commerce and even art and letters flourished. The people were thoroughly Latinized. Eminent poets, savants, generals and statesmen, Seneca, Lucan, Pomponius, Martial, Quintilian, Trajan, Hadrian and Marcus Aurelius, were born in Spain. The strong ties of common speech, religion, laws, customs, interests and culture bound Spain firmly and organically to Rome.

This, however, was true only in the southern provinces; in the Basque districts Roman influence diminished with the proportion of Latin blood in the veins of the natives.

Spain was virtually a Roman colony and rose, prospered and perished with the mother country. They grew old together. Decadence set in about the beginning of our era. Patriotism and public spirit disappeared; trade, industry and agriculture languished; intellectual force vanished; morals deteriorated, and the great public buildings went to ruin. The people drifted irresistibly into the decrepitude of old age. Christianity failed to regenerate them, but participated in the general decadence.

Suddenly the storm of the great Migrations burst upon them in A. D. 406. Vast hordes of Vandals, Suevi and Alani, rushed across the Rhine, swept through Gaul like a tempest, crossed the Pyrenees and conquered the Iberian peninsula. The Goths coming a little later from Italy overthrew Vandals and Suevi, their kindred, and founded the Visigothic kingdom, which, in 484 A. D. under Euric, extended from the Strait of Gibraltar to the Loire in Gaul. The enfeebled, nerveless, aged, native race, composed of effeminate nobles, an incompetent clergy and cowed and spiritless serfs, offered no serious resistance to the young and energetic invaders.

Then followed three centuries of incessant friction, strife, turmoil, revolts and feuds, the concomitants of fusion. The Goths, thanks to their superior physical, intellectual and moral vigor, formed a ruling, aristocratic class. They divided and distributed the land in accordance with the feudal principles, then coming in vogue, and reduced the natives to serfdom.

But these subjugated Latin and Iberian natives were in possession of a cultivated language, a noble literature, an imposing art, a well ordered civil administration, a refined manner of living, and a religion well calculated to awe and fascinate the savage mind with its mystic creed and its gorgeous ceremonial. The huge, rude and uneducated Gothic barbarians contemplated the superior culture of the conquered with dread, reverence and admiration. The bold, youthful, vigorous Gothic nation became the willing, docile pupil of the prestige-crowned, aged Latin-Iberian people.

The invading Goths were Ayrians. Missionaries of this heretical belief had first brought the gospel to them. First come, first served! The ignorant Goths could not follow the finely drawn theological distinctions. At last, confounding civilization and religion, as is done frequently, they accepted orthodoxy at the hands of the vanquished, but culturally superior natives.

The Goths strove hard at first to maintain their race, language, laws, customs and manners, in their purity. Intermarriages were prohibited. But love mocks at such decrees. Race-prejudices and antipathies vanished rapidly, and about 700 A. D. fusion was fairly complete. The Goths and Suevi were Romanized. The numerically much stronger Latin-Iberian natives had absorbed and assimilated the Teutonic invaders, and the aged, stagnant and decrepit race had been rejuvenated by the infusion of young blood. A new nation was born.

The substratum of the new nation consisted of natives of Iberian, Celtic and Latin descent, overlaid by a thin stratum of aristocratic Goths. The Teutons furnished the active, motive, and constructive force to the new organism. Teutonic leaven and ferment injected new life and motion into the inert and passive native mass. This dominant, directive and constructive Teutonic force was strongest during the early centuries of Spanish national life, it diminished in proportion to the absorption and assimilation of the Gothic by the Latin-Iberian element.

The new Spanish nation was yet in the formative phase of tender infancy, when, in A. D. 711, the Arabs, in the flush and vigor of youth, dashed across the Straits of Gibraltar, and carried the victorious crescent over the peninsula, and even over the Pyrenees into Gaul. It was a combat between a mature man and a boy.

The Goths were still in the primitive tribal state and had not reached the stage of nationalism. The authority of the kings was weak; the nobility was recalcitrant; the clergy was more cosmopolitan than national; ease and luxury had made the upper classes enervate and effeminate; and the downtrodden laboring masses contemplated with stolid indifference the danger to their race, nationality, language and religion. The Moslem invaders, with their higher civilization and their nobler ideas of justice, equity, equality and tolerance, were welcomed as liberators by the oppressed serfs.

Spanish national and intellectual life flowed thenceforth in two separate but parallel channels the Moorish-Islamitic and the Gothic-Christian from the eighth to the close of the fifteenth century, when the two streams merged into one.

The Arabs occupied three-fourths of Spain immediately after the conquest. They formed a ruling class, and devoted themselves exclusively to government, war and the cultivation of letters, art and learning.

The Moslems of Spain evolved a high civilization, which, as we have seen in a preceding chapter, reached its point of culmination about 1000 A. D., remained there until the thirteenth century, and then gradually paled and lost lustre, until it was forcibly extinguished by Ferdinand and Isabella.

Goths, Iberians, Celts, Latins, Arabs and Moors, formed the Spanish nation. The effect of each factor is readily traceable in the physical, moral and intellectual character of the people. In regard to age, the Goths were still in their childhood, the Arabs in their youths or early manhood, and the Iberians, Latins and Celts in their old age, at the time of the confluence. As a result of fusion, and in obedience to the law of the parallelogram of forces, the new nation passed rapidly and almost imperceptibly through its phases of infancy and childhood and began its national career at the stage of youth.

The civilization was developed faster in the south, where Arab and Berber blood predominated, than in the north, where the Gothic prevailed. The former stood in its zenith in the tenth century, the latter in the sixteenth. The young Gothic blood in the north retarded evolution. It exhausted its energy in the rejuvenation of the aged Latin-Iberian race.

Vast numbers of Christians were converted to Islam. Justice and tolerance characterized Arab rule. Goths, Latins, Iberians, Arabs and Berbers intermingled freely. This fusion is readily traceable in the physical types and the character of the Spanish nation.

A large part of the Goths had fled before the Moslem invaders to the inaccessible mountain regions of the north. There, sheltered by their strongholds, surrounded by want and poverty, and removed from the scenes of enervating luxury and refinement, they slowly recovered their wonted simple virtues and warlike spirit.

A marked political progress occurred there and then. The people prepared to emerge from the tribal stage and rise to the national. Tribes coalesced with tribes into larger organizations. Tribal chiefs grew into petty kings. Interminable border warfare with the Moslem led to centralization of military power. The small kingdoms of Leon, Castile, Navarre and Aragon were already firmly established in A. D. 900.

Feudalism, chivalry, love of adventure, epic song, religious fervor and enthusiasm, and hatred of the Arab and his civilization, were the characteristic features of the civilization springing up in Christian Spain. They were the same symptoms that marked the youth of all the European nations. Growth was accelerated in Italy, Spain and France, due to the infusion of old blood. For this reason they led the van of general progress.

Slowly, city after city, province after province, the Christians recovered territory from their adversaries. The Moslem power began to show signs of decline and disintegration at the end of the twelfth century, and could have been swept out of the land if the Christians had been united. But the old Teutonic tribal spirit did not permit any one kingdom to gain complete ascendancy and enforce a systematic and persistent advance. Such well-planned, methodical work cannot be expected of juvenile nations.

The Christians fought bravely but irregularly and spasmodically. This retarded the reconquest of Spain. If the Arab statesmen of that age had with due foresight provided for a large Semitic and Hamitic immigration and colonization, the Pyrenees would today form the boundary between Christianity and Islam. They failed in that, and they lost the fair peninsula.

When, as in the sanguinary battle of Tolosa in A. D. 1212, the Christians did unite, their foes were defeated. The Moslems retreated to Granada after this battle, and all the rest of Spain submitted to Christian rule and returned to the Christian faith.

Intellectual life of a higher order began to unfold itself among the Christians as soon as the northern kingdoms established order, and gained in wealth, power and prestige. The cities, the natural breeding grounds of culture, public and progressive spirit and democratic ideas, grew in importance. They demanded and were accorded a large share in public affairs. General assemblies or Cortes were convoked regularly to discuss public affairs and to shape the policy of the state in conjunction with the crown. Medieval Spain was politically more progressive and farther advanced than any contemporary nation of Europe.

Literature, also, began to shoot forth its earliest buds and blossoms in the form of popular epic and lyric songs. The first poets were mere imitators of the troubadours of Provence; but Spanish poetry soon assumed a distinctive national and religious character. Chivalry, the wars with the Moslem, love, the adventures of heroes, and miracles performed by saints, formed the popular themes of the poets' songs. The poem of "Cid Campeador," "The Book of Appolonius," "The Life of Our Lady St. Mary of Egypt," and "The Adoration of the Three Holy Kings" all composed by unknown authors, appeared in the twelfth century. Gonzalo of St. Milan (1220-1250), a writer of voluminous verse, is recognized as the first known poet of Spain. Alfonso, the Wise (1221-1284), himself a noted scientist and renowned writer, promoted literature and science.

The nation was in its vigor of youth, and the time had arrived for its display of conscious strength and creative genius. In heroic adventures, in the contest with the Arabs, in the feuds of chivalry, in the struggle for and against privileges of the Cortes with the crown, in the upbuilding of the power of democratic cities and in epic verse, it gave vent to its expanding power. A strenuous, juvenile desire for learning pervaded all classes. The intellectual horizon widened amazingly. Universities were founded in rapid succession; at Salamanca in 1242, at Valencia in 1245, at Sevilla in 1256, at Palma in 1280, at Montpellier in 1289, at Alcala in 1293, at Lerida in 1300 and at Valladolid in 1304, A. D.

That was the springtime of the Teutonic and semi-Teutonic nations of Europe. The adolescent people became conscious of their growing strength. From the Atlantic to the Adriatic, and from the Mediterranean to the boreal seas, the youthful nations were impetuously struggling onward and upward. It was the era of the scholastics, the troubadors, trouveres and minnesingers; of the creation of the great epics of Beowulf, Gudrun, Edda, the Nibelungenlied, the Cid and the Divine Comedy; of the insane enthusiasm of the crusades; of the efflorescence of knighthood; of the rise of a new art in painting, sculpture and architecture; of the expansion of municipal power; and of the rise of democracy in powerful confederacies or leagues of cities.

In many of these upward movements Spain led the van. The epidemic fever of the crusades, however, did not cross the Pyrenees. The Iberian Peninsula had its own crusades. The constant wars with the Moslems monopolized attention, zeal and energy of knight, burgher and peasant. Dominic de Guzman in 1215 founded the religious-military order, named after him, for the purpose of fighting the infidels and of stamping out the heresy of the Albigenses.

This epoch of strenuous physical, intellectual and moral activity was followed, in Spain as well as throughout all Europe, by an age of stagnation and retrogression, lasting about a century. It was the period which witnessed the decay of medieval chivalry, the centralization of royal power, the rise of money power, the temporary decadence of literature and learning, and the spread of feuds, brigandage and anarchy.

Only a few authors of merit, among them the infant Don Juan Manuel (d.1347), the priest-poet Juan Ruiz, and Pedro Lopez de Ayala, poet and historian, dimly illuminated the age. They represented the transition from the heroic, popular, natural and spontaneous style of poetry to the more artistic and studied. The vivid imagination and fervid enthusiasm of youth gave way to the sober reason of mature manhood. One redeeming feature of these turbulent and anarchical times is to be found in the conduct of the proud, independent, sturdy burghers of the growing democratic cities. They organized the Hermandad for mutual protection against the lawless raids of a demoralized chivalry. This organization restored law and order.

The cities of Spain and, to a large extent also the peasantry, enjoyed at that time a greater amount of liberty, independence and self-government than those of the rest of Europe. Feudalism and serfdom did not take deep root under the liberal rule of the Arab Emirs in central and Southern Spain. Spain served as pioneer in the social and political advance of the continent.

The fifteenth century brought an intellectual revival and the inauguration of the national spirit to supersede the tribal. The period of transition was ended. The nation had entered the phase of early manhood. Henry of Aragon (1384-1434), translator of the classics; Inigo Lopez de Mendoza, a natural and original poet; Perez de Guzman, a celebrated biographer, and Ximenes, famous statesman and cardinal, ushered in the new epoch of national greatness.

A long procession of illustrious rulers, statesmen, generals, churchmen, explorers, poets, historians and artists, followed: Ferdinand and Isabella; Torquemada (1420-1498), inquisitor general; Gonzalvo (14531515), famous general; Pizarro (1471-1541), conqueror of Peru; Las Casas (1474-1566), historian; Oviedo (1478-1557), historian; Cortez (1485-1547), conqueror of Mexico; Loyola (1491-1556), founder of the order of Jesuits; Garcilasso de la Vega (1503-1536), author; Mendoza (1503-1575), statesman and classic writer; Xavier (1506-1562), renowned missionary; de Leon (1528-1591), poet; Herrera (d.1589), poet; Mariana (1537-1624), savant and historian; Cervantes (15471616), humorist; Lope de Vega (1562-1635), dramatist; Ribera (1588-1656), painter; Velasquez (16011681), celebrated painter; Calderon (1601-1681), great dramatist; Cano, artist; and Murillo (1618-1682), illustrious painter, illuminated Spanish history from the close of the fifteenth century to the middle of the seventeenth. These men represent the Spanish nation when it stood at or near its zenith.

Ferdinand and Isabella, yielding to the universal desire, created or organized the Spanish nation. They forced the recalcitrant feudal nobles into submission, fastened and strengthened royal authority, promoted literature and art, aided to make the Castilian dialect the national language, conquered Granada, united all Spain under one crown, and added America to the Spanish dominion.

At the beginning of the sixteenth century Spain held the championship among the nations of Europe. She had the opportunity to hold the leadership for centuries, but she failed to utilize it. She halted and stepped to the rear when the inquisition suppressed reform and heresy with brutal force; when Ferdinand, Isabella, Charles and Philip stamped out the democratic spirit in the cities; when arrogant nobles reduced the free peasantry to the condition of abject serfs; and when the clergy became the custodian of education, learning and public opinion.

Spain participated but slightly in the general movement of that age for social, political and religious reform. She suffered from a certain dualism in her blood. The progressive Gothic and Suevic blood struggled with that of the ultra-conservative Iberian, Latin and Moor for the mastery, and failed. The Gothic leaven had exhausted its force, and the heavy and inert mass began to sink and settle.

The time when Spain stood at its point of culmination was very brief. The impetus given to intellectual life at the beginning of the 16th century had spent its force at its close. Decline set in then and the nation sank rapidly. Premature decay and old "age was the lot of the people. Originality and creative force dwindled away. Spain lost the Netherlands, her Armada, her merchant marine and many colonies, and even the enormous treasures from Peru and Mexico became a curse to her. Two generations sufficed to reduce her from the rank of a first class power to that of third class.

Decadence permeated public and private life. Sterility succeeded to the fertility of the classical epoch. With Murillo disappeared the race of giants. Dwarfish epigoni took their places in art, letters and learning. Despotic kings, imbecile nobles and ignorant, fanatic priests hastened the downward course. Aranda (1738-1788) and Campomanes (1723-1802), two enlightened and patriotic statesmen, made futile attempts to check further deterioration. They could not resuscitate the former spirit of progress, invention and originality.

Spain had had her day. In her prime she produced great generals, poets and artists, but few philosophers and scientists. Her unsymmetrical civilization was the joint product of progressive thinkers, narrow-minded and devout kings, a fanatical and bigoted clergy, and an arrogant and unprogressive nobility. There was a strong leaven of social and religious reform in Spain, at the close of the fifteenth century. But when the inquisition was introduced, when Charles V extinguished all free, democratic life in the cities, and when a selfish and haughty aristocracy reduced, the peasantry to dull and brutalizing servitude, a fatal blight fell on the land. When the inquisition exterminated the men of free thought and inquiry, Spain lost her best and most progressive blood. The loss was irreparable. It was the inquisition and not the Catholic faith that wrought the downfall. Religions have very little to do with the rise and fall of nations. Spain enjoyed the same religion in her rise to power, wealth and fame, as she did in her rapid descent to premature old age.

Incited thereto by their neighbors, the Spanish people at the present time enjoy a revival of intellectual life. It is not of their own creation. Their poets, artists, scientists and statesmen copy after foreign models. Remove the impulse and influence from abroad, and they would at once sink into the marasmus of national old age.

The Spanish colonies share the fate of the mother country and keep pace with it on the down grade.

16. The French.

When the Romans conquered Gaul they divided the province into Gallia Celticae and Gallia Belgae; recognizing the marked contrast between the two branches of the Gauls or Celts. Related dialects and uniform cults, customs and manners prevailed throughout the broad zone inhabited by the Celts, extending from the Atlantic to the Balkan, but physically the distinction between the Belgae and the Celts proper was striking. The former were tall and blond like the Germans, the latter swarthy and of short stature like the Mediterranean nations to the south. The blond Celts, occupying a wide zone along the German frontier, were Celticized Teutons, or people of mixed Celtic and Teutonic descent.

The Celts had advanced to a higher degree of civilization than their Teutonic neighbors, at the time when European affairs were first revealed in the early dawn of history. They were the conquerors, heirs and descendants, in part at least, of that great Mediterranean race which had evolved a notable civilization in the south of Europe; erected mounds, cromlechs, dolmens and cyclopean structures; and used tools and implements of polished stone and bronze. The Celts lived in organized communities. They had developed a mysterious cult with an organized priesthood and an elaborate ceremonial of worship. They were experts in mining, metallurgy, founding and smithing, and had advanced agriculture, horticulture, stock raising, industry and commerce to a fair degree of perfection.

The Celts, due to the strong infusion of old Iberian or Etruscan blood, were farther advanced in age than the Germans; and their superior civilization gave them a certain advantage in their dealings with their rude and more barbarous northern neighbors. The germs of a higher culture were carried from the Celtic South to the Teutonic North. The Teutons, as evidenced by their early epic poetry, looked with friendly and admiring eyes upon their dwarfish, swarthy, intelligent, mischievous, mining and metal-working neighbors; and deemed them beings gifted with super-human powers. The heroic poetry of the ancient Germans reflects a long struggle between Teutons and Celts, but, upon the whole, the relation between the two races seems to have been rather pleasant and friendly.

The two Celtic branches the fair and the swarthy had not been fused into a homogeneous race at the time of the conquest of -Gaul by the Romans. The development of a purely Celtic race and civilization was arrested by the presence of the Roman legions. The Celtic race, while in its early formative stage, was ground to pieces between the Latin and Teutonic millstones. It ceased to exist; only fragments of that once extensive and promising race are to be found in Brittany, Wales, the Scotch Highlands and Ireland. The bulk of the Celtic population was absorbed and assimilated by the Romans on one side and by the Germans on the other. The Celtic race suffered a premature extinction; but by absorption and assimilation its racial traits were transmitted to the conquerors, and thus became a strong factor in shaping the character and history of the French, the British and the southern Germans.

The Romans colonized Gaul extensively. The Gauls, recognizing a strong affinity between themselves and the Latins both being descendants, in part at least, of the ancient Iberian, Etruscan or Pelasgic races, submitted to thorough romanization without much opposition, friction or delay. The Gauls adopted Latin speech, laws and customs. Marseilles, Nimes, Langres, Bordeaux, Rheims and Paris, became great centers of Latin life and culture as early as the reigns of the first emperors. Romans and Celts speedily fused into a new homogeneous people of a distinct and characteristic Latin type. Gaul was the most thoroughly Latinized of the imperial provinces.

Gaul, being essentially a Latin colony or province, rose, prospered and declined with the mother country. Mother and daughter kept pace in their march as they crossed the meridian of their national existence, and on their descent toward old age. The unavoidable decline, with its diminution of physical, intellectual and moral strength and energy, affected them simultaneously. When Rome, in its dotage, fell an easy prey to the invading hosts of the Heruli, Goths and Langobards, aged Gaul succumbed without resistance to the hordes of Franks, Alemanni, Burgundians and Visigoths.

Old Celto-Latin Gaul perished in the fifth century, and the invading German tribes took forcible possession of it. The Visigoths took southwestern Gaul, the land between the Loire, the Rhone and the Pyrenees; the Burgundians occupied the valleys of the upper Rhone and the Saone; the Alemanni settled in Elsass and Lorraine; and the Franks pushed their frontier from the Rhine to the Somme. The Celto-Latin natives retained control of Brittany and of a region of undefined extent in the center.

Such was the ethnic condition of Gaul or France at the close of the fifth century, when the shifting and transpositions of tribes and nations, due to the great Migrations, ceased, and when stability returned. There has been no material ethnic change since then.

During the next four centuries, or until the treaty of Verdun in A. D. 843, France was a seething, ebullient, fermenting mass of humanity. The heterogeneous Celtic, Latin, Iberian and Teutonic elements struggled fiercely and turbulently with each other for supremacy. They strove to adjust themselves to the new conditions, and to attain homogeneity in language, laws, customs and religion.

The Teutonic element, here as well as in Italy and Spain, although vastly outnumbered by the Celto-Latin natives, constituted the leading and dominant factor in the formation of the new nation and in shaping its destiny and character. It became the active leaven of the new mixture. It supplied the new organism with physical, intellectual and moral force. The infusion of young Teutonic blood rejuvenated the decaying, sterile, inert, fossilizing Celto-Latin mass, which was in a moribund state from the effect of old age. Without fusion with younger and rising nations, the Latin world would have sunk deeper and deeper into the torpor and impotence of old age.

French culture, therefore, is essentially Teutonic in character. The spirit of the youthful conquering nations gave shape and form to the life of the new nation; the Celto-Latin substratum, old and passive, could only modify and color the work achieved. The Teutonic invaders made French history and created the ideals in art, literature, science, philosophy, religion and statesmanship. The elite of intellect and society, long after the invasion, bore a strong Teutonic impress, and this is noticeable even at the present day. The regions of France where Franks, Alemanni, Burgundians and Goths settled in large numbers produced proportionately a larger number of great men of inventive and creative genius than the provinces where the native Celto-Latin element retained the hegemony.

The history of France during the formative period, from the invasion of the German tribes to the Treaty of Verdun, is properly a part of the history of the German people. The invading Teutonic tribes had spent their childhood at the old common home on the shores of the Baltic and the North Sea. They resisted stubbornly the absorption and assimilation by the natives in their new home for many generations. They strove tenaciously to maintain intact their language, laws, traditions, social and political institutions. They formed a distinct social and political class or caste and, although cast adrift, their social, political and intellectual evolution ran parallel with that of their kindred nations which remained at home.

But, while in the normal development hereditary kingship slowly supplanted tribal chieftainship; while the national idea gained upon the tribal spirit; while feudalism and serfdom superseded the old patriarchal and tribal equality; while a national literature began to take root; while Christianity drove out the old Teutonic gods and established a new cult; and while the nation was passing from childhood into youth; a quiet, steady and thorough ethnic transformation of the lower and middle classes took place.

Four centuries of uninterrupted amalgamation of Teuton, Celt and Latin sufficed to create a fairly homogeneous nation. In the storm and stress of the period a new nation had been born. Charlemagne, like Theodoric, the Great, before him, dreamed of a great Teutonic world-empire; but differentiation and amalgamation had silently created and evolved three distinct and separate nations, in the realms ruled by kings of Teutonic extraction. The dreams came to naught. Fusion was an accomplished fact in the age immediately succeeding Charlemagne, and this fact was recognized in the Treaty of Verdun, when Italians, French and Germans were treated as three distinct and separate nationalities.

The Treaty of Verdun, in A. D. 843, was the real birthday of the French nation. At that date it began its separate and independent existence.

The commingling of aged Latin with young Teutonic blood revivified the Roman and Celtic element and accelerated the development of the Teutonic. The consequence was that France passed through the phases of youth and manhood a century or more in advance of the unadulterated Teutonic nations of the North, and assumed the role of a guiding elder sister in the family of European nations. In company with Italy and Spain, who for the same reason matured faster, she took and kept the lead in all intellectual movements of Europe from the sixth to the nineteenth century.

France also constituted the bridge by which Christianity entered the North. Roman orthodoxy gained the ascendancy over Arian heresy when the Franks championed its cause. France formed the connecting link between the effete, stagnant and refined Orient and the crude, barbarous but progressive North and West of Europe. The germs of Latin civilization, the ideas of Christianity and the principles of the Roman law passed through Prankish channels into England and Germany.

Feudalism was the characteristic social, political and economic feature of the age when France seceded from Germany. It grew out of the relation existing between conqueror and subject. It was a natural and necessary phase in the evolution of Teutonic political life in the conquered lands. It sprang forth spontaneously in Italy, Spain, France, England and eastern Germany. It is also associated with a nation's transition from the tribal to the national stage; from chieftainship to kingship; from childhood to youth. France took the initiative and lead in this social and political evolution.

Hard times, general distress and insecurity of life and property favored the growth of feudalism. The large estates absorbed the small; the small, independent freeholders were eliminated from society, and sought refuge and protection under the walls of the feudal castle.

Feudalism caused and fostered an intellectual awakening. The castle became a center of social, political and intellectual life. Luxury and refinement entered the baronial halls, and minstrels and bards, the harbingers of a new literature, wandered from stronghold to stronghold, from monastery to monastery, to sing their inspiring songs of war and love, of adventures and heroic deeds.

Epic and lyric poetry, allowing full play to the imagination, is characteristic of youth, be it that of the individual, of a nation or of all humanity. The Troubadours of the South and the Trouveres of the North were the genuine representatives of the glorious morn, the happy springtime, the merry youth of France. The joyous, light-hearted and knightly Troubadours of the beautiful Provence, where the Visigoths had established their new home, filled the castle halls with their charming melodies, until the ruthless and brutal persecution of the Albigenses silenced the poets, stamped out all free and progressive thought and filled the land with gloom.

The more sober and less passionate and elegant Trouveres of northern France, the descendants of the Franks and Alemanni, continued the work of the Troubadours. Their poetry of love, religion and chivalry was imitated, remodeled and improved by the Mirnesingers of Germany.

The Troubadours inaugurated medieval epic and lyric poetry, but were unable to create masterpieces in this line. They were the descendants of the Goths, and between them and their distant past, rich in myths, legends and traditions, Christianity had been driven like a separating wedge. The Goths, in their long wanderings through steppes, woods and mountains, had lost all recollection of the adventures and conflicts of their ancient national gods, goddesses, demigods and heroes. The Troubadours, lacking this material, the soil from which true epics must spring, resorted to the stories of biblical characters and Christian saints, as substitutes. The blending of Jewish patriarchs and prophets, Christian saints and martyrs and pagan heroes resulted in poetic creations, fanciful, incongruous and grotesque. No great national epic could spring forth under such conditions; it must be rooted in the myths, sagas and legends of a nation's own heroic past.

Scholasticism made its debut in France at that time. It indicated that fusion of the race was as yet incomplete. In it we find a mixture of the contemplation of the Celto-Latin sage and the vivid imagination and unrestrained speculation of the Teutonic youth. It was the strenuous, intellectual sport of youth, restrained by classical and ecclesiastical authority. Gerbert of Aurillac, afterward Pope Sylvester II (about 980 A. D.), Berengarius of Tours (998-1088), Abelard (1077-1142), St. Bernard, and others, were the typical representatives of this strange intellectual movement. Scholasticism was a futile attempt to unite the aged, contemplative Latin hermit and recluse with the playful, imaginative and boisterous Teutonic youth into one person.

In the field of art, less hampered by tradition and ecclesiastical authority, the French national mind manifested originality and inventive power at an early date. It created the Gothic style of architecture, which is well adapted to give full expression to the sublime religious conceptions and aspirations of that era.

The passionate, fanatic, uncontrollable religious frenzy of that age found vent in the insane crusades. It was the folly of the nation's youth. No mature nations would have ventured on such mad adventures. France took the initiative, led in the delirious movement and bore the brunt of the disastrous wars for the recovery of the holy sepulchre.

It was the heroic, juvenile age of France. Her youthful intellectual life exhausted itself in lyric poetry, scholasticism, chivalry, the crusades and the beginnings of modern art.

A long era of exhaustion and inactivity set in after this period of strenuous life. The Troubadours. Trouveres and Scholastics vanished. France failed to produce a national epic, like the Iliad, the Mahabarata, the Edda, Gudrun or the Nibelungen song. She had no Homer or Dante. A phenomenal paucity of great names in poetry, art and learning characterized the period that intervened between the thirteenth century and the great revival that began in the sixteenth. Only the historian Joinville (1224-1318), and the poet and historian 'Froissart (1337-1410), faintly illuminated this dark age, between the height of chivalry, scholasticism and song and the Reformation.

But the French national mind was not dormant and entirely inactive during this epoch. It participated in the general European decline which succeeded the unusual intellectual activity of the Middle Ages. It shunned art, letters and philosophy, and devoted itself almost exclusively to political affairs. Foreign conquests and the development of internal social and political institutions engrossed public attention. It was an era of marked political activity, growth and expansion. The French had conquered England and southern Italy and were recognized in the Orient as the champions of Christianity. At home they evolved a strong, centralized kingship, a growing national spirit and a municipal democracy, in a long struggle with the independent, arrogant, and oppressive feudal lords.

Socially and politically, the French people made uncommon progress. The complete triumph of a national kingship over haughty, insubordinate and mighty vassals, the victory of the national over the tribal spirit, the rapid growth of the democratic cities as centers of wealth, power, patriotism and intelligence, the decay of chivalry, the ascendancy of the money power in the hands of sturdy burghers over the power of the soil as monopolized by a decadent aristocracy, fully compensated them for any loss in the fields of art, letters and learning.

A new era dawned upon France about the middle of the sixteenth century. The long period of exhaustion, of rest, and of the storing of intellectual and moral forces, came to an end. An intellectual life of a new order and of a higher type made its appearance. The realism and materialism of the practical burgher made room for the idealism of the poet, artist and philosopher. A happy alliance between the democratic cities and royalty created an organically united nation.

Humanism and the New Learning which so deeply stirred up life in Italy, Germany, the Netherlands and England, at the close of the fifteenth and at the beginning of the sixteenth century, made only a slight impression on France. The Reformation, however, which left Italy and Spain almost completely undisturbed, sent its turbulent waves clear across fair France, from the Rhine to the Pyrenees. The clarion call of the German and Swiss reformers found a responsive echo in France. For the first time in her history did France attempt to follow in the wake of Germany, and reverse the old order. Both nations were now approaching full maturity, and France was on the point of losing her position as a leading and guiding older sister.

But at that very moment, so auspicious for the German nation, it was struck down and paralyzed by the short-sightedness, narrow-mindedness and folly of the German reformers and princes; while France continued in her normal development, and thus retained her leadership for two centuries more.

The Reformation set adrift many new ideas, many more than Luther and his co-workers anticipated and desired. A spirit of inquiry, independence, emancipation and revolution, in art, literature, philosophy, science and government, as well as in religion, permeated the whole Teutonic and semi-Teutonic world. This race had arrived at its majority. It dismissed its tutors and guardians of the church and of classic Greece and Rome, and was determined to follow its own course in every department of human endeavor. That is the true interpretation of the deep, strong and reformatory, intellectual and moral movement of the sixteenth century; which was central in Teutonic Germany, Switzerland, the Netherlands, England and Scandinavia, and extended into the semi-Teutonic countries of France, Italy, and Spain; especially where Goths, Suevi, Franks, Burgundians, Alemanni and Langobards had settled in large numbers.

The French reformers followed the broad-minded Zwingli and Calvin rather than Luther, who strove to confine the great movement within the narrow limits of the church. The French, like the Swiss, Dutch, Scotch and English, could not dissociate religious from social and political reform. The reformation to them meant universal emancipation from bondage and absolute authority, and greater freedom of thought and action in the state as well as in the church.

More than one tenth of the French people adopted the new, progressive and revolutionary ideas, and, as might naturally be conjectured, the Protestants were largely located in the departments occupied and settled by the early Goths, Burgundians, Alemanni and Franks; and where, three centuries before, the Albigenses and Waldensians, the forerunners of the Reformation, had preached reform in church and state, and suffered cruel martyrdom in consequence. The departments peopled by Celto-Latins adhered tenaciously to the old faith and the old order of things. The nobility, more Teutonic in its extraction than the other social classes, favored the new thought from the beginning and only halted and hesitated when the Peasants* War of Germany disclosed aggressive, democratic principles. The Reformation in France, as elsewhere, was essentially a Teutonic movement.

The French Protestants, or Huguenots, as they were called, like the Swiss, Dutch and English reformers, were strongly animated by democratic principles. They were the active, intellectual and moral leaven of France, in every domain of human activity, and their country suffered an irreparable loss when they were banished or exterminated. It was the Teutonic blood in the veins of the French people which brought forth the Huguenot, with his progressive ideas; and which created the brilliant era of Louis XIV, the Revolution and the modern republic.

The Celto-Latin population, aged, inert, unprogressive and passive, adhered loyally to priest and king through all the vicissitudes of religious and political strife. Blood will tell. Catholicism and Caesarism, which had sprung from the character of the decadent Romans, was best suited to the ideas, sentiments and tastes of Latin and Celt; and Protestantism and Democracy were more in harmony with the nature of the Teuton.

The sixteenth century is justly famous for the many great artists, poets, scientists, philosophers, statesmen and reformers which Italy, Germany, Switzerland, the Low Countries and England produced. France did not share in the general revival. Only a few rose above mediocrity. With Rabelais (1495-1553), the bold, witty and extravagant writer; Calvin (1509-1564), the austere reformer; Marot, Rousard and the "Pleiads" as poets; Montaigne (1533-1592), the philosopher; Casaubon (1559-1641), the savant; Conde, Coligny and Henry of Navarre, generals and statesmen the list of great names is about exhausted.

But beneath the calm exterior it was seething, fermenting and germinating in the soul of the French nation. Great things were preparing. In the period of the transition from a comparatively quiet youth to a glorious manhood, the nation was silently equipping itself for its grand achievements of the seventeenth century. France approached the meridian of its national existence, and during the whole seventeenth century a brilliant and imposing procession of great poets, artists, historians, philosophers, scientists, orators, generals and statesmen, passed across the stage of history.

Duchenne (1585-1642), the celebrated historian, inaugurated the great epoch, and was quickly followed by Richelieu (1585-1642), cardinal and statesman; Claude Lorraine (1600-1682), the painter; Corneille (16061684), the tragedian; Descartes (1606-1650), the philosopher; Duquesne (1610-1688), the admiral; Turenne (1611-1673), the famous general; Colbert (1619-1683), the statesman; La Fontaine (1621-1695), the poet and fabulist; Conde (1621-1686), the general; Moliere (16221673), the illustrious writer of comedies; Pascal (16231662), the philosopher and scholar; Bossuet (1627-1704), the orator; Boileau (1636-1711), the poet; Malebranche (1636-1715), the philosopher; Racine (1639-1699), the dramatist; Bayle (1647-1706), the scientist; Fenelon (1651-1715), the author; Lesage (1688-1747), the novelist; Massillon (1683-1742), the pulpit orator; Watteau (1684-1721), the painter; Montesquieu (1689-1755), the political philosopher; and many others of minor importance.

These men of talent and genius placed France at the head of the progressive and civilized nations. Their masterpieces became the models of all aspiring minds, at home and abroad. France had entered upon the phase of manhood, and, in consequence, the vivid and luxuriant imagination of youth was guided and restrained by the reason, tact and good taste of maturer years. It was an era of great originality, invention, bold, creative genius, daring investigation, masterly diplomacy, splendid victories on land and sea, unprecedented expansion of power and extraordinary development of the national spirit and pride.

Under a normal development the republican form of government should have been established in France during the seventeenth century. But, while the nation enjoyed a healthy growth in art, science, literature, philosophy and foreign politics, it remained stunted and atrophied in internal statesmanship and religion. While reaching full maturity in art, literature, philosophy and science, it remained a child in religion and politics. It could not emancipate itself from the absolute control of princes and priests.

French culture of that age was for this reason unharmonious and unsymmetrical. Obsequiousness and servility cast an ugly shadow upon the otherwise brilliant scenes of French life. Poets, artists, philosophers and statesmen vied with each other for favors bestowed by king and cardinal who ruled by divine right. The charming muses were degraded to ladies in waiting at the court. Sycophants crowded the royal and episcopal palaces. French national life was devoid of that proud, manly, sturdy, independent, democratic spirit, without which no modern nation can become truly great.

The seventeenth century harvested what the sixteenth had sown and planted. The progressive ideas that germinated, budded and sprouted in the soil of France in the times of Henry of Navarre and the Huguenots attained their efflorescence and fruitage under Louis XIV.

The Huguenots and their sympathisers gave the impulse to a higher, nobler and grander national life, and when, at the close of the seventeenth century, the force of this impulse had spent itself, a sharp, general decline set in. Prosperity vanished, taxation became a grievous burden, civil and religious liberty took wings, individual initiative disappeared, and pigmies took the place of intellectual giants.

The last years of Louis XIV were disastrous to France. The country was exhausted; commerce and industry paralyzed; art, literature and learning decaying; greatness slumbered in the cemeteries; armies and navies suffered humiliating defeat; and a frivolous, profligate and servile nobility surrounded the throne. The haughty Louis and his contemporaries had squandered the rich inheritance left them by their more democratic ancestors.

Decadence continued unabated after the demise of the "Grand Monarque." The long reign of Louis XV (1715-1777) is characterized by the haughty and extravagant nobility and clergy monopolizing all the honors, wealth and remunerative offices of the nation; by the pauperization of the masses; by the shameless licentiousness, prodigality and corruption of the upper classes; by their cynic contempt of the aspirations for greater freedom and enlightenment of the proletariat; and by a constant decline of political and military power and prestige.

But in spite of the decay of aristocracy and clergy above, and of the degradation and brutalization of the proletariat below, the great middle class of the French nation remained sound and strong, intellectually and morally. And here were gathering and training the great forces for the impending crisis, to which all looked forward with a gloomy or cheerful presentiment.

A great internal change took place at this time. The tribal spirit was completely eliminated; the exuberant imagination of youth, which to some extent yet ruled the genius of France during the seventeenth century, was superseded by the cool, clear, calculating and investigating reason of ripe manhood. The renaissance gave way to classicism. The personnel of the procession of great representative men changed decidedly; the poets and artists of the previous age made room for the scientists, the logical thinkers, the inventors and the bold investigators. France was approaching closely to its point of culmination.

Voltaire, the poet and satirist (1694-1778); Buffon, the naturalist (1707-1788); Boucher, the artist (17041770); Rousseau, the poet and novelist (1712-1778); Diderot, the scientist (1713-1784); Helvetius, the philosopher(1715-1771); D'Alembert, the scientist (171 7-1 783); Beaumarchais, the poet (1732-1799); Lagrange, the scientist (1736-1813); Lamark, the savant (1744-1829); David, the artist (1748-1825); Jussieu, the botanist (1748-1836); Mirabeau, the statesman (1749-1791); Delambre, the astronomer (1749-1822); Laplace, the scientist (1749-1827); DeMaistre, author (1753-1824); Petion (1753-1793), Brissot (1754-1793), Lafayette (1757-1834); Robespierre (1758-1794); Danton (17591794), and Desmoulins (1762-1794), statesmen of the Revolution; Mme. de Stael, authoress (1766-1817); Bonaparte, general, consul and emperor; Chateaubriand, romantic poet (1769-1848); Saint Simon, social philosopher (1760-1825); Cuvier, the scientist (1769-1832); Fourier, the social reformer (1772-1844); Goeffry Saint Hilaire, the scientist (1772-1844); Ampere, the scientist (1775-1836); Gay Lussac, the scientist (1778-1850); Beranger, the poet (1780-1857); and Decandolle, the botanist (1778-1841); made the France of the eighteenth and of the early part of the nineteenth centuries resound with their well merited fame.

The center of gravity of French intellectual life shifted from the domain of imagination to that of reason during the eighteenth century. The foregoing lists of great names reveals this truth. The scientists superseded the poets and artists. Among the great men of the seventeenth century, there were eleven men famous by their works of the imagination to four celebrated by their achievements in science; and among those of the eighteenth we find seventeen immortal scientists to eight poets, artists and speculative philosophers; not to speak of the statesmen of the Revolution and of ante-revolutionary days, who used their reasoning faculties rather than their imaginative. The French civilization of the seventeenth century bore the imprint of poetry and speculation; that of the eighteenth the stamp of pure science. Painting and sculpture had degenerated into mere prettiness; decadent rococo ruled in architecture; Voltaire and Rousseau excelled rather in keen criticism, cutting satire and bold negation, than in positive, creative work; but the men of science, with their bold and firm investigations, conclusions and convictions, gave to the France of the eighteenth century its distinctive character.

This metamorphosis affected the whole people, of whom the famous men were but the living representatives. The achievements of science widened the intellectual horizon of the masses, and the disparity between modern, progressive thought, and the fossilized ideas, laws, customs and institutions, handed down from hoary antiquity, became more apparent from day to day. The old order of things had become untenable. The French people were progressive, they could not stand still nor retreat, they had only to choose between normal growth and a violent explosion of compressed forces; between evolution and revolution. The latter was forced upon them.

The Revolution was unavoidable. Royalty, nobility and clergy, the ultra-conservative classes, interested in the maintenance of the established, "divine" order of things, endeavored frivolously and foolishly to stem by the masses and produced a strong fermentation. The nation's soul was filled with a new understanding, new desires, hopes, aspirations and life. Tremendous explosive material was gathering beneath the rigid social upper crust. Premonitory quakings pointed to an approaching catastrophe; but the blind, thoughtless and profligate upper classes disregarded the prophetic warnings, and kept up their wild orgies on the top of the volcano.

Then came the eruption. The long-suppressed forces of social, political and religious reform found vent in the Revolution. France, of a sudden, became a vast crater, filled with a superheated, boiling, seething and foaming mass.

The violence and explosive force of the Revolution was in exact proportion to the force employed in repressing progressive ideas. Had princes and prelates yielded to the moderate demand of the people for greater freedom of thought and action, the catastrophe would have been averted. The moral responsibility for the excesses of the revolutionary movement rests with the selfish, arrogant and unprogressive princes, nobles and priests, who would not recognize the justice, fairness and necessity of the people's demands. In their blind folly they imagined that the French nation would always remain a child and had to be treated and governed like a child; and they were dumbfounded when they found that this child had grown and expanded into lusty youth and manhood; had ripped and torn to shreds the time-honored institutions which it had outgrown as a youth outgrows the habiliments of childhood; and was now making feverish haste to clothe itself with new institutions, fitted and suited to its present mature age, stature and condition.

What the Revolution wrought had to come, sooner or later. The transformation caused by the great upheaval was really due in the sixteenth century, when the Huguenot reformers were in the ascendant, and when the nation passed from childhood into youth. The normal development, however, was retarded by autocratic kings, an egotistic and frivolous nobility and an ambitious clergy. When in spite of all oppression, the republic, with its free institutions, did come, it came in the nature of a violent, volcanic eruption.

Every phase in the life of a nation has its characteristic representatives. The Revolution brought a new type of men to the surface. The old type was unfit to meet the present crisis, and was ruthlessly swept aside. The terrific energy of an awakening nation, unleashed in a moment, and concentrated upon the destruction of the old, and the immediate upbuilding of new social, political, religious and economic institutions, demanded men of quick perception and comprehension, self-sacrificing spirit, noble courage, daring resolution, warm patriotism, love of freedom and progress, the genius of invention, fertility of resource and disregard of authority, Such men sprang forth in abundance when the times and their country called for them Mirabeau, Brissot, Lafayette, Danton, St. Just, Robespierre, Desmoulins, Petion and others. As if impelled by some demoniac force, they shot up from the dark, boiling and seething mass, enjoyed an ephemeral existence of unparalleled destructive and creative power on the crest of the tidal wave of popular enthusiasm and confidence, and then subsided as suddenly as they had risen.

Take them all in all, the men of the Revolution were men of gigantic mould. Without any preparation they were called upon the stage, and extemporaneously played a leading part in a grand world-tragedy. The work aca leading part in a grand world-tragedy. The work accomplished by them was phenomenal. The labor of generations, under ordinary conditions, was condensed into the space of five years. Every nerve and muscle oi France was strung to the utmost tension, and the aggregate amount of strenuous labor performed was astonishing.

The fatal spell of the divine right of kings and prelates was broken, privileges were brushed aside, equality of all men before the law was proclaimed, and the fetters of absolute authority were rent asunder. In spite of all excesses committed, the French Revolution was a great blessing to humanity; it raised the race to a higher level. A new code, of a nobler humanity, with liberty, equality and fraternity as its leading tenets, was promulgated amid fierce lightning and roaring thunder. A new decalogue from a new tempest-riven Sinai!

The Revolution marked the point of culmination in the life of the French nation. The people, enjoying the originality, the inventive genius, the creative power and the expansive force of the full prime of manhood, stepped across their meridian in the midst of a fierce social and political cyclone.

The storm subsided. The revolutionary fervor cooled. Most of the heaven-storming titans had perished under the knife of the guillotine. Napoleon, the child and heir of the Revolution, made his debut. He was undoubtedly a man of genius in the art of war and in statecraft, but his phenomenal success was chiefly due to the enormous quantity of latent, democratic energy, stored in the hearts of Frenchmen during two centuries, and which became potent and was organized through the efforts of the revolutionists. It was an easy task to lead the patriotic and enthusiastic republican armies to victory against slavish and stolid foes. Armies, even if poorly fed, equipped and disciplined, when filled with high ideals and animated by the spirit of freedom and independence, are nearly always invincible.

The democratic tidal wave lifted Napoleon to power and honor. When it subsided he vaulted on to an imperial throne. He betrayed the spirit that had made France and him great. Under his rule France drifted rapidly from democracy to oligarchy, and from oligarchy to monarchy. But the empire retained many of the democratic principles and forms.

It was the first downward step of the nation. The fever of the Revolution was succeeded by a season of exhaustion and lethargy. The republican spirit, which alone had made Marengo, Austerlitz, Jena, Wagram and Friedland possible, evaporated. The champions of democracy were nearly all dead, and the aspiring youths of the nation, the young men to whom democracy looked for succor, slumbered in the graves of a hundred battlefields. Exhaustion dulled the national spirit. Napoleon erected the empire on the ruins of the first republic; but the imperial army fought no more for the high ideals and with the enthusiasm, courage, fortitude and self-sacrifice that had animated the soldiers of the republic. The grand army dwindled away before the boreal blast of the Russian steppes, and suffered disastrous defeats at Leipzig and Waterloo, and Napoleon was sent an exile to the lonely island of St. Helena.

Then reaction stepped in to undo all that the Revolution had achieved. The ultra-conservative Bourbons, the Congress of Vienna and the Holy Alliance sought to extirpate the spirit of reform, progress and freedom throughout the world.

A half century of frequent and rapid changes in the form of government, and of an endless struggle between democracy and monarchy, between progress and reaction, followed. Despotism, liberal kingship, republic and constitutional empire, were tested in quick succession until the third republic was proclaimed during the debacle of 1870 and again brought peace, liberty, progress and prosperity to France.

In spite of evil predictions of short-sighted politicians, the republic has endured four decades. It seems to rest on a solid foundation, and is well able to cope with external and internal foes. Most Frenchmen have developed into true republicans and the reactionary forces are in the minority. The republic is the form of government best suited to the age of that nation. Democratic institutions are the concomitants of the prime of manhood among Aryan nations.

Under a normal evolution the advent of the republic should have occurred in the seventeenth century, when the nation passed from youth into manhood. But, in France, as elsewhere in Europe, an alien spirit of law and an alien religion, imported from the effete, stagnant and decrepit Orient, and engrafted upon the people of the Occident, retarded intellectual, political, social and religious development.

The French republic was a belated product of French social and political evolution. Under normal development the republic belongs to a nation's later youth and manhood; never to infancy and old age. The evolution of Hellas and Rome was fairly normal, and the Hellenic and Latin republics flourished at the time when those nations produced their greatest artists, philosophers, poets, orators and constructive statesmen, in great numbers. The social and political progress of the Teutonic and semi-Teutonic nations, on the contrary, has been abnormal. The sixteenth century should have witnessed the laying of the foundations of enduring republics. Strong efforts were made in that direction by Savonarola and the city-republics of Italy, by the democratic cities of Spain, by the Huguenots of France, by the Peasant War in Germany, and by the revolutionary movement of the Reformation in all the Teutonic countries; but a crystallized alien religion and a petrified foreign judicial system, both rooted in the institutions of the despotic Orient, crushed the liberal and progressive movement. The advance to republican institutions was retarded.

Italy and Spain never reached the height of democratic self-government; the Low countries enjoyed an ephemeral republic; the Anglo-Saxon and Swiss enjoyed fairly normal growth and created democracies; and the French, after many trials, finally established the belated republic on a permanent basis.

France reached its zenith during the Revolution. More greatness, more originality and more creative and inventive energy, was condensed into the last decade of the eighteenth and the first decade of the nineteenth century, than into any period of even much greater length in the history of that country. This is especially manifest in science and government, the domains where mature reason dominates. Scientists, statesmen and social reformers were the true representatives of the national spirit of that epoch.

A decline of physical, intellectual and moral force became perceptible after the restoration of the Bourbons. The succeeding generations, although they could still boast of a Beranger (1780-1857), a Lamartine (1792-1869), a Balzac (1799-1850), a Hugo (b. 1802); a Dumas (1803-1870), a Sand (1804-1876), and a de Musset(1810-1857), in literature; an Arago (1786-1853), in science; a Guizot (1787-1874), a D'Aubigne (1794-1872), a Michelet (1798-1874), and a Taine (b. 1828), in history; a Vernet (1789-1863), a Delaroche (17971877), a Delacroix (1799-1863), and a Dore (1832-1883), in art; and a Compte (1795-1857), a Cousin (1792-1869), and a Jouffroy (1796-1842), in philosophy; have to admit that these eminent men did not measure up to the high intellectual standards set up by the men of the two preceding centuries.

The classicism of the eighteenth century was superseded by the romanticism of the early nineteenth, and this again by the decadent realistic school, of which Merimee, Balzac, Flaubert, Sardou, Daudet and Zola were and are the true representatives. They point to two downward steps in literature.

The impressionist school in art also indicates a downward tendency.

Literary France is also growing reminiscent and garrulous; turns her eyes from the present and future to a glorious past, and fills the book stalls with memoirs, a sign of decadence and approaching age.

Symptoms are evidently accumulating, pointing to the, fact that the French nation has recently crossed the meridian of its life and has entered upon the descent to old age. However, it is still near its point of culmination, and, although creative and inventive power will diminish as old age advances, it may, for several centuries to come, continue to be an important factor in the world's progress.

17. The Anglo-Saxons.

The men of the Palaeolithic, Neolithic and bronze ages have left their footprints behind them in the British islands. There too, as well as on the continent, one primitive race followed another; each conquering a decadent and aging people; each building up a civilization superior to that of its predecessor; each, in its turn, rising, flourishing, declining and sinking into the impotency and decay of old age, to be subdued, and exterminated, or absorbed and assimilated by a younger, more progressive and higher developed race.

We do not know whether these early races were dark or fair. Certainly, any race developing in the soft, mild, cloudy and foggy climate of these islands must have been blond; but it is quite probable that races of dark complexion invaded the country from Spain and Gaul.

When the Romans conquered England they found two types of aborigines: the tall blond, and the swarthy of short stature. Amalgamation had not yet resulted in homogeneity. The dark and fair races lived side by side, and constant fusion would have produced a homogeneous, Celtic race in the course of time. The process of assimilation was arrested by the Roman conquest.

The Roman conquerors of England forced Latin speech, customs, religion, social and political institutions upon the natives. The island became a Roman colony and province. A new ethnic element was injected into the heterogeneous mass. Rome sent her legionaries, civil officers, merchants, mechanics, colonists and camp-followers, in great numbers. They ruled the island and built roads, forts, border walls, castles and cities. They also introduced Christianity when that cult became the state religion of the empire. The island was fairly Latinized as early as the second century of our era.

The British population of that time was of a very diverse origin. Fragments of Latin itself highly mixed Celtic, Iberian, Palaeolithic, Neolithic and Teutonic peoples, were jumbled together within a very limited space. Nearly all these fragments belonged to races which had left their zenith behind them, and were old or approaching old age.

This Latin colony shared the fate of the mother country. The same century, which saw the overthrow of the empire at the hands of the Goths, Franks, Burgundians, Alemanni, Suevi and Vandals, on the continent, witnessed the conquest of England by the Angles, Saxons, Frisians and Danes. The invasion began about 450 A. D. Hordes of warriors and colonists rushed across the North Sea annually, and in a few decades Britain, with the exception of the Scottish Highlands, and the mountains of Wales, was in the possession of the Teutonic invaders.

The natives offered a stubborn resistance, but were overpowered, annihilated or forced to seek refuge in the hilly regions of the west and north. The few, scattering remnants were readily absorbed by the conquerors, who began to form a homogeneous nation of almost pure Teutonic extraction.

Goths, Heruli, Gepidae, Langobards, Vandals, Suevi, Burgundians and Franks, whom the Great Migration had set adrift, had each conquered a fragment of the collapsing empire, but, readily fusing with the subjugated natives, lost their national identity, and sacrificed their language, laws, traditions, myths, legends and religions. It was different in England. Angles, Saxons, Frisians, Jutes and Danes were all closely related, and brought their dialects, gods, cults, customs, myths, sagas, traditions, folk lore and civil institutions with them to their new home. Teutonic life was bodily transplanted from the banks of the Rhine, Weser and Elbe and from the Danish islands to England, and there kept in its normal development. England, proper, became a purely Teutonic country; as much so as western Germany, the Netherlands and Scandinavia.

The Anglo-Saxons, as this conglomerate of Teutonic tribes soon began to be called, commenced their separate national existence at the identical stage of development, at which all Teutonic tribes stood at the time of the Great Migration. All had passed through the phase of infancy at their common home on the shores of the Baltic and North Sea, and all were still in their childhood, when some unknown cause scattered them south and west.

The evolution of national life in England ran along parallel lines with that of the Teutonic tribes which remained at home. The differentiation in speech, thought and institutions was very slow at first, so that four centuries after the invasion the inhabitants of the valleys of the Thames, Humber, Rhine and Elbe could communicate with each other without much difficulty in their, native dialects. The ties of kinship were recognized by all the tribes and nationalities that dwelt on the shores of the German Ocean.

The transition from the primitive tribal to the higher national stage was of comparatively short duration in England. Anglo-Saxons, Frisians, Jutes, Danes and Norsemen were thoroughly mingled in the colonization of the island; the lines of demarcation between the different settlements were soon obliterated; dialects, customs, laws, traditions, myths and religious beliefs and cults, blended readily and assumed new forms; and everywhere was manifest a strong drift toward homogeneity. Tribes merged with tribes into larger organic groups, and these groups finally coalesced into a nation. Tribal chieftains and petty kings rose and fell, and out of the turmoil emerged the national king. The heterogeneous mass of the invaders was organically united into the English nation, with hereditary kingship at its head, as early as the eighth century.

The normal development of the English nation was arrested, and diverted in a new direction in the seventh century, through the introduction of Christianity. The young and thriving Teutonic sapling was polled of its twigs and branches, and a foreign cult, with foreign gods, and foreign ideas on religion, government, society, law, art and poetry y was engrafted on its stem. Zealous and fanatic missionaries tore up the native religion with its popular deities, and the national poetry, art, myths, legends, customs and institutions, interwoven therewith, and substituted for it the ideas, ideals, conceptions and institutions of classic and decadent Jerusalem and Rome. Strange gods, with a large retinue of alien ideas on right and wrong, on the true and false, took possession of the land. The Semitic Yahweh, in his Hellenized and Latinized form, accompanied by his suite of patriarchs, prophets, apostles, saints and angels, expelled the Teutonic Wotan with his Walhallan court. The "Ragnarok," the evening twilight of the Teutonic deities, of which the native seers had a presentiment, had come.

It produced a radical revolution. The intellectual and moral development of the nation received a violent shock. The Christian priests and missionaries not only brought a new religion, they came also as the representatives of a higher civilization. They were men of learning and at once became priests and tutors of the barbarians. They conducted the new, symbolic worship, taught the people, administered the affairs of the court and state, and introduced Latin as the official language of the Court, of the church and of literature. The nascent, native literature, of great promise, and of which a few fragments, such as "Beowulf" were saved from the vandalism of a jealous and intolerant priesthood, was nipped in the bud, and suffered a premature death.

The whole social, political, religious and literary life of the Anglo-Saxons was rooted in its Teutonic past. A sound, normal and vigorous development was possible only on this soil. The organic connection with the pagan past was almost totally severed by the introduction of the new religion. The juvenile Anglo-Saxon nation was suddenly abducted from the sphere of its native gods and heroes, and installed as the pupil, apprentice and slave of Roman, Greek and Semitic masters, and subsequent English history is but a continuous struggle to shake off this foreign yoke.

Undoubtedly, without this deforming and stunting foreign influence, the Anglo-Saxons would have built up a civilization, stronger, more advanced, more progressive and more symmetrical, than the one they now enjoy. The strong blast from degenerate Rome, Athens and Jerusalem, sweeping uninterruptedly across England for over a thousand years, has bent, twisted and warped the British oak.

However, the influence of the Orient was never as strong and complete in England as on the continent. The insular position and the distance from Rome afforded some protection. The Civil Law, for instance, which followed in the wake of Christianity, the product of the degenerate Orient, and well suited to oriental society, but poorly adapted to a community of sturdy, independent and progressive Teutonic freemen, was generally adopted on the continent, but gained only a slender foothold in England. The Common Law of the Anglo-Saxons, on the contrary, is the natural evolution of the ancient Teutonic ideas of right and justice; and to these ideas and principles the Anglo-Saxons owe their freedom, their sturdy citizenship, their progress and their power. The ancient Teutonic ideas of personal and civil liberty vanished from Europe in proportion as the principles of the Civil and Canon Law were incorporated in the codes.

It is also readily observed that in art, literature, philosophy, learning, economic and political life, the Anglo-Saxons always manifested a stronger individuality and initiative, and a more pronounced national independence than their more Romanized kindred on the continent.

But, nevertheless, the introduction of Christianity with its retinue of Roman and Oriental ideas, manners and institutions, exerted a disturbing and baneful influence on the growth of the English nation. The Latin language, and with it Latin thought, ruled in the royal court, in the church, in judicial proceedings, in the schools and hi literature, from the middle of the seventh to about the middle of the thirteenth century. All intellectual life of a higher order was Latinized. The old bards and minstrels, who had celebrated the deeds of pagan, national gods and heroes in epic song, grew suddenly mute, and a new class of poets, priestly and monkish in their ideas, substituted Roman, Hellenic and Semitic deities and saints for the old heathen divinities, and sang in Latin verse of their adventures and miracles. The native literature, grand in its promise, which reflected the spirit of the heroic age and of the phase of infancy of the Teutonic race, sank into complete oblivion. Rulers and judges turned from the fountain head of ancient Teutonic customs and laws, and sought wisdom in the codes of Moses and Justinian.

Genuine intellectual life of the Anglo-Saxons from about 650 to 1250 A. D. was mainly confined to the hut of the peasant; a poor refuge for a tender, budding civilization.

The Norman conquest, A. D. 1066, did not seriously affect the normal development of English national life. True, Norman kings and vassals ruled the land, Norman French became the language of polite society, Normans developed the power of kings and barons to a higher degree than had been done by Anglo-Saxons rulers and thanes, but the conquerors themselves were of Teutonic lineage, they, too, thought, felt and acted like Teutons, and as they constituted only an insignificant minority of the whole people, they were speedily absorbed and assimilated by the natives. They made only a slight impression on the English language, literature, social and political institutions. The Norman conquest wrought no ethnical change, and the Normans never became an important factor in the shaping of England's destiny and the English character.

The true genius of the Anglo-Saxon nation had found refuge in the peasant's humble hut during this long period, and there, silently and undisturbed by the strifes of feudal lords, the bloody wars with France, the picturesque life of chivalry, the craze of the crusades, the alien learning of the monastery, the speculations of scholasticism, and the revival of literature by Troubadours, Trouveres and Minnesingers, it quietly and unobtrusively prepared itself for its great and peculiar mission.

The higher intellectual life of England, during the earlier part of the Medieval Age, was an exotic, and was almost exclusively confined to royalty, feudal nobles and churchmen; most of them of foreign birth and ancestry, and nearly all of them following foreign models. They wrote chronicles, religious and legal treatises, in Latin, but the great, subdued and oppressed Anglo-Saxon masses did not participate in that life. With the exception of a few folk-songs, transmitted verbally from generation to generation, no real English literature existed in that age.

The thirteenth century witnessed the tardy and belated awakening of the national genius. The Anglo-Saxon passed from a dull and dreary childhood into a more cheerful early youth. He became conscious of his own native vigor, and manifested symptoms of insubordination under the rigorous restraint of foreign tutors. Literature drifted away from castle and monastery to the unpretentious dwellings of peasant and burgher, and became secular and popular. Poets rose to address the commons in the vernacular. Latin fell largely into desuetude. Norman kings and nobles became imbued with the national spirit and began to think and feel as Englishmen.

The Roman clergy and Norman kings and knights suppressed Anglo-Saxon literary activity from the seventh to the thirteenth century. This wide, dismal gap of nearly seven centuries is almost destitute of national literary efforts. It was the nation's childhood and early youth and, under normal development, should have been filled with great epics, the natural production of a nation's youth and heroic age.

The national intellect was chiefly occupied, during that age, in the upbuilding of better social and political institutions. The growth of the cities in wealth and power and the decay of feudal chivalry, were the characteristic features of the latter part of the Medieval Age. The cities, as the new ganglia and nerve centers of the political organism, superseded palace and castle. There the new intellectual force and activity was concentrated.

The soil, the sole source of wealth and influence in that early age, was monopolized by the aristocracy and the church. The small, independent freeholder had been eliminated from the social structure, and, about 1200 A. D. when knighthood was at its height, the country knew only feudal lords, abject serfs and the burghers of the democratic towns and cities.

The phenomenal increase in commerce and industry wrought a corresponding social and political change. Political power always follows material wealth. Money, in the hands of the burghers, became a new social and political factor. The thriftless, profligate knight, in his crumbling castle, looked with disdain and apprehension upon his industrious and opulent rival in the city, whose rights he denied, but whose money he was compelled to borrow. The center of gravity of political power shifted from baronial stronghold to the guild hall and market place of the cities.

The English towns and cities had silently grown up under the old Teutonic ideas, customs, laws and usages. The feudal lords, bent upon adventure, gaiety and foreign wars, had paid very little attention to the internal management of the cities, which now sprang up as important and growing centers, in which a new national life was stirring. At these centers, and there only, dominated a democratic progressive and aggressive spirit, and to this spirit, slowly but steadily spreading from the city to village, castle, palace and monastery, Britain owes its greatness.

All progress, inventions, original ideas, creative force, enlightenment and liberal policies, which have made England justly famous, emanated from her democratic towns and cities. Princes, nobles and prelates, the natural champions of existing conditions and of a conservative past, strove in vain to suppress and curtail this rising, revolutionary power. The cities were generally triumphant in the struggle for civil liberty. The rise and fall of democracy in England, since the beginning of the Middle Age, is a good barometer to mark the rise and fall of British civilization.

This is true of Europe generally. A strong democratic spirit moved all the Teutonic and semi-Teutonic nations, as they advanced from childhood into youth. It was a sign of adolescence. The Hansa of Germany and the city leagues of France, Italy, Spain and the Low Countries, were all animated by an intense desire for progress and larger freedom. They all failed eventually and had to succumb to the power of kings and nobles, which resulted in intellectual stagnation. In England, alone, were the democratic cities victorious.

This fact gave the English nation the lead in social and political evolution. The social and political organs of the body politic were atrophied and crippled among the Continental nations when democracy was struck down, but in England they attained healthy development by proper exercise. It is for this reason that the Anglo-Saxons enjoyed a more complete and symmetrical civilization than their neighbors.

This democratic spirit was not confined to any class; it pervaded all social classes. Almost every Briton of note, from Roger Bacon to Gladstone, recognized the plain citizen as an important factor in all affairs of state, and sought his approval by a direct appeal to his sentiments, passions and judgment. Public opinion was always a great power in England, and this fact lent stability and solidity to progress.

The English nation stepped from childhood into early youth during the thirteenth century. A notable social and political transformation took place. Democracy gained ground. The national spirit, personified in the king, was triumphant over the feudal barons, representing the old tribal idea. The democratic cities were the allies of royalty and found recognition. King John granted them some seats in Parliament in 1215 A. D. Henry II subdued the feudal nobles and called two representatives of every borough to Parliament. The Statute of Mortmain checked the absorption of land by the church. The first Statute of Westminster (1275 A. D.) codified all previous charters, decrees and ordinances, and confirmed the right of each city to send two members to Parliament. London rose to the first rank as a center of wealth and' power, which no king, noble or prelate dared to ignore.

The poets gave voice to the new life now beginning to pulsate through the nation. Layamon (about 1220 A. D.), and others gave utterance to their thoughts and feelings in the undeveloped, unrefined, rustic English of the age. Roger Bacon (1214-1272), Occham (1270-1347), and Duns Scotus (d. 1308), represented the transition from the authoritative scholasticism of France and Italy to a daring and independent inquiry. The young British nation was growing restive under the hitherto absolute rule of foreign tutors and masters.

The fourteenth century saw a continuation of progress and a yet greater intellectual revival. Parliament grew more democratic and wrested one popular right after another from the crown. The decadent nobility and clergy grew weary of parliamentary struggles, and the knights of the shire a lower aristocracy allied with the burghers formed the "Commons," a new, rising, progressive and aggressive force in the government of the realm. Monasticism and knighthood were on the decline. The well-attended universities became influential centers of learning and bold investigation.

The land was rife with revolt. The nation had outgrown its old habiliments. Laborers, peasants, burghers and yeomen rose to demand greater rights for themselves, and the curtailment of the privileges of the few. The "Black Death" (1348-1356), and a general famine, decimated the populace, and fanned the general discontent into an open insurrection. The frightened feudal lords endeavored to quell the uprising by harsh laws, fettering the laborer to the glebe, fixing his wages and stamping him a criminal if he left his master without permission. Futile endeavor! The movement could not be stemmed. Popular leaders sprang up. John Ball (1360) preached the rights of man; Langland, in his socialistic and realistic poem "Piers Ploughman," proclaimed the gospel of equal rights; and Wycliffe (1324-1384)", and the Lollards, maintained a stubborn fight for freedom of conscience, social rights and untrammeled investigation. The peasants rose in open rebellion to demand the abolition of serfdom. The uprising was crushed, but the victorious nobility, perceiving the grim determination of the masses, granted many concessions, and the aim of the revolt was attained.

This first genuine outburst of intellectual life of the youthful Anglo-Saxon nation culminated in Chaucer, the poet (1328-1400 A. D.), and in Wycliffe, the reformer.

Chaucer represented the past and the present; Wycliffe the present and future. Chaucer was the poet of chivalry and of the medieval church, both in their decline then; Wycliffe was the realistic, bold reformer. The vivid imagination of youth predominated in Chaucer; clear reason and sound judgment of manhood in Wycliffe. Both brought the English language to a high perfection and made it popular.

The overshadowing influence of the Latin clergy and of Norman kings and nobles, although it did not affect the normal growth of the English nation seriously, was fateful in the development of the English language. Anglo-Saxon speech, being confined to laborers, peasants and burghers, for centuries, and having served her proud sisters as the despised Cinderella of the nursery tale, had been crippled during its most important, formative phase, and had emerged from the Dark Ages in a much-stunted condition. Living languages grow by derivatives and compounds, and new words are created and coined, to give expression to new ideas as they arise in the progress of nations. The

Anglo-Saxon tongue had lost this capacity for growth at the time of Chaucer. It was unable to send forth new buds, leaves and branches. To meet the demand for new terms and expressions, recourse was uniformly had to borrowing words from the Greek, Latin and French. The purely Anglo-Saxon vocabulary of Chaucer has not changed much. Modern English is the old Anglo-Saxon trunk, entirely overgrown by Greek, Latin and French terms engrafted upon it. And as man thinks in words, it might be a very interesting inquiry to determine how far, and in what form, the excessive adoption of foreign words has influenced modern English thought.

The youth of the Teutonic and semi-Teutonic nations of Europe, which lasted from about the seventh to the fifteenth century, and which reached its greatest height in the twelfth and thirteenth centuries; the age of strenuous, intellectual activity, originality, creative force, exuberant fancy, restless vigor and picturesque life; the era of scholasticism, of a new architecture, of a new art, of chivalry, of the crusades and of the rise of real kingship and city-republics; the epoch in which rose Dante, Petrarch and Boccaccio in Italy, Alfonso, Gonzalo and the anonymous author of "The Cid" in Spain, the Troubadours and Trouveres in France, Langland and Chaucer in England, and the Minnesingers and the unknown writer of the "Nibelungen" epic in Germany; the heroic age of the race; came to an end, and was succeeded by an era of exhaustion, stagnation and sterility. It lasted for over a century. It was an era of transition from youth to early manhood; an era of rest and preparation for a grander effort to reach a still higher level.

England participated in this general but temporary decline. Lollardism, originally a healthy movement in favor of liberal government in state and church, but later transformed into a wild and fanatic socialism, was extirpated by brutal force. Free thought was stunned for over a century. The exhaustive wars in France and of the Roses, the centralization of power in the crown, the deterioration of the nobility, the imbecility and corruption of the clergy, a pusillanimous Parliament, the degeneration of democracy in the cities, and the poverty and distress of the masses, prevented men of talent and genius from rising to fame. The paucity of great names in art, letters, science and statesmanship, between the death of Chaucer (1400), and the reign of Henry VIII is surprising. The nation seemed to suffer from a lingering malady.

Reconvalescence came at the close of the fifteenth century. External influences gave a new impulse to intellectual life. The revival of the study of the Greek and Latin classics, the invention of printing and gunpowder, the discovery of new worlds, the opening of new channels of commerce, the Humanism and Renaissance imported from Italy, and the German Reformation, stimulated the then sluggish British mind to renewed efforts.

The Reformation, from its very incipiency, divided itself into two currents. The one faction, headed by Luther, strove to confine the revolutionary movement within the church; the other, led by Zwingli, Calvin and Knox, was strongly imbued with democratic principles and aimed at social and political as well as at religious reform and liberty.

The feudal and the semi-Slavic part of Germany, as a rule, followed Luther; but the western Germans, the Swiss, the Dutch and the English, among whom the democratic ideas were deeply rooted, and where city-republics and small free-holders were still powerful social and political factors, leaned toward the broader doctrines of the Swiss and Scotch reformers.

The legal maxim *"cujus regio, ejus religio" ("Whose realm, his religion")* made the reformation in Germany the exclusive affair of the princes; it remained in the hands of the people in Switzerland and the Netherlands, and in England crown and Parliament combined to direct and control its course. The scope and thoroughness of the movement depended upon the extent to which the common people participated in it.

The English reformation, in consequence, was a compromise. The teachings of Zwingli and Calvin, especially after the Peasants' War of Germany, were deemed too radical and democratic by the British crown and nobility, and the common people did not favor Luther's alliance with the conservative princes. So a golden mean was selected, and the English reformers halted midway between Zurich and Rome.

The Reformation was essentially a Teutonic emancipation from foreign rule. The English compromise, however, did not satisfy the masses; it was the work of statesmen and churchmen. The established Anglican church is neither wholly Teutonic nor Roman. It maintains itself through the community of interests of crown, nobility and clergy, and the inertia of the masses. As a rule, whenever the Briton emigrates and when the force of habit and tradition is materially lessened, he withdraws from the established church, and allies himself with sects which, in doctrines, tenets, and organization, harmonize better with his inherent, democratic ideas, and more truly represent progressive Teutonic thought.

The England of the sixteenth century made rapid progress in every domain of thought. Parliament, representing the people, gained steadily in power and prestige. Many political reforms were inaugurated. Serfdom disappeared silently. Prosperity returned. British merchants, taking advantage of the new order of things the opening up of America, the new route to India and the paralysis of Germany reached out for the control of the world's commerce. English sailors swept the Spanish navy and merchant marine from the ocean, and the gold and silver of Peru and Mexico, filched from the natives by the conquistadores, found its way to British coffers. Britain rose at once to a commanding position in the councils of nations.

The English nation was in the full flush of youth or early manhood in the sixteenth century. Its literature unfolded its swelling buds. More, Wyatt and Surrey, still laboring under the overshadowing influence of the Italian Renaissance, ventured forth as the harbingers of approaching spring. An epoch of glorious efflorescence followed. Sidney (1554-1586), the romantic, sentimental and chivalrous poet; Spenser (1553-1599), with his vivid imagination and his songs of love, loyalty and puritanism; Marlowe, Greene, Beaumont, Fletcher, Marston and Jonson, with their youthful fire, fervor and volcanic force, and, greatest of them all, the immortal Shakespeare, appeared.

It was England's period of "storm and stress"; a grand, spontaneous, majestic outburst of genius, daring originality, creative power, innovation, invention, and of irresistible physical and intellectual energy; an era full of unrest, curiosity, passion, energy, virility, riotousness, extravagance, exaggeration, bold fancy, exulting ambition and consciousness of titanic powers; and her writers of gigantic mould found their peers in the talented queen, the gifted Cecil, and in the adventurous Raleigh, Drake and Frobisher.

The poetic phase of youth ended with Shakespeare, and calm reason, the attribute of riper manhood, began to sway the scepter. The national genius diverted its attention from the poetic flights of the imagination to philosophical reasoning, exact sciences and practical politics. Bacon (1561-1621), who opened the way in scientific and philosophical research; Hobbes (15881679), who sought to apply the laws of nature to social organisms; Locke (1632-1704), who based all knowledge on experience; Harvey (1578-1657), Boyle (16261692), Hooke (1635-1703), Newton (1642-1727), Flamstead (1646-1719), and Halley (1656-1742), were pathfinders in the field of science, and, by their original investigations and great discoveries, enriched the stock of human knowledge.

Poetry, especially epic poetry, which is always associated with the childhood and heroic youth of nations, retired modestly from the front of the stage in the seventeenth century, and gave way to reason and science. Scientists, philosophers, jurists, statesmen and national economists, the true representatives of a nation's full maturity, crowded to the footlights.

Still, the century produced some poets of merit; Milton (1608-1674), with his bold fancy, gorgeous imagery and sublime thoughts; Butler (1512-1680), coarse, licentious and cynical; Bunyan (1628-1688), highly imaginative and puritanic; and Dryden (16311700), intellectual, calm, argumentative and critical, represented the poetic side of the nation's work. Milton and Bunyan, with their exuberant imagination, were belated spring flowers, an aftermath of the preceding poetic age; Butler reflected the profligate, corrupt and chivalric court of Charles II; and Dryden was the poetic interpreter of the new age of reason and science.

The poetry of this epoch was not the natural, spontaneous outburst of juvenile passion and fervor, like that of the sixteenth century. It was written for the purpose of championing a social class, a political party* or a religious sect. It was aimed at the understanding of man rather than at his heart. Reason held the reins of Pegasus.

It was not a poetic age. Public attention was riveted on practical social, political and religious reforms. Problems of this kind absorbed the intellectual force of the nation. The nation had outgrown kingship, and the established church satisfied neither the aristocracy nor the common people. The majority of the people was Calvinistic at heart, and the nation longed for democracy in church and state.

The intellectual activity of the sixteenth century was mainly confined to the upper strata of society. The broad masses, like the depth of the storm-beaten Atlantic, remained undisturbed. The champions of English liberty and progress, previous to the seventeenth century, had been recruited chiefly from the patrician classes. Poets rarely portrayed the life of the husbandmen or the proletariat of the cities. They knew humanity only down to the baron, and ridiculed the plain people with the haughty contempt of the courtier.

But a new religious and political force began to stir the hearts of the people to the very bottom, in the first half of the seventeenth century. The common people now became conscious of their own strength and importance. They demanded their rightful share in the administration of political and religious affairs; they felt that the nation was of age. The crown resisted these claims. James and Charles I, infatuated with the belief in the divine rights of kings, endeavored to make their 'personal will the law of the land. The aroused people sent their champions Eliot, Pym, Hampden, Cromwell and others, to the Parliament. Charles continued obdurate. The contest waxed hot. The higher nobility, the Anglican clergy and the Catholics, stood by the king; but the yeomen, the small freeholders, the burghers of the cities and the Puritans espoused the cause of Parliament. The clash was inevitable. Civil war ensued, and on the sanguinary field of Naseby, in 1645, chivalry and monarchy went down before the intrepid onset of Cromwell's Puritan Ironsides. Democracy was triumphant; the commonwealth was established; Charles, unable to understand the new spirit of the times, lost his crown and head; and England, free and united at home, strong and victorious abroad, acquired a renown and prestige, unprecedented.

The nation had arrived at maturity; had entered the phase of manhood. The republic, the culminating point, the keystone in the arch of the Aryan nations' political life, was established. Every man, high or low, was now a recognized, full-valued factor in the state. Every man could now exercise and develop his faculties without hindrance, and the stupendous aggregate force thus generated and employed was the main cause of England's subsequent greatness in every department of thought and action.

The commonwealth was founded in accordance with the age and normal development of the nation. But it did not endure long. The change from absolute monarchy to a free republic was too abrupt, and disconcerted the masses. They could not shake off at once the weight of habit, tradition and ingrained ideas. And the Puritans, the real republicans of the land, could not sever the affairs of state from those of religion. They were very pious and looked upon the Bible as the source of all wisdom. But the Bible cannot be taken as a textbook on political science. It was written, in its present form, nearly three thousand years ago, and reflects the political condition and ideals of primitive Asia, with its autocratic rulers and submissive subjects. The kings ruled by divine right; the subjects' duty was to obey. Of the modern ideal of self government not a word is to be found in Holy Writ. These political ideals were first introduced by the Greeks and Romans.

To the mind of the Puritan the commonwealth was an innovation, not sanctioned by divine ordinances. Two opposing forces in his breast made him a caricature politically. With one foot he stood in the progressive England of the seventeenth century and with the other in the stagnant, primitive and patriarchal Palestine of the prophets or even of Moses. He was unable to advance; he stumbled and slid back. The republic of Cromwell, after a brief trial, failed, and monarchy was restored.

That the English people were ripe for democracy is established by the fact that an offshoot of that nation found lodgement in the wilds of America at that time, and there, unencumbered by the weight and shackles of class interests, musty traditions and tenacious habits and customs, laid the enduring foundations of a progressive and mighty republic.

In England reaction set in when the great leaders of the republican movement were gone. The pendulum swung back violently from austere and progressive Puritanism to cynical, arrogant, licentious and reactionary royalty. The cavaliers triumphed. Servile and corrupt courtiers, poets, and savants vied with each other in adulations of a worthless king. Court and clergy strove to undo the work of Cromwell and his compatriots.

They did not succeed. In one generation after the exhaustive wars of Cromwell did the people recover their old spirit. They rose again to demand their rights, dethroned James, called William of Orange, a citizen of a republic, to the British throne, and in the Declaration of Rights, sanctioned by the king and queen, secured substantially everything for which Cromwell and his confederates had fought and labored. England was virtually a republic again.

Reaction had celebrated an ephemeral success; but the consciousness of youthful strength, the sound judgment, the practical, good sense, the determined will, the progressive spirit, and the sturdy independence of the Anglo-Saxon race, were bound to reassert themselves, and come out triumphantly in the end. Indeed, English progress and liberty were never seriously jeopardized by the profligate Charles, or the obstinate James.

The eighteenth century was for England an epoch of quiet, healthy growth rather than of brilliant and picturesque deeds. It could not boast of its Voltaires, Rousseaux, Laplaces, Goethes, Schillers, Kants, Bachs, Fredericks, Dantons and Napoleons; but England was great in every department of human endeavor, and created a civilization which, if in some points overshadowed by some neighbor, is superior to all in its symmetry and general excellence.

Clive and Nelson as soldiers and sailors; Walpole, Pitt and Burke, as statesmen and orators; De Foe, Swift, Addison, Pope, Fielding, Smollet, Sheridan and Burns, in literature; Hogarth, Reynolds, Gainsborough and Leslie, in art; Butler, Wesley and Whitefield, as reforming churchmen; Berkley, as philosopher; Adam Smith, as the pioneer of the science of political economy, Hunter, Priestly, Cavendish and Herschel in science; Arkwright and Watt, as inventors; and Hume and Gibbon, as historians, present an illustrious array of genius and talent. The intellectual life of the nation was strong, sound and well rounded out; not a field was left uncultivated. The genius, the talent, the energy, of the nation, were not directed exclusively to a few departments, such as poetry, philosophy, art and music, but extended also to internal politics, political economy, commerce, industry, agriculture and colonization, and herein they were eminently successful.

The British nation was now in the prime of manhood. The leading men of a nation are always the representatives of the phase of life through which it is passing. The personnel of the procession of eminent men changes in character as the nation advances from childhood to youth, from youth to manhood, and from manhood to old age. At full maturity, in its age of reason, the English nation brought forth as its true representatives, its Newtons, Pitts, Priestleys, Cavendishes, Humes, Watts and Adam Smiths.

British intellectual life of the eighteenth century manifested a strong democratic, realistic and materialistic tendency. All thinkers kept in close touch with the masses, and strove to elevate them. They discovered the truth that a state is powerful in proportion to the freedom and material welfare enjoyed by each individual member. Every leading statesman, from the elder Pitt down to Asquith, has exerted himself to improve the condition of the people in this direction. This policy bore splendid fruit. Patriotism, national pride and manly independence pervaded all strata of society; personal initiative was fostered; skill in handicraft was promoted; invention followed invention; commerce and industry flourished; and Anglo-Saxon rule expanded over large parts of all the continents.

The England of the sixteenth century followed in the wake of Italian Humanism and Renaissance; at the beginning of the seventeenth century she copied the Dutch; at its close she was the pupil of France; but during the eighteenth she forged ahead and conquered the position of standard-bearer of European culture. Her social, political, judicial and economic institutions were universally accepted as models. The greater part of all inventions, innovations and reforms in government, laws, judicial proceedings, commerce, industry, agriculture, transportation and colonization, from the commencement of the eighteenth to the middle of the nineteenth century, was of Anglo-Saxon origin. And originality, invention and creative power are the true tests of progress, civilization and of a nation's maturity. Every individual, every nation can imitate, but a few only can invent and create. This truth is usually lost sight of in fixing an individual's or a nation's cultural position. The creator, inventor and originator is frequently under-estimated and the imitator over-estimated. To create new light, to extend the bounds of knowledge into unknown fields, is the true touchstone of civilization. The inventor of the friction, match, for instance, although scarcely known, achieved more for the enlightenment of mankind than the famous author of a highly entertaining novel.

England experienced a check in her progress during her conflict with the French republic and the Napoleonic empire. She took an illogical position. The traditional champion of human rights and liberty, she allowed herself to be drafted into opposition to democracy in France. She suffered in consequence. Progress was brought to a full step, and did not resume its advance until the first quarter of the nineteenth century had passed. The aristocracy of birth and wealth was again in the ascendant. All reforms ceased. Industry was paralyzed. Finances were in a deplorable condition. The laboring masses sank into the state of a hopeless proletariat. The land was filled with a spirit of unrest, discontent and mutiny. Literature, although represented by eminent writers, such as Wordsworth, Coleridge, Scott, Moore, Byron, Keats and Shelley, bore an unhealthy look and showed the hectic flush of the degenerate, romantic school.

A revival of intellectual life began in the third decade of the nineteenth century. Every nerve, every muscle, every brain was strained to the utmost in the final ascent to the culmination point in Anglo-Saxon national life. Every department of knowledge, every field of human activity, found its representative men of the highest order. Canning, Peel, Cobden, Bright, Palmerston and Gladstone, in statesmanship and oratory; Turner and Landseer in art; Carlyle, Macaulay, Tennyson, Thackeray, Dickens and George Eliot, in letters; Milman and Grote in history; Mill, Buckle and Herbert Spencer, in philosophy; Hooker, Sir Humphrey Davis, Lyell, Tyndall, Huxley, Geikie and Darwin, in science; and a host of inventors, explorers and great captains of industry, commerce and finance, covered the England of the nineteenth century with imperishable glory.

We may designate the sixteenth century as the Italian and Spanish, the seventeenth and eighteenth as the French, and the nineteenth as the Anglo-Saxon. These nations successively enjoyed the leadership of Europe in the periods named, when they, respectively, crossed their meridians.

England stood at her zenith about the middle of the nineteenth century. Her navy ruled the sea; her dominion had reached its greatest expansion; her merchant marine very nearly monopolized the carrying trade of the world; her industry supplied the markets; her capital inaugurated, maintained and controlled innumerable and gigantic enterprises of all sorts on all the continents; her literary men were the peers of the best in other countries; her statesmen promoted democracy and fostered free institutions; her scientists led the way in bold conceptions and thorough, original investigation; and her citizens had more useful, practical and epoch-making inventions to their credit than all the rest of Europe combined.

With Mill, Spencer, Dickens, Tennyson, Buckle, Peel, Gladstone, Huxley, Tyndall and Darwin, the English nation crossed its meridian.

The last decades of the nineteenth century furnished many symptoms to indicate that the nation has begun its downward march. A growing paucity of great names in politics, science, art and literature is manifest. The epigoni of today do not measure up to the standards set up by the intellectual giants of preceding generations, Originality, inventive and creative power, the attributes of the prime of manhood, seem to have spent their force. The expansive power is exhausted. Colonization is growing weak. The prestige of the British soldier suffered grievously in the Boer War. Commerce and industry are losing ground relatively. Life is growing more conservative and stereotyped. The people grow averse to innovations and reforms. They are becoming nervous, oversensitive and even hysterical. A pessimistic consciousness of waning strength pervades all strata of society. Extravagance, profligacy, effeminacy, immorality and corruption, the concomitants of approaching old age in nations, are on the increase.

It is difficult or impossible to fix the exact point of culmination in the life of a living individual or nation. We can only say that the individual is in his prime within a certain decade, and the nation within a certain century. It is quite probable, however, that, under normal conditions, the zenith point of the British nation would be still in the future, but the irresponsible rule over hundreds of millions of alien subjects, the conscienceless exploitation of vast colonies, the constant stream of enormous wealth flowing to the island from all directions, and the centralization of this wealth and power into the hands of a few, have accelerated the gait of the nation, and are bringing on premature decay and old age. But, be that as it may, whether the nation is now on this side or beyond its meridian, it is in its vicinity, and, in obedience to the laws of nature, has already begun or will soon begin its descent to the imbecility, sterility and unprogressiveness of old age.

If this diagnosis be correct that England has begun her descent from the apex of her power and glory, she is in a very critical situation. She will have to fight her life's battle to retain her present world's championship, or voluntarily relinquish it. It was always thus. The earth is but the enlarged arena of the prize ring. Here champion follows champion in quick succession. The young athlete rises through a series of successful battles, until he confronts the acknowledged champion, who has enjoyed the honors and emoluments of championship for a brief period, and whose vigor the passing years, and the dissipations incident to the position, are silently sapping. A rising and a falling star collide in the ensuing battle, and a championship is lost and won. In the world's great prize ring, nations and races also contend for the championship. Champions rose and fell. China, India, Egypt, Babylon, Assyria, Persia, Greece, Rome, Arabia, Italy, Spain and France, when in the full vigor of youth and early manhood, successively defeated the preceding champion, basked for a while in the glories of the world's championship, until advancing age, profligacy and corruption weakened them to such an extent, that they lost it in the next decisive struggle to a new and rising athlete, who, in the course of time, was to meet the same fate. The great decisive battles of history are those which were waged for the supremacy and the championship of the world; and from the date of which the course of history took a new turn.

Until recently the England of the nineteenth century has been the acknowledged champion and arbiter of the world. She now must defend the title against all comers, or relinquish it voluntarily. Conscious of her wasting powers, she views with alarm and trepidation the growing strength of the younger athlete from the Rhine and the Elbe, who, fresh from Sadowa, where he defeated the German champion, and from Sedan, where the continental champion went down before him, is certain to dispute with England the championship of the world. England is in no condition to contend successfully with her younger, more formidable and more progressive rival. If she is wise, she will not run the risk. If, however, she ventures upon it, the world will witness another memorable contest, in which the championship of the world is lost and won; a pivotal battle, from the date of which the current of events will flow in another direction.

The enormous expansive force incident to the prime of nations led to the successful foundation of a number of vigorous and promising Anglo-Saxon colonies in America, Australia and Africa. These offshoots began their separate national existence at a stage in which the mother-country stood at the time of the separation. With it they are marching abreast through the phase of national manhood toward decline and old age. Indeed, freed from the hampering burden of tradition, habit and custom of thought and action, they are outrunning the mother-country. The United States, Canada, Australia, New Zealand and South Africa, in the development of their political, social, religious and economic institutions, are advancing faster than Old England. But, whatever they may think, invent, create and evolve, it is all on the line of Anglo-Saxon progress. They all form a group of states organically united by common speech traditions, laws, ideas, ideals, aspirations and social, political and religious institutions.

18. The Germans.

The Teutons, at the time of Caesar and of Tacitus, peopled all the region bounded by the North Sea, the Baltic, the Vistula, the upper Danube and the middle and lower Rhine. The left bank of the Rhine, most of what is now southern Germany, and the German provinces of Austria and Switzerland, were inhabited by Celtic tribes.

The Teutonic tribes of that age were all united in their old home. They were then passing from the phase of infancy into that of childhood. The family, as a dominant social and political unit, had given way to the clan or tribe. The tribal form of government had superseded the patriarchal. Myths, legends and gods grouped themselves into larger clusters, to conform to the new tribal arrangement. Tribal bards sang of the exploits and adventures of tribal heroes and deities; and the people passed slowly from the primitive, nomadic and pastoral to the agricultural and more settled life.

Shortly thereafter, a fierce tornado, having gathered its forces on the borders of distant China, swept through northern Asia, rushed across the eastern confines of Europe, and only when it had reached the heart of Germany and of France, had it spent its destructive force. When quiet returned, Europe was radically changed. The terrific impact of the ethnical storm had torn the eastern Teutonic tribes of the Goths, Vandals, Gepidae, Suevi and Burgundians, from their moorings and sent them adrift to find new anchorage in the provinces of the Roman Empire; had pressed the western tribes against the shores of the North Sea, and forced Franks and Alemanni into Gaul, and the Anglo-Saxons, Jutes and Danes across the German Ocean into the British Isles.

All these tribes took possession of and established new homes in the Roman provinces. Ostrogoths, Heruli and Langobards conquered Italy; Visigoths, Franks and Burgundians settled in Gaul; Goths and Suevi occupied the Iberian peninsula; the tribes along the eastern shore of the North Sea invaded and colonized England; Marcomanni and Alemanni founded new homes in the Celto-Latin provinces of what is now German-Austria, Bavaria, Wurtemberg, Elsass, Lorraine and Switzerland; and the Slavs inhabited the eastern half of ancient Germany.

Goths, Vandals, Suevi, Langobards, Burgundians and Franks were absorbed and assimilated by the conquered Celto-Latin peoples, and with them formed the neo-Latin nations of the Italians, Spaniards and French. The Anglo-Saxons maintained their purity of blood. Slavs and Germans of eastern Germany fused into a new German people. Around the headwaters of the Rhine and the Danube, a region originally occupied by Celts, and subsequently held in possession by the Romans for five centuries, new nationalities of mixed Teutonic, Latin and Celtic origin sprang up. Celtic aborigines, Roman soldiers, traders, officials, laborers and colonists and German invaders, met in this borderland, amalgamated, and became the ancestors of the modern Austrians, Bavarians, Suabians and Swiss.

The new tribes thus formed were German in speech and sentiment, but always exhibited strong physical, mental and moral evidence of their triple ancestry.

The Slavs, crowded westward beyond the Elbe and Saale in Germany by the hordes of Mongol-Tartaric invaders behind them, undoubtedly absorbed the residue of German tribes which had remained at home; and, in the German reconquest of the territory, were not exterminated, but, as was customary in those days, were reduced to servitude, and in their turn absorbed and assimilated by the Germans.

Only the tribes of western and central Germany retained their purity of blood and their Teutonic character.

The German nation, therefore, is a conglomerate of Teutonic, Celtic, Latin and Slavic elements, and the knowledge of this fact furnishes the key to its history. No two races think, feel and act alike, and besides that, the ideas, ideals and aspirations of each race undergo a radical change as the race or nation passes through the phases of life, from infancy to old age. Only when we have acquainted ourselves with the value, in regard to numbers, age and character, of each ethnic factor that enters into the formation of a nation, can we understand that nation's position in history.

The German tribes of the west and center and of Alemannic Suabia, Elsass and Switzerland, being of pure Teutonic extraction, enjoyed a normal development. Those of the south and along the west bank of the Rhine, where much old and decadent Latin and Celtic blood had been infused, evolution was accelerated; and in the northeast, in the Prussian provinces, where the inferior Slavic element, mainly of Mongolic and Tartaric extraction, formed the substratum of the people, progress was retarded.

From the writings of the Romans and Greeks, an4 from the preserved fragments of an incipient native literature we obtain a fairly good picture of the condition of the Germans at the commencement of the Christian era.

Agriculture, carried on by women, serfs and slaves, formed the main occupation. Iron, in the manufacture of tools and implements, had superseded bronze and polished stone. Epic poetry was cultivated by the tribal bards. Families merged into clans, clans into tribes and tribes coalesced into ephemeral leagues, governed by an elective leader; kingship appeared in a sporadic and tentative manner; the tribal gods and cults followed suit. It was the transition from childhood into early youth.

The degree of civilization attained by the different tribes varied greatly. The Teutonic-Celtic-Roman south had adopted much of the old Latin culture; the Slavic northeast seems to have manifested no higher intellectual life; but the great poems of "Beowulf," "Gudrun," and the "Edda," at that time growing out of scattered songs into grand organic epics, furnish us with a fairly good picture of life among the upper classes of north-western Germany and Scandinavia.

From them we learn that the German people, at that date, were passing from childhood into the phase of early youth. The heroic epoch with its fierce conflicts with the stupid, uncouth, mongolic giants of the East, and the less sanguinary struggles with the shrewd, intelligent, swarthy, diminutive race of the South, had come to an end, and the great epopees, the Iliad and Odyssey, of the Teutonic race, celebrating the deeds and adventures of its gods, demigods and heroes, were in the process of formation.

Christianity, as a disturbing element in the nation's normal evolution, was introduced into Germany a few centuries later.

This religion was then in a very critical condition. Of Semitic origin, it had been transformed into an Aryan cult by Hellenic and Latin Church fathers, and thus made acceptable to the Graeco-Latin mind. Its fate was inextricably interwoven with that of the Latins and Greeks. It lost ground among the Semites, Hamites and Turanians of Asia and Africa as soon as its Aryan character was established. The disintegrating Roman Empire was its only support, and that support was near its collapse. The new religion was incapable to stem the downward course of the empire. It could not reform, revivify or rejuvenate the decadent and rapidly aging nations. It participated in the general degeneracy. Indeed, the missionaries mainly followed the flight of the imperial eagles, and rarely accomplished anything beyond the line of Roman sentinels. With the moribund Greek and Roman nations, it would have suffered extinction, if at that critical moment the young rising Teutonic race had not come to the rescue. The palsied arms of Rome could not shield the new religion, and the new faith could not renovate the people; but the vigor and enthusiasm of the Teutonic converts saved Christianity from annihilation, by becoming its stout defenders.

If the Teutonic nations and tribes had adhered to the gods and cults of their ancestors, Yahweh, with his Semitic and Graeco-Latin cult, would have disappeared on the same trail on which Zeus, Jupiter, Osiris, Bel, Ahura Mazda and thousands of other national gods had previously vanished. Deities without strong and aggressive worshippers waste away and perish. If the Goths, Vandals, Suevi, Burgundians, Langobards, Franks and Anglo-Saxons had clung to the worship of Wotan, Thor, Balder and other tribal and national divinities, modern Europe would not be Christian, but another religion, rooted completely in the character, the traditions, the history, the conceptions, the ideals and the usages of the ancient Teutons, would have been evolved.

But the Teutons discarded their gods and accepted in their stead the Graeco-Latin-Semitic gods and cults, and the course of history was diverted in another direction.

It was not the intrinsic merit of the new cult, but chiefly the person of the missionary which secured victory to Christianity. The barbarian, even in the hour of triumph, pays homage to the higher culture of the conquered. The spiritual message was incomprehensible to the savage mind; but the refined speech and manners, the trained and clever reasoning, the gorgeous vestments and ceremonials, the artistic and symbolic rites, the appeal to a childish and vivid imagination, and, above all, the imposing and mysterious structure of Roman civilization, back of the Christian missionaries, fascinated the untutored minds of the simple Germans, and filled their souls with awe and admiration.

Men of antiquity credited their own achievements to their gods, and the unsophisticated Germans, perceiving what great things the mighty, magnificent and mysterious deity of the missionaries had wrought in Christian and Jewish lands, readily transferred their allegiance from Wotan and Thor to Yahweh. The "Ragnarok," the "Gotterdaemmerung," the evening twilight of the Teutonic gods, came to pass. The old pagan gods perished or were outlawed and condemned to lead a precarious existence as devils, demons, imps, kobolds, nixes and other mischievous beings of supernatural power.

The introduction of an alien religion already complete, hardened, rigid and petrified in its dogma, tenets, rites and ceremonials, worked a radical change. It was fitted for the decaying, aged mind, and not for the growth of vigorous youth. Intellectual growth was stunted. The old bards and minstrels became mute. The national gods and heroes, and the epic literature of great promise, which had sprung up around them, were banished to oblivion by narrow-minded, fanatic and zealous missionaries. Foreign priests conducted a strange worship of alien gods in a foreign tongue.

The gods are human conceptions; are idealized men. They spring spontaneously from the hearts and brains of the people, and conform to their character, age and culture. The god-ideas of the missionaries were the products of the refined, effete, decadent, autocratic Orient; but the deities of the Germans were the ideals of young, hopeful, aspiring and progressive nations.

The unprejudiced observer will admit that the god-ideas and god-ideals of the ancient Germans were conceptions of a higher order than the conceptions introduced by the missionaries. The Asiatic gods, like Oriental despots, were cruel, intolerant, partial, unjust and suspicious and inspired only fear and awe; the Teutonic deities, as they are depicted in the ancient epics, exhibited courage, fortitude, honor, tolerance, dignity, justice and cheerfulness, as their characteristic traits; they were loved and not feared by their worshipers.

A reciprocal relation exists between man and his ideals. Young men and young nations of great promise have lofty ideals, and as they advance their ideals are constantly exalted and beckon them on to nobler conduct. The characters and deeds of Wotan, Freya, Frigg, Thor, Heimdal and Balder, and of the deified heroes Siegmund, Helge, Beowulf and Siegfried, as sung and rehearsed at the people's firesides, were well calculated to foster the manly virtues of courage, fortitude, honor, truthfulness, honesty, loyalty and justice, in the hearts of the German youths.

The missionaries ruthlessly brushed away these high ideals and substituted their own. But from the glorious battlefield to a gloomy cell of a monastery; from Helge, Beowulf and Siegfried to the fasting, meditating and ascetic hermit; from mirthful Walhalla to an insipid heaven; from restful Hel to a terrible hell; from cheerful, active and brave Valkyries to doleful, resigned and apathetic madonnas; from daring, lofty heroes to austere and gloomy saints; was not a step onward and upward. "Enjoy life" sang the pagan poet; "remember death" responded the monk. The change wrought meant a lowering of national ideals.

The degenerate Greeks and Romans, in the garb of priests, became the tutors and guardians of the juvenile German nation; an event fraught with dire consequences. The young, pliant German soul was checked in its normal and symmetrical development in accord with its own nature and environment, and was twisted and distorted, in order to conform to the ideals and standards of nations of a different race, living in different surroundings, at a different age, and belonging to a different and more primitive phase in the life of humanity. The German mind was forced to break completely with its past, from which only it could develop normally. The foreign tutors stripped the young tree of its twigs and branches, and engrafted upon it alien ideas and institutions.

We can imagine what would have taken place in Germany if an alien religion with its retinue had not been forced upon its people, and if they had not been exposed for upward of a thousand years of the formative period of their national life to a sharp, bending and warping breeze, blowing incessantly from the Latin, Hellenic and Semitic East. In this respect man is like the woods upon the seashore, where a constant blast from the same quarter bends and distorts everything, and where scarcely a tree of straight and symmetrical growth can be found. We can well picture to ourselves how the Germans, undisturbed by foreign influence, and standing firmly on the foundation of their own native religious, social and political ideas, ideals and institutions, would have evolved a civilization, characteristically Teutonic, and bolder in thought and deed, broader in sympathy, nobler in ideals and conceptions, greater in achievements, and more harmonious in all its parts than the one they now enjoy. It would have been a civilization symmetrical and strong like that of ancient Hellas. German civilization, as finally evolved under such untoward conditions, is a caricature only, and resembles a temple erected after the plans of many architects, and constructed of incongruous material brought from the ruins of Rome, Athens, Jerusalem and Alexandria. If the Hellenes, like docile and servile pupils, had submitted for centuries to the tutorship, guardianship and authority of Egypt and Babylon, their civilization, so admirable for its vigor, scope, originality and symmetry, would have been but a blurred copy of that of the Nile and the Euphrates.

Feudalism appears to be a characteristic feature of nations in their youth. It grew logically out of the relations existing after the great Migrations between conquerors and conquered.

The earlier patriarchal and tribal conditions in the age of infancy of the nation were characterized by a strong sense of equality among the members of the social units. The heads of families, clans and tribes were regarded only as the first among equals. The soil was held in common. Property was justly and equally distributed. Enormous wealth and abject poverty did not exist side by side.

This social, political and economic condition was disturbed when a tribe conquered a foreign territory and appropriated the land. The invaders formed a ruling class, divided the land among themselves according to rank, and degraded the natives to servitude. Landholders, holding directly from the tribe, enjoyed social and political equality. Military service rendered to the tribe was the usual consideration of the holding.

A transformation followed quickly. Wars and revolts necessitated the strengthening of the military and executive power. The tribal chieftains gradually assumed the prerogatives of hereditary royalty. The allegiance which the freeholder originally owed to his clan or tribe, was transferred to the king or duke, and became the personal relation between ruler and subject, between lord and vassal.

The Roman civil law accompanied Christianity on its march to the North. This famous system of law had sprung up and been codified during Rome's degenerate days. It was well suited to a decadent society which knew only absolute rulers and subservient vassals, clients and slaves. A spirit of oriental autocracy, entirely foreign to the Teutonic sense of justice, equality, independence and personal liberty, pervaded the whole system. The missionaries, imbued naturally with the spirit of the civil law, and called to leading positions among their converts on account of their learning, ingrafted Latin and Semitic ideas of right, justice and social order on the native institutions of the Germans. It was a misfit. Much of the harshness of feudalism may be traced back to the maxims and principles of the Civil Law.

The Germans were mainly an agricultural people in the fifth century of our era. They had no cities and very little industry and commerce. There existed no social classes. All members of clan or tribes, except a few slaves, were freeholders. Feudalism, however, transformed communal into private ownership and created an aristocratic class, based on the possession of large landed estates. Wars, feuds, hard times and general distress favored the centralization of wealth. The large estates swallowed up the small holdings; the freeholders became the tenants, retainers and serfs of a noble lord paramount, who assured them of peace and protection.

Feudalism was really the natural outgrowth of existing economic conditions. The class of free, independent farmers dwindled away rapidly, and had been eliminated from the social structure at the beginning of the tenth century. At that time the country knew only feudal lords and serfs.

The transition from tribal government to national kingship, from communal to private ownership of land from free farmers to a landed aristocracy and serfdom, the desuetude of public assemblies for the administration of public affairs, the complete ascendancy of an alien religion, the introduction of a foreign legal system with its strange maxims of right and justice, and the almost complete extirpation of a native, comprehensive and promising literature, mark the radical transformation of German national life in the period between the fifth and the ninth centuries.

It was an era of exhaustion and stagnation, following an epoch of unusual activity in war, colonization and upbuilding of states. Foreign masters smothered the native progressive spirit of the people. They had cropped the vigorous young sapling, and it required generations for young shoots to bud forth and develop.

The native spirit, however, could not be extinguished completely, and began to reassert itself in the age of Charlemagne (768-814). This enlightened ruler, a true representative of a youthful, rising and aspiring people, fostered education, letters, art and general progress. He inaugurated a notable intellectual revival. A literature began to flourish, but it was not popular; it did not reach the masses; it was not rooted in the rich soil of native myths, legends and traditions; it was clerical, was composed in Latin and chose the adventures and miracles of Semitic and Roman patriarchs, heroes and saints for its themes. But the national idea made progress in spite of these obstructions.

Under normal conditions, the social and political change from tribal to national institutions and from chieftainship to kingship would have been accompanied by a metamorphosis from patriarchal and tribal to national cults. In the change incident to the transition from childhood to youth, families and clans merged into tribes, and tribes, voluntarily or by force, coalesced into nations, and, if the introduction of a foreign religion had not disturbed the normal growth, the various tribal cults would have participated in the general evolution. As soon as one tribe would have secured the hegemony in the battle for existence and supremacy, its tutelary deity with its cult would have become supreme and national. This supreme national god, known and worshiped as Wotan, Thor, Balder or any other deity, would have been an idealized German, and the national conceptions of his being, character, purpose and decrees would have kept pace with the general progress of the nation.

But the German nation has repeatedly essayed to throw off this foreign spiritual yoke, and to establish religious conceptions in harmony with its character, its traditions and the times in general, but has not met with complete success.

The Carolingian empire included Germany, France and Italy. The dream of a great Teutonic world power, cherished by Charlemagne, came to naught through the disintegrating influence of the new and growing national spirit. New homogeneous nations were rising in Italy and France through the fusion of Latin, Celtic and Teutonic elements. The classic language of Cicero and Virgil was dead, and vulgar dialects of dual origin took its place. The sentiment of kinship follows the common speech, and this sentiment grew stronger with every decade, and drove Italians, French and Germans further apart.

The Alps form a natural boundary between Italy and the other two nations, but between the Germans and the French there existed no natural line of demarcation. From the Rhine to the Loire the percentage of the Teutonic element of the population diminished steadily and that of the Celto-Latin elements increased. A differentiation in speech, laws, customs and sentiment brought about an estrangement between the two people. A secession was unavoidable. The Treaty of Verdun in 843 A. D. recognized the already established natural cleavage along ethnic lines, and from that date the two nations led a separate existence.

The youthful German nation experienced a great intellectual revival in the tenth, eleventh, twelfth and thirteenth centuries. It advanced with firm and steady steps and became conscious of its powers. A new, intensely active life began to pulsate through Europe at that time. Great schools were founded, and thousands of eager students flocked to the feet of celebrated teachers. Scholasticism, that strange compound of aged reason and juvenile fancy, fascinated teacher and pupil alike. Artists invented a new style of church architecture. Magnificent castles and palaces arose on the sites of former dingy, feudal strongholds. Nobler ideals lifted up the chivalry. The resuscitated bards and minstrels again strung their lyres and in popular songs celebrated the heroic adventures of knights and the miracle-working saints. Epic and lyric poetry was again cultivated. The Saxon "Helyand" (about 890); the "Krist" of Ottfried of Weissenburg (9th century); the works of Luitprand (about 946); of Wittekind of Corvey (973); of Ditmar of Merseburg (1015); and of Adam of Bremen, mostly written in Latin, appeared as the harbingers of spring. Commerce and industry were revivified. Cities, the ganglia and nerve centers of a higher social and political organism, the breeding spots of democratic ideas, were founded and grew in importance. And when the church sent out its appeal for the redemption of the holy sepulchre, fervent piety rose to the highest pitch; religious enthusiasm knew no limit to sacrifice; and wave after wave of frenzied, delirious humanity rushed toward the Orient, to be lost in the burning sands of Syria.

That was the spring-time, the morn, the youth, the first awakening of the German people. The period from about 1000 to about 1300 A. D. was one of extraordinary activity in all the domains of culture, but all the achievements of the age bore the stamp of juvenility. Lack of originality, hasty, spasmodic and impulsive action, inconsistency in ideas, sentiments and convictions, naivety in expression and conduct, faith in miracles and supernatural phenomena, marvelous religious enthusiasm, great inquisitiveness, picturesque language, fondness of symbolism, extravagant speculation, vivid, unbridled imagination, exaggeration, irresistible love of adventure, a keen propensity for gay dress, spectacular festivals and gorgeous processions, and unquestioning credulity, all the characteristics of nations in their youth indicated that the German people were passing from childhood into youth.

It was the adolescence of the German nation. It was the epoch of Albertus Magnus, the famous scholastic philosopher; of the renowned Minnesingers; Heinrich von Veldecke (about 1180), Hartmann von Aue (1140-1210), Walter von der Vogelweide (11651230), Reimar von Hagenau (d. 1190), Gottfried von Strassburg (about 1207), Wolfram von Eschenbach (about 1200), Ulrich von Lichtenstein (1200-1275), Frauenlob von Mainz (1270-1318); and the unknown author of the Nibelungen epic (about 1200 A. D.). It was the era when the democratic Hansa rose and flourished; the age of the great

Saxon and Hohenstaufen emperors; of the erection of celebrated gothic cathedrals; of the efflorescence of romantic and resplendent knighthood, a period full of poetry, romance, fancy, color, light and life. A vast amount of work of a high order was crowded into the space of two centuries. It was the first outburst of the long-suppressed energy and passion of the youthful nation. It was the incipient struggle for independence of thought and action; for emancipation from foreign bondage in religion, philosophy, poetry, art and science; but the day of freedom had not yet arrived.

The first impulses of these intellectual and moral movements feudalism, genuine kingship, nationalism, scholasticism, democracy in cities, knighthood, the poetry of chivalry, the fervor of the crusades, and gothic architecture, came from Italy and France to Germany. Due to the fusion of aged Latin with young Teutonic blood, the semi-Teutonic nations of the south passed with hastened speed through the earlier' phases of their national lives, and reached the stages of youth and manhood a century or more in advance of the northern nation of purer blood, larger mass and slower growth. Like older sisters in relation to younger, they assumed the lead and took the initiative in all movements of reform and innovation in art, literature science, religion, statesmanship, and political economy, down to the time when their decline set in. Germany copied the work of her older sisters, but gave to the copy an original tone and a national character entirely her own.

The reconquest of eastern or Slavic Germany, begun by Charlemagne, was continued throughout the Middle Ages. The German conquerors advanced steadily from the Elbe to the Oder, and to the Vistula. The reconquered territory, according to feudal custom, was granted to military chiefs and their retainers, and the Slavic natives reduced to servitude. Fusion of the two races progressed unabated and without much disturbance. The Slavs were Germanized readily and formed the substratum of the new, homogeneous people of that section. Feudalism, in its crassest form, was the rule. No middle class of importance intervened between feudal lord and serf, and, due to the docile, ultra-conservative and fossilized character of the Slavo-Mongolian elements, intellectual progress was scarcely perceptible. The German leaven was not strong enough to permeate and stir to action the passive Slavic mass.

The national idea, as distinguished from the tribal, which under the banner of kingship made phenomenal progress in England and France during the Medieval Age, remained stunted in Germany.

The Emperors, in league with the democratic cities, fostered the national idea; but the high nobility frustrated every attempt at complete national union, and Germany remained backward in its social and political evolution.

The intellectual life of the early part of the Medieval Age was confined almost exclusively to the upper social classes; the common people, mostly down-trodden, stupefied serfs, did not participate in it. Poetry, art and learning flourished only in castles, palaces and monasteries.

The growth of the cities was a fact pregnant with great consequences. These nuclei', in and around which German national and intellectual life was to find refuge and fostering care, rose into importance in the tenth century.

They increased rapidly in population, wealth and power, and soon made themselves the leading factors in commerce, industry, wealth, politics, art and literature. With the decay of chivalry, in the thirteenth century, the center of gravity of German intellectual life shifted from the feudal castle to the democratic city hall, and from that day to the present, the rise and fall of democracy marked the rise and fall of German civilization.

A decline of intellectual activity set in about the middle of the fourteenth century; almost simultaneously with the general European decadence. Picturesque knighthood deteriorated, scholasticism died out, literature grew silent, imperial power was only a shadow, anarchy prevailed, and the nation was exhausted by interminable feuds, crusades and disastrous foreign wars. German history, from about 1250 to the middle of the fifteenth century, mentions but few names famous in art, letters, learning, war and statesmanship.

This era of apparent decay embraced the transition from early to a riper youth. It was an age of rest, of storage of force and of preparation for greater activity. The ideas, ideals and aspirations of the people underwent a change in the meantime; sober reason of manhood began its contest for supremacy with the luxuriant imagination of youth. But the early part of this period of transition bore still the stamp of juvenility. Gross superstitions, characteristic of nations in their credulous youth, filled the realm. The childish belief in the supernatural powers of priests, devils, demons, saints, sorcery, magic, relics, miracles and pilgrimages held the minds in bondage. Flagellants, mystic and ecstatic visionaries crowded highways and marketplaces.

The age was devoid of picturesque men and spectacular events. No broad and deep intellectual and moral movements hurled men to the crest of popular tidal waves. Intellectual life was confined to the cities and grew realistic and materialistic. The sturdy burghers aimed chiefly at the accumulation of wealth and political power; art and letters were of secondary importance, and money now became a dominant factor in the social, political and intellectual evolution of the nation. The agile coin of the republican burgher was pitted against the immobile soil of the nobility in the battle for supremacy, and won.

In this age of transition the representatives of early youth, the men of luxuriant fancy, of sublime, unquestioning faith and of fervent religious enthusiasm, the men who raised knighthood to its romantic apex, built the magnificent cathedrals, composed the great epics, and rushed in frenzied hordes to their graves in the Orient, all passed away, and their greater successors, the men of sober reason, the heroes of science, were yet unborn.

The fifteenth century was full of that unrest and ferment which invariably precedes a great crisis. The German nation was fast approaching the day when it would be of age, and pass from youth into mature manhood. A radical change, external and internal, transpired. The invention of gunpowder and firearms hastened the downfall of chivalry. Geographical discoveries promoted commerce and industry, and widened the intellectual horizon. Printing was invented and made self-culture general. An inordinate thirst for knowledge took possession of all classes. Sixteen universities were founded between 1365 and 1506 A. D., and tens of thousands of eager students crowded into the lecture rooms. Natural science received unusual attention. The study of the Greek, Latin and Hebrew classics was revived. Humanism radiated its mild light. The doctrines preached by the Waldenses, Albigenses, Wycliffe and the Lollards penetrated the masses.

Signs of an impending revolt against absolute authority in. church and state multiplied. Heretics, although persecuted, incarcerated or burned, increased on all hands. The councils of Constance and Basel, frightened by the rising tide of reform and insubordination, attempted a mild reform of the most glaring abuses, but failed. The Humanists: Kuess (1401-1472), Agricola (1443-1485), Reuchlin (1453-1522), Erasmus (1466-1536), and Kirchheimer (1470-1530), assailed disintegrating orthodoxy. And even the oppressed, brutalized peasant raised his head to demand greater rights and freedom for himself, and a curtailment of the privileges of the nobility.

Into this fermenting, seething, surging and foaming mass of humanity Luther flung his bold challenge and precipitated the Reformation. That act was the German nation's declaration of independence. It was of age. It was desirous to originate, invent and create. It had grown conscious of its strength, and was determined to carve out its own future, free from the restraint of alien tutors and guardians. Foreign masters, from the time of Boniface to that of Luther, had exercised almost absolute sway over the juvenile German mind; but now, the mature Teuton dismissed tutor and guardian, and assumed the right and responsibility to think and act as suited him best. That is the true meaning of the Reformation.

That great movement, however, was originally not an exclusive affair of the church. The desire for religious regeneration was inextricably interwoven with keen longings for social and political reform and liberty, and for the extension of art and science into new domains. The revolutionary movement embraced the whole social, political, religious and economic life of the nation. It aimed alike at the despotism of potentates, feudal lords, prelates and authoritative masters in art and learning. Luther and Melanchthon in the church, Reuchlin and Sachs in literature, Durer and Cranach in art, Copernicus and Paracelsus in science, and Muenzer and Geyer in politics all endeavored to lead their people into new, untrodden paths. It was an age of great originality and creative force. Germany was ripe for a great revolution, and, in regard to age, hers may be compared to that of Hellas at the time of Solon.

Luther, unfortunately, failed to comprehend the full scope of the movement. He always remained a stubborn, narrow-minded monk. He stepped from the gloomy cell and the secluded cloister of the monastery into the wide, bright, active world, full of strange, complex and jostling forces, and was immediately accepted as the central figure of a great movement. He was bewildered. He was a theologian and saw only wrangling theologians. He thought he could cure all evils and redress all wrongs, by a reform of doctrines and cults. He forced a broad stream, destined to fertilize a parched country, into the narrow channel of a theological dispute. It was a fatal error. He robbed the movement he had inaugurated of its legitimate fruit.

Luther's clarion call to arms found a responsive echo in all parts of Germany. The people rose in a universal revolt, but they could not separate religious from political and intellectual freedom. The democratic cities grew louder and bolder in their demands for abolition of class privileges, and the cowed serfs began to tug at their galling fetters. The oppressed masses believed that the day of their deliverance had come. The peasantry of the center, south and west of Germany rose spontaneously, and with great moderation demanded their rights as citizens, as Christians and as human beings. Democracy was on the point of triumphing. The justice of the peasants' demands was conceded by all except the princes, the feudal lords and the higher clergy. They were seconded by the burghers of the cities and by the lower nobility. The petition was coldly denied. Arbitration was haughtily refused. No concession, no alleviation, was offered to the mutinous serfs.

Disappointment, anger, despair and a pent-up desire for revenge then fanned the revolutionary flame into a holocaust. Castles and monasteries were stormed and sacked. The princes and feudal lords were panic-stricken. They unsheathed their swords in defense of their privileges and prerogatives. They appealed to Luther for aid. The famous reformer took his stand by the side of the oppressors, and vehemently urged upon prince and noble the extirpation of the rebel peasants. Disciplined troops were sent against the poorly led and equipped mob, and in the memorable battle of Frankenhausen, in A. D. 1525, the cause of liberty and democracy in Germany collapsed.

This battle was a turning point in German history. In its results it ranks with the battle of the Teutoburg Forest, with Leipzig, Waterloo and Sedan. It deflected the course of social, political, religious and intellectual evolution from the normal.

The Peasant War decided the fate of Germany for centuries. The German nation, by ruthlessly crushing that uprising, relinquished its claim of leadership in Europe, and stepped to the rear and remained there until the nineteenth century. The emperors were weak; the dukes and princes became arrogant and insubordinate; the recalcitrant cities were cowed into submission and lost their rights, liberties, energy, spirit of progress and prosperity; the peasantry was crushed into insensibility. The Reformation, which had commenced as a general, popular upheaval with marked democratic tendencies, lost its force and ended in a movement solely in the personal and dynastic interests of princes. The peasants turned from it in disgust and the burghers looked upon it with indifference.

Germany spurned a glorious future from her. She had just entered upon an era of great originality, creative and inventive power. She was in the heyday of exultant maturity. In point of wealth, population, extent of territory, political power, education, commerce, industry and general progress, she held the first place in Europe. With Reuchlin, Erasmus, Hutton (1488-1523), Sachs (1494-1576), Luther 1485-1546) and Melanchthon (14971560), as pathfinding pioneers of literature; with Holbein, the Elder (1460-1524), Durer (1471-1528), Cranach (1472-1553) and Holbein, the Younger (1497-1543), in art; with Regiomontanus (1436-1476), Copernicus (1493-1543), and Paracelsus (1493-1541), in natural science; a promising epoch opened, and a new continent invited German colonization on a grand scale.

If Luther, who was the most potent force in Germany at that time, had been in full touch with the masses; if he had possessed the experience, the practical insight and the broad human sympathy, of a Zwingli, a Calvin or a Knox; if he had understood the intimate relation existing between religious and civil liberty; if he had placed himself resolutely on the side of the people, the cause of freedom would have triumphed in the Fatherland, and normal intellectual and moral growth would have continued.

The people were ripe for the initial forms of democratic self-government. The cities had formed a preparatory school for republican self-government for centuries. A constitutional monarchy, permeated by a bold, progressive, democratic spirit, the abolition of serfdom, the curtailment of class privileges, a united and mighty empire, the Germanization of the Slavic and Magyar borderlands, the complete victory of the Reformation from the Baltic to the Alps, the founding of powerful and progressive German colonies in the New World, and an age of extraordinary activity in all the fields of human endeavor, would have resulted if Luther had comprehended his people and his age. He failed in this and Germany lost her great opportunity.

The Reformation made progress notwithstanding these drawbacks. The momentum given to it during the first decade of its existence was so powerful as to carry it -onward three decades longer. The year 1558 saw its high-water mark. Nine-tenths of the people had declared in favor of the Reformation. Protestantism was in control of nearly all educational institutions; it was generally regarded as the champion of progress and culture. Beyond the German border it had swept like an inundation over the Teutonic countries of Scandinavia, Holland, Switzerland, England and Scotland.

Then the tide turned. The Counter-Reformation, favored by the legal maxim *"cujus regio, ejus religo,"* and skillfully directed by the Jesuits, began its victorious march northward.

Ethnical causes help to explain the progress of the Catholic Counter-Reformation. We know that Celtic clans and tribes originally occupied large districts in western and southern Germany and in Switzerland. We also know that from about 50 B. C. to 450 A. D. vast numbers of the Roman legionaries, officials, mechanics, traders, laborers, camp-followers and colonists, occupied a broad zone along the frontier of the Rhine, Main and Danube, with spurs of Latin settlements projecting into the interior of Germany. These Latin and Celtic elements were completely absorbed and assimilated by the invading and conquering German tribes, and a new people, German in speech and sentiment, but in physical appearance, temperament and character, betraying in part its Celtic and Roman origin, sprang from the fusion.

Due to the admixture of aged Latin and Celtic blood with the young German, the South-German tribes experienced a hastened development and led the van of German culture down to the Reformation.

The religious schism forced the German people to choose between Roman and Teutonic conceptions and ideals. Blood decided the choice. The Teutonic blood spoke for Luther; the Latin and Celtic blood in the veins of some southern and western tribes was attracted to Rome. Religions are always national or racial. Catholicism had sprung from and was suited to the Latin character; Protestantism to the Teutonic. The Reformation swept southward along the path which the Alemanni, Marcomami and Burgundians had taken a thousand years before, and gained a permanent foothold in Wurttemberg, Baden, Elsass and Switzerland; the Catholic Counter-Reformation pursued the trail northward of the ancient Roman legions, traders and colonists and Celtic settlers. The cleavage between the sects ran along ethnical lines and has practically remained unchanged down to the present day.

As a truth, however, Teutonic blood preponderates also in the Catholic provinces of Germany, and if the Reformation had been made broad and popular, these provinces would have been permanently attached to the reformed faith, especially as southern Germany was farther advanced politically and more democratic than northern and central Germany. But the course pursued by the reformers and princes estranged many of the southern Germans from the cause.

The German nation was divided into two hostile camps. One was eager to battle for selfish princes; the other in the interest of a coterie of alien prelates; the interests of the people were ignored.

An era of decline, deterioration and disintegration set in after the failure of the Peasants' War. The emperors were powerless; over a hundred territorial lords decorated themselves with the tinsel of sovereignty. The commerce of the world opened new channels to the detriment of German trade. The proud democratic cities were humiliated and began to decay; and intellectual life was paralyzed for two centuries after Luther. Only Kepler (1571-1630), the astronomer; Leibnitz (1646-1716), the philosopher; Opitz (1597-1639), the poet; Schlueter (1664-1714), the architect, and the inventors, Guericke (1602-1686) and Papin (1647-1714), rose above the German horizon as stars of the first and second magnitude. Germany contributed very little to the cause of civilization during this period. The stunning and stunting blow to German intellectual life, administered by princes and reformers, was terrific.

To fill the measure of misfortunes to overflowing, came the Thirty Years' War in A. D. 1618. The embattled hosts, frenzied with religious hatred and fanaticism, rushed to the fray. Grim visaged war devastated the country for three decades. The population shrank to almost nothing; cities dwindled to the size of villages; hundreds of villages disappeared entirely; prosperous communities were converted into horrid wastes, and brutalized armies stamped out the last vestiges of intellectual life and culture. Germany resembled a sturdy oak, riven and seared by lightning; a man disabled by a stroke of paralysis.

The Peace of Westphalia in 1648 ended the frivolous war between the Christian sects. The nation was completely exhausted, humiliated and demoralized. Foreign statesmen and generals shaped its destiny.

Then the tide turned and reconvalescence came slowly. It took several generations to repair the ravages of the civil war, and to secure a fair degree of order and prosperity as a foundation for a revival of a higher intellectual life.

The nation grew vigorous again, and the revival came in the early part of the eighteenth century. Leibnitz (1646-1716), Wolf (1679-1754), and Reimarus (16941768), in philosophy; Bodmer (1698-1783), Gottsched (1700-1766), Kleist (1715-1759), and Gellert (17151769), in poetry; Haendel (1685-1759), Bach (16851750), and Gluck (1714-1787), in music; Fahrenheit (1686-1736), Haller (1708-1777), and Winckelmann (1717-1769), in science, represented the rosy dawn of a new era. They were the precursors of the classic age. Most of them, except the composers, lacked originality still, and contented themselves with copying after French and English models.

With the advancing light of morn came the poets of the period of "storm and stress"; Buerger (1747-1794), Lenz (1751-1792), and Klinger (1752-1831). Conscious of their power and filled with the youthful, exultant, turbulent, volcanic and revolutionary spirit of the age, they ushered in the classic period.

Then came the long procession of eminent and illustrious poets, artists, composers, philosophers, historians, educators, statesmen and scientists, which filed across the stage of German history, from the middle of the eighteenth century down to the present day.

Klopstock (1724-1803), Lessing (1729-1781), Wieland (1733-1813), Herder (1744-1803), Goethe (1749-1832), Schiller (1759-1805), Richter (1763-1825), Arndt (17691860), Brentano (1777-1843), Uhland (1787-1862), Koerner (1791-1813), Heine (1789-1856). Hauff (18021827), Freiligrath (1810-1876), Reuter (1810-1874), Geibel (1815-1854), Freytag (1816-1895), Marlitt (18251887), Scheffel (1826-1886), Heyse (b. 1830), Rosegger (b. 1843), Sudermann (b. 1857), and Hauptmann (b. 1862), in literature; Kant (1724-1804), Fichte (1762-1814), Hegel (17701831), Schelling

(1775-1854), Schopenhauer (17881860), Hartmann (b. 1844), and Nietsche (1844-1900), in philosophy;

Haydn (1732-1809), Mozart (1756-1791), Beethoven (1770-1827), Schubert (1778-1828), Wagner (18131883), and Brahms (1833-1897), in music; Rauch (1777-1857), Cornelius (1783-1867), Kaulbach (1805-1874), Menzel (1815-1904), Defregger (b. 1835), Lenbach (b. 1836), and Makart (1840-1884), in art; Foster (1729-1798), Herschel (1738-1822), Bode (1747-1826), Werner (1750-1817), Blumenbach (17521840) Hahnemann(1755-1843), Gall (1758-1828), Olbers (1758-1840), Humboldt (1769-1859), Buch (1774-1853), Ritter (1779-1859), Fraunhoffer (1787-1826), List (1789-1846), Encke (1791-1865), Bopp (1791-1867), Struve (1793-1864), Liebig (1803-1873), Bunsen (18111899), Mayer (1814-1878), Virchow (1821-1904), Helmholtz (1821-1894), Kirchhoff (1824-1887), Koch (b. 1843), Haeckel (b. 1834), and Roentgen (b. 1845), in science; Basedow (1723-1790), Pestalozzi (1746-1827), Froebel (1782-1852), and Diesterweg (1790-1866), in education; Niebuhr (1776-1831), Ranke (1795-1886), Mommsen (1817-1903), Treitschke (1834-1896), and Lamprecht (b. 1856), in history; Stein (1757-1831), Hardenberg (1750-1822), Bismarck (1815-1898) and Bebel (b. 1840), in practical statesmanship; these men of talent, genius and world-wide renown, and hundreds of artists, poets, composers, historians, scientists, statesmen, generals, political economists, inventors, educators, and promoters of commerce and industry, of great merit but less known to fame, constitute Germany's splendid contribution to the galaxy of gifted men who have built up our modern civilization.

The German nation had at last recovered from its sickness and stupor. The native, long suppressed powers and energies issued forth with great vehemence. The nation's achievements which, under normal conditions, should have consumed three centuries, were compressed into the space of one. German genius, like the belated vegetation of a tardy and frosty spring, stimulated into uncommon activity by the warm sun of June, endeavored to make up for lost time by more strenuous efforts. German representative men, although belated, appeared in a regular and normal order of succession. A close examination of these representative men in regard to their genius, achievements, aspirations, character and place of birth reveal the following facts:

The center of gravity of intellectual national life shifted rapidly from the field of imagination to the domain of reason. The personnel of the procession changed markedly in the space of a hundred years. The men of exuberant fancy; the poets, composers, artists and speculative philosophers, led the van. They were belated flowers of spring. Under normal development they should have appeared a century or two earlier. The brief but highly productive springtime culminated in Lessing, Goethe, Schiller, Kant, Hegel, Handel, Mozart, Beethoven, Rauch and Cornelius. It was the classic age of German literature, art, music and philosophy.

Then followed a steady decline in letters. The romantic school at the beginning of the nineteenth century was a step downward. The realistic school that succeeded the romantic bore the mark of continued decadence. Its authors, when compared with Goethe, Schiller, Kant and Hegel, are but weak epigoni. Poetry belongs to youth, and Germany's youth had passed. At best, the writers of the romantic and realistic schools are but a good aftermath of German literature.

But in one respect the romantic school rendered signal service. It opened up connection with the almost forgotten glorious pagan past. The childhood days of the nation were resurrected. Richard Wagner, in his grand trilogy of the Nibelungen, brought the grand old conceptions of gods, goddesses, demigods and heroes, on the stage. From the way Wagner's creations were received, we can readily infer the wonderful effect that would have been produced, if these lofty Teutonic conceptions and ideals had been constantly kept before the people, as they grew up from childhood into youth, from youth into manhood.

But, while the German Pegasus was tottering down the descending path with palsied limb and wing, the genius of the nation dismounted from the poetic steed, and began the ascent to still higher levels by another trail. It shifted to the steep and laborious path of science. It grew rational, realistic and practical. The men of science, of fearless investigation, of statesmanship, of practical invention; the Humboldts, Mayers, Helmoltzs, Virchows, Haeckels, Roentgens, Kochs, Mommsens, Lamprechts, Bismarcks and Bebels, and the captains of industry and princes of commerce and finance, became the true representatives of the nation during the nineteenth century. The age of reason had succeeded that of imagination; the people had outgrown their youth and had entered the phase of mature manhood; they are now approaching their zenith.

Secondly: in regard to their place of birth, the men of genius and talent were massed in vast numbers in the purely Teutonic provinces of Sleswic-Holstein, Hanover, Brunswick, Friesland, Westphalia, the Saxon and Thuringian states, Hessia, Wurtemburg, Baden, Elsass and Switzerland, while in the Rhine province, in Bavaria and Austria, where the population is of mixed German, Celtic and Latin origin; and especially in the provinces of Brandenburg, Mecklenburg, Pommerania, Silesia, Posen, East and West Prussia, where the population is predominently Slavic, there is a startling paucity of great names.

The reason is not far to seek; it is in the blood. The tribes with a large admixture of Latin and Celtic blood in their veins crossed their meridian sometime ago along with the neo-Latin nations, and with them are on the down grade; the Germanized Slavs of the northeast, belonging mainly to the Mongol-Tartaric stock, which was in its prime and began its descent over two thousand years ago, are old, unprogressive, sterile and ultra-conservative; and only the people of unadulterated Teutonic blood, in the enumerated provinces of the north, southwest and center, are today in the full prime of their manhood. And there only, originality, inventive and creative force flourished. There only, men of genius and talent were born to any large extent during the last four centuries.

It is also worth noting that the Catholic provinces, as compared with the Protestant, exhibit a dearth of great names in science and letters.

This apparent backwardness of the Catholic provinces is not due to the Catholic faith. They advanced and matured under the same belief. It is simply due to the fact that the sterility of old age has crept upon them, and that they have lost all initiative and force to emancipate themselves from the rule of foreign masters. Old age has made them inert and passive.

The Slavo-Germanic northeast never participated to any notable extent in the progressive movements of the German people. It took no part in the poetry of chivalry; it did not promote democracy in the cities of the Mediaeval Age, except in the colonial towns of the Hansa on the shores of the Baltic; it remained indifferent to Humanism, Renaissance and the Reformation; it adhered tenaciously to medieval feudalism, even to this day; it held aloof from the democratic, revolutionary and progressive currents of the nineteenth century; and even yet loyally and unswervingly supports its reactionary and ultra-conservative feudal lords. The aged, unprogressive blood of Mongol and Tartar tells.

Thirdly: democracy kept pace with the general advance. It began to stir feebly when literature, art, philosophy and science commenced their great revival. All these branches are by nature democratic and must exert a stimulating influence on democracy in politics. Even such far-seeing statesmen as Stein and Bismarck accepted its services, to a large extent, in their work of regenerating and reconstructing Prussia and Germany. Democracy is gaining steadily in Germany. The great majority of the people is democratic at heart, and this is especially true at all the centers and foci of greatest intellectual activity. Democracy and culture are inseparable in advance and retreat. German democracy, with its advanced social ideas, theories and ideals, leads the world. It ought to triumph soon. The German republic, under normal development, was due two centuries ago. It is the only form of government fully suited to an Aryan nation in the phase of manhood and prime of life. It is the only form that can secure full play to all the intellectual and normal forces of the nation.

Fourthly: the national idea, always very backward in Germany, has come to the front during the intellectual revival. Germany continued in the tribal state longer than any other European nation. We cannot speak of a German nation as we do of the English and French nations, where tribal lines of demarcation were obliterated long ago, and where the whole people are organically united into one compact mass. Germany has not yet fully outgrown the old tribal state. A German union was the long hoped for, fondly cherished ideal of the people for generations; and Bismarck realized the ideal and welded the tribes together by force. He created a common executive, foreign policy, army, navy, legislature, judiciary, legal code and internal administration, for the whole country; but there are still a score of sovereign princes, who place their dynastic interests above everything; the spirit of class and caste is still unusually strong; and tribes, classes, parties and sects are yet separated by deep fissures.

German civilization owes very little to the Slavo-Teutonic northeast; and yet, paradoxical as it may appear, from that region had to come the political regeneration of the Fatherland. No philosophers, poets and savants could bring order out of chaos; semi-Slavic Prussia accomplished it. We have here a repetition of the history of Sparta. The Spartan was a peculiar blending of Aryans and Pelasgians into a new nation, intensely monarchical and oligarchic, hostile to democracy, indifferent to civilization, and devoted to war and politics. The fusion of Slav and German in Prussia seems to have been in nearly the same proportion of similar elements, and produced similar results. The peculiar national character resulting from this blending made Sparta the natural champion of Hellenic independence, and Prussia of Germany. Both excelled in war and civil administration, and both were highly deficient in higher culture.

Society as organized in semi-Slavic Prussia, outside of the large cities, consists of an able, haughty, powerful, landed aristocracy, devoted exclusively to arms and politics, and the docile, brave, submissive and unprogressive substratum of laborers and tenants of Slavic or mixed ancestry. They fight and vote as dictated by their more intellectual Aryan masters.

As remarked before, Germany was reconvalescent at the beginning of the eighteenth century, at least in art, philosophy, poetry and science. But in regard to social and political evolution, the nation suffered still from the desuetude of these respective organs. The national and democratic spirit seemed to be extinct.

A slight political awakening, which made Frederick and his victories possible, took place at the beginning of the great intellectual revival, in the middle of the eighteenth century, but it soon subsided again into dull and stolid indifference.

The thunders of the French Revolution awakened no audible echo in Germany. The princes with their battalions and obsequious officials stamped out every dangerous spark and inflammatory idea that was wafted across the Rhine.

Then came the catastrophe of Jean in 1806. The nation awoke from its stupor. The old Prussian system had failed utterly. All recognized the necessity of beginning a new political life. The enlightened Stein and Hardenberg became convinced that an injection of democracy into the body politic was absolutely necessary for its recovery. In this spirit they began to reorganize Prussia. Many reforms were inaugurated. New blood and new life began to pulsate through the atrophied and paralyzed political organism. The result was Leipzig and Waterloo.

Brutal reaction reared its head again as soon as the foreign danger was past. The sacred promises were ignored by the princes. The spirit of freedom and national union was to be extirpated. But this spirit could not be extinguished. Civil liberty and national union became the inspiring ideals of the masses. Poets, savants, students, burghers and peasants dreamt, sang and talked of a free, united Fatherland. They were answered with dungeons, gallows and exile; but the spirit of progress and reform moved on.

Then came the memorable year 1848. Germany caught the revolutionary infection. The uprising was successful at first, and the alarmed princes yielded. A parliament met at Frankfurt to frame a constitution in harmony with modern, progressive ideas. Germany was on the point of becoming a strong, united, progressive and constitutional state. But in the mean time the princes recovered from their fright. The loyal battalions of Prussia marched up, and political reaction was triumphant once more.

But the lessons taught by the revolution could not be ignored. And when Bismarck, the sturdy aristocrat with a strong strain of good plebeian blood in his veins, the man of a wonderful comprehension of all the social and political forces that shape the modern state, the man of "blood and iron," was placed at the helm, he saw clearly what was to be done. After three successful wars he established German unity on a firm basis, and he gave the new state an organization, in which democracy, as an upbuilding force, is fully recognized. The Reichstag is elected by universal suffrage.

The dream of the people was realized at last. An era of unequalled intellectual activity was inaugurated. The Fatherland made rapid strides in advance in science, education, industry, commerce and political power. Democracy gained in numbers, higher ideals and clearness of purpose from decade to decade. Germany assumed the place that belonged to her among the foremost nations.

In art, literature and science, in originality, invention, creative power and expansive force, the peer of the foremost nations; with victory almost within reach of its progressive and aggressive democracy; and with the national idea triumphant; the German nation stands today in the full prime of manhood, and has almost reached the point of culmination in its life. She will reach the goal of her highest ambition if she does not permit Prussian militarism to monopolize and exhaust all the national energy to the detriment of the growth of civilization.

Of all the European nations that aided in the upbuilding of our magnificent civilization, each nation or group of nations had a peculiar part to perform. The Latin excelled in art, belles-lettres and in all matters of taste; the Anglo-Saxon surpassed in epoch-making, practical inventions, in building up trade and industry, and in constructive statesmanship; and it seems to be the mission of the German to encompass all by his broad generalizations, to establish fully the rule of law in the universe, to deepen philosophy, to widen the channels of religious thought, and to raise mankind to a higher level of ideas, ideals and sympathies.

The Scandinavian, Dutch and Swiss, although enjoying a separate and distinct national existence, but belonging to the same ethnic stock with the Germans and Anglo-Saxons, passed simultaneously with these through the phases of infancy, childhood and youth into manhood.

19. The Slavs

The Slavic race has sprung from a fusion of Mongolic-Tartaric elements with Teutonic and others. It occupies a broad zone filled with mongrel nations, between the Teutons in the west and the Mongols and Tartars in the east It is a gigantic block of conglomerate in which fragments of prehistoric, Mongolian, LJral-Altayan, Turanic, Hellenic, Latin, Illyrian, Celtic and Teutonic races lie imbedded.

The wide steppes of eastern Europe form a natural thoroughfare for migrating peoples. Nomadic nations, like huge tidal waves, swept to and fro across these plains in historic and prehistoric times, and most of them left a sediment behind.

It is safe to assume that, in prehistoric times, forced by a strong pressure from the south, a number of eastern Teutonic tribes were compelled to migrate eastward through the Scythian plains. Eventually we find them as Greeks in Hellas, as Hindus in India, and as Iranians on the plateau of Iran. We may also assume that detached fragments were left behind, and were absorbed and assimilated by the natives of the steppes.

Later, but still in the dim, early dawn of history, did Mongolic-Tartaric hordes fling themselves against the eastern boundary of Germany, and sent the tribes of the Goths, Vandals, Burgundians and others adrift toward the Euxine, the Danube and the Rhine.

And again the Hunnic inundation, a few centuries later, which reached its high-water mark at Chalons in France, and then receded.

Out of the layers of sediment of various color and texture, broken, jumbled and cemented together, left by these different inundations, the Slavic race was formed. The substratum of this race is decidedly Asiatic. The bulk of the population is composed of Mongolic, Tartaric md Turanic elements, which has received a slight Graeco-Latin admixture in the south, and Teutonic in the north and west.

Out of this fusion of such varied, heterogeneous elements resulted the type, the character and the history of the Slavs. They nearly all passed their zenith at least three thousand years ago and nearly all of them live in the phase of extreme old age. They gave to the Slavic racial character the stamp of Asiatic unprogressiveness, sterility and fossilization. Temperament, physical type, and many social, political and religious institutions of the western and southern Slavs, however, point to the fact that they received an infusion of Roman, Illyrian and Hellenic blood. All along their western border, from the Danube to the Polar Sea, the Slavs mingled with the Teutons; with Germans in the south, and with Scandinavians in the north; and the effect of this mixture is manifest in the physical, intellectual and moral character of the Slavs along this boundary.

The early history of the Slavs is hidden in obscurity. Centuries of constant amalgamation must have elapsed before a perceptible degree of homogeneity was attained. The old German epics speak frequently of the constant wars of the fair Teutonic gods and heroes with their swarthy, huge, uncouth and savage neighbors in the East. The fusion of these heterogeneous races in the broad border zone brought forth the Slavic race. The race, as a rule, remained stationary at the stage of the family or clan. It did not develop tribal organization, let alone national. In the early part of the Medieval Age, when the Slavic race first steps into the light of history, it was a wild, disorganized, anarchic mass of families and clans, not united by tribal or national ties.

The Slavs had pressed forward during the Great Migrations into the heart of Germany. The tide turned with Charlemagne. The Slavs were slowly forced back across the Elbe, the Oder and the Vistula, and the center of gravity of the race was shifted to the Dnieper and Volga.

The adventurous Vikings of the north, who extended their piratical raids to the shores of the North Sea, the British Channel and even to the Mediterranean, had at that time secured a foothold on the Gulf of Finland and Ladoga Lake. They brought law, order and prosperity. The Russian Slavs, weary of anarchy and interminable feuds, invited the warlike Scandinavians to govern them. Three brothers, Ruric, Sineus and Trouvor, answered the call, and, with their retainers, established an orderly government in A. D. 862, with one capital at Kiew and another at Novgorod. That event was the birth of the Russian nation, which from that time forth may be considered as the typical leader and representative of the Slavic race.

The Varangian invaders constituted a ruling class. They belonged to a juvenile, progressive nation, and they endeavored to keep pace with the advance of the western nations. The great Slavic mass, on the contrary, the descendants of the aged and ossified Asiatics, were ultraconservative and adhered tenaciously to their inherited ideas, customs, manners and traditions. This dualism of progress and stagnation runs through all subsequent history of Russia.

The civilization of the Russian Slavs, and of the Slavs in general, at the time of the advent of the Varangians, was of a low and primitive order. Agriculture was the leading occupation; commerce there was none; and industry consisted only of the fashioning of crude tools, implements and utensils of wood, iron, bronze and clay. The family, or the mir or clan, formed the highest social and political unit. These units owned the land. The religious ideas conformed to this low development; every clan was in possession of its tutelary deity and local myths and legends. A vast horde of lesser divinities peopled trees, grottoes, springs, mountains, etc. The Slavic heaven mirrored the social and political organization of the Slavic earth.

The progressive Varangians built cities, opened the country to foreign trade, promulgated a Teutonic code of laws, and were instrumental in the introduction ot Christianity from Byzantium. They organized the state in the spirit of feudalism. They divided the land into large estates for the chief vassals, and into smaller holdings for the rank and file of their retainers. The consideration for the holdings was personal allegiance tu the lord paramount. The natives were reduced to a state of serfdom. The organization of the clan or *mir,* however, remained intact.

The patient, passive, docile, simple, improvident, credulous, superstitious and unprogressive Slavs, like resigned and spiritless octogenarians, submitted readily to the reforms and innovations inaugurated by their superior foreign rulers. Like the aged, fatalistic races, of the Orient, they bowed stolidly to inevitable fate. They were too old to either resist or initiate reform.

And so it has remained since the days of Ruric. The Slav has contributed very little to the cause of human civilization. Very few original ideas, new discoveries or epoch-making inventions can be traced to him. His whole intellectual life, as it manifests itself in art, religion, science, government, literature, architecture, war, commerce, industry and agriculture, is but a slavish imitation of Hellenic, Latin, French, German, English, Dutch and Scandinavian models. Without foreign impulse he would speedily revert back to the condition of Asiatic barbarism or semi-civilization.

The Varangians reformed the political, social and economic conditions, and Greek missionaries introduced a new religion and cult. The Slav accepted the new ideas only superficially; they never became ingrained with him; he continued to be a stagnant Asiatic.

Kiev was the political and intellectual center of the Varangians until the twelfth century, when it lost its hegemony, and the center of gravity of national life was transferred to the Volga. This change enabled the democratic cities of Novgorod, Pskow and Viatka to rise into prominence. These cities, with their magistrates, senates, common councils, guilds, militia, laws, usages and general management, were faithful copies of the Hansa towns. There were quite a number of such towns in Russia.

Indeed, the Russia of the twelfth century, with its growing, progressive and aggressive democratic cities, its weak central power, its feudalism, its rebellious territorial lords, its internecine feuds and its oppressed peasantry, resembled Germany of the same period. But the German people, from serf to emperor, were progressive and had created these conditions; while in Russia it was all imitation, and the progressive spirit was confined strictly to a thin layer of Varangian aristocrats, and to the Hanseatic merchants, mechanics and colonists in the cities. The great mass of the people remained inert.

The slow progress which Russia had enjoyed under Varangian and Hanseatic influence was halted abruptly by the Tartar conquest, in the thirteenth century. Genghis Khan had founded a mighty empire in the far East, and his invincible armies swept across Asia like a huge tidal wave. Russia felt the brunt of the collision and suffered disastrous defeat at Kalka, near the Sea of Azov. The Tartar hordes invaded Russia in 1237 A. D. and in a brief time conquered all the country up to the vicinity of Novgorod. They built their capital at Sarai on the lower Volga, and soon extended their rule to the Danube, and to the swamps, fens and forests of north-western Russia.

Russia paid tribute to the Khans; Russian princes swore allegiance to them; but the common people were left unmolested in their possessions, religion, language, customs and laws. The nobility adopted Tartar ideas and manners. Kinship was readily recognized between the Russian bojar and the Tartar chieftain.

The two related races soon affiliated and fused, but to what extent the mingling took place during the 250 years of Tartar rule is difficult to determine. If we bear in mind the facts that Batu, the Tartar Chief, commanded a half a million of warriors; that several millions of Tartar, Mongolian and Turanian soldiers, merchants, officials and colonists found their way to Russia between 1237 and 1480 A. D.; and that all this vast material was absorbed and assimilated by the Russian people, the conclusion is unavoidable that the fusion was extensive, and that it made the nation yet more Asiatic in blood and character.

Among the cities of Russia, during the troublous time of Tartar rule, Moscow gained the ascendant. It became the rallying point of all patriotic Russians. The energy of the Varangian nobility had spent itself at that time. Stern, cruel, sinister, vindictive princes, of Asiatic lineage, thought and manners, superseded them.

Ivan, the Great (1462-1505), a cruel, cold and calculating tyrant, enlarged the principality of Moscow; annihilated progress and democratic rule in Novgorod, Pskow and Viatka; encroached upon the Tartar empire, then already in a state of decay, disintegration and decomposition; made Moscow the heir of Constantinople in the championship of the orthodox church; compiled and promulgated a new code which bore strong traces of Byzantine and Tartar influence; and drew Greek, Italian and German artists, artisans, engineers and diplomats to his court.

Ivan, the Terrible (1533-1584), further centralized power in the hands of the Grand Princes of Moscow. He subdued the recalcitrant nobles, reconquered most of Old Russia from the Tartars, and began the conquest of Siberia.

Russia, at that time, was almost completely isolated from the active, progressive, intellectual life of the rest of Europe. Even the channels of commerce between the Hanseatic and Russian cities, through which some new and progressive ideas had occasionally percolated into the Slavic empire, were narrowed and filled with obstructions. Princes, nobles and people grew more and more Asiatic in thought, tastes and manners. They adhered tenaciously to the primitive patriarchal forms of government, and the Czar was simply the head of the great Russian family, magnified to enormous dimensions.

Humanism, the Renaissance and the Reformation, made no impression on the Russians. They remained impervious to the new ideas. The national idea, however, made some progress The national and religious ideas became practically conterminous in the realm of the Czar when the protectorate of the orthodox church was transferral from Constantinople, after its fall, to Moscow.

The rulers of Moscow maintained a stout defense of their land against Swedish, German, Polish and Lithuanian encroachment. The ceaseless wars with their western neighbors were invaribly struggles for supremacy between races and religions. The Russians adhered tenaciously to the beliefs and tenets brought to them from Byzantium; the Poles clung stubbornly to Rome; and the Germans, Swedes and Lithuanians followed the Saxon reformers. Race and religion were inseparable. The Russians were orthodox; the Poles, with evidently much Latin blood in their veins, fought for Catholicism; and the others, largely of Teutonic lineage, upheld Protestantism.

Intellectual life stood at a low level. Nobility, clergy and the common people, were steeped in the grossest ignorance and superstition. No literature existed. The poorly educated upper classes were content with the Bible and the biographies of saints; and, among the common people, a number of epic and lyric folk-songs were handed down orally from generation to generation.

The close of the seventeenth century gave evidence of some intellectual activity and progress. A few poets, orators and historians Polotski, Kotochikine and Krijanitach, the forerunners of a revival appeared; Peter the Great, talented and imbued with the spirit of reform, rode to fame on the rising wave.

Peter (1869-1723) was an energetic, autocratic reformer. He journeyed abroad to gather new ideas and surrounded himself with foreign advisers. He opened the Baltic gates for intercourse with the cultured West, reorganized the army, created a navy, built his new capital in a swamp, abolished the oriental seclusion of women, commanded religious toleration, promoted education, science, commerce, industry and agriculture, fostered the national spirit, and reformed the civil administration.

His work was an imitation of German, Dutch and English models. He endeavored to engraft the young twig of Teutonic culture on the old Mongol-Tartaric trunk, and met with only indifferent success. His subjects did not second him in his arduous labors.

He had to force innovations upon them by his despotic and imperious will. His whole life was an incessant struggle with a reactionary aristocracy, an ossified and stagnant clergy, and an inert and ultra-conservative people.

German masters guided Russian intellectual life during the first half of the eighteenth century. French classicism, as represented by Voltaire, Rousseau and the encyclopaedists, took the lead during the reigns of Elizabeth and Catherina (1741-1796). The French Revolution alarmed autocrat, aristocrat and clergy, and German and English patterns came in vogue again. The Russian changed his tutors, but never had the innate force to emancipate himself intellectually, and carve out his own destiny.

The Russians were good imitators, and made fair progress in art, literature and learning during the last two centuries. A number of eminent poets, historians and scientists arose. Lomonossow, savant and poet (1712-1765), Derschawin, poet (1743-1818), Demitrijewn, poet (1760-1837), Karamsin, great Russian poet (1766-1826), Krylow, the Russian La Fontaine (17681844), Oserow, dramatist (1770-1840), Koslow, an author of the romantic school (1779-1840), Shukowski (1783-1852), and Pushkin (1797-1837), the greatest of Russian poets, shed immortal lustre on their country. But they all lacked originality, invention and creative force. They followed alternately in the wake of German, English or French classics. Nowhere, neither in art, literature, science, religion, trade, industry, nor government, did the Russians attempt to hew out their own path. They shone in reflected light; glowed in a foreign flame, and cultivated exotics only.

The reactionary reigns of Alexander I and Nicholas I stifled free thought and speech, and the unsatisfied longing of the people for freedom and civilization, found expression in gloomy, melancholic and pessimistic songs, novels and dramas.

Gogol, Herzen, Turgenieff, Kolzow, Lennontow, Dostojewski, Askarow, Tolstoi and Gorki all of the middle and the last half of the nineteenth century laid bare the terrible ignorance, superstition, brutality, vice and utter misery of the masses with a naturalistic and realistic truthfulness that fascinates as it offends. It is the mournful elegy of a feeble sage, regretting that he can no more participate in the sports of youth, nor in the exalting activity of manhood of other nations.

Two souls the Teutonic and the Mongol-Tartaric dwell in the Russian organism. The one, young, optimistic and progressive, strives to lift itself up to the heights reached by other nations; the other, aged, pessimistic, feeble and unprogressive, clings to primitive conditions. And in this regard Russia is only typical of the whole Slavic world. All progress there has been imported, or is due to Teutonic colonists. The missionaries from Constantinople, the Varangians, the Scandinavian invaders of Finland, the Hanseatic traders, the German knights and their retainers in the Baltic provinces, the German colonists, teachers and mechanics, and the court of German descent these were and are the active and progressive elements which have made Russian history and supplied the great empire with what civilization it has. The great mass, of Asiatic origin, is sterile and fossilized, and can only be galvanized into the semblance of life by contact with an organism highly charged with a progressive spirit. That contact, that foreign impulse withdrawn, and the inert mass sinks back immediately into the former lethargic state.

The same observation may be made in regard to the Finns, Esthonians, Livonians, Poles, Magyars, Bohemians, Slavonians, Servians, Bulgarians and Roumanians of the east of Europe, in so far as the old, unprogressive blood of Mongols, Tartars and other Asiatics courses through their veins. They are all stagnant nations, and what little civilization they enjoy, they owe to their neighbors. And over a half a million of immigrants per year, of this undesirable class, find their way into the United States.

20. The Japanese.

The Aryan race has almost exclusively held the stage of history for upward of twenty-five centuries. Hindus, Persions, Greeks, Romans, Italians, Spaniards, French, Anglo-Saxons, Scandinavians, Dutch and Germans, have successively played the leading roles in the great drama of humanity. The parts acted by other races were subordinate and insignificant. The Arab episode was only an interlude between the acts of ancient and modern Aryan civilization. Empires rose and fell among other races, but the foci of real, progressive culture were found only in Aryan lands. Here only was bright light; everywhere else it was either the murky night of barbarism, the dawn ot races in their infancy, or the evening twilight of decaying and aging peoples. The Aryan race was in its prime; all the rest, with one exception, were either undeveloped infants or decrepit sages; that one exception was the Japanese nation.

This uninterrupted phenomenal success, unavoidable under such conditions, made the Aryans haughty, arrogant and regardless of the rights of other races. They deemed themselves the favorites of Providence, the born rulers of the earth, and fancied that the yellow, brown or black races were created for their service, and must accept their social, political and religious conceptions and institutions as standards.

The civilized Aryans, well equipped with cannons, machines, Bibles, firewater, etc., took forcible possession of all the continents and reduced the native, colored population to the condition of servants, serfs and slaves. The history of the Aryan conquest of America, Australia, Africa and Asia is written in the blood and tears of the subjugated native races.

But "might makes right" is the law of nature. The earth belongs to that race which is best able to utilize it. The young, strong, progressive and superior races always crowd out the aged, feeble, unprogressive and inferior peoples. Fortunately, no individual, tribe, nation or race, can maintain itself at the height of championship and mastery for any great length of time. All great historical nations and races have for a brief period enjoyed the glories of supremacy; after which they stepped down and made room for others.

The Aryans encountered only weak infants in Africa and the Malay Archipelago, and races in their dotage in America, Australia and Asia, and their victory was easy. They began to dream of universal dominion.

Then, all of a sudden, like a medieval knight, with closed visor, entering the lists abruptly, and throwing down his gauntlet as a challenge in defence of the oppressed, an unknown, mysterious champion of the maltreated non-Aryans races dashes into the arena, and in a few tilts hurls the biggest defender of Aryan supremacy to the ground. That knight was Japan.

The sudden apparition surprised the civilized world. The idea, that progress and civilization were synonymous with Aryan race and Christian belief, had become an ingrained dogma with the Aryan, and he was astonished and baffled when a brown nation of Mongol-Malayan extraction, of pagan faith, and which had not enjoyed the training of Christian missionaries, traders, soldiers and officials, stepped up in the full vigor of national manhood, and demanded recognition as the peer of any Aryan or Christian nation.

The demand could not be denied. The young aspirant had earned his spurs on a dozen bloody battlefields. We were compelled to revise our musty theories on history, religion and civilization. We were forced to admit that superior intellectual and moral strength are not confined to the group of Aryan-Christian nations.

All eyes were turned with surprise and admiration to the little islands which fringe the eastern coast of Asia. The world wanted to learn, how, contrary to all long cherished and deeply rooted hypotheses, a non-Aryan nation, far removed from Aryan and Christian influences, could create and evolve a civilization of a superior order.

The Japanese are a people of mixed origin. Mongolian and Malay blood courses through their arteries. There is increasing evidence of the fact that successive waves of primitive peoples and civilizations swept over these islands before the advent of the Japanese. The early race of pit-dwellers, of a very low grade of advancement, is extinct. The Ainos, a race superior to their predecessors, succeeded them, rose, flourished and sank into the petrifaction of old age. Then followed inundation after inundation of Mongolian invaders and colonists via Korea, and of Malayan by sea from the Malayan archipelago. The Palaeolithic and Neolithic natives were either exterminated or absorbed and assimilated.

These early invasions from the south and west took place in prehistoric times, and only vague traditions tell of them. The conquerors, of various types and races, and the degenerated natives fused, and a fair degree of homogeneity in type, language, customs, religion and laws had been attained when the early dawn of history bathed Nippon in its rosy light. A new and young nation had been born and was entering upon a long and glorious career. A remnant of the Ainos, unabsorbed and unassimilated, and adhering to the habits of primitive barbarism, still inhabits some of the bleak regions of the northern islands.

If the qualitative and quantitative values of the different ethnic factors that entered into the make-up of the young Japanese nation were ascertainable, much that now appears enigmatical in the character and history of the Japanese would readily explain itself. We know that the aboriginal natives, as to age, were in their dotage; that the Mongolians from Korea, China and Manchuria, had passed their zenith and entered upon their decline; and that the Malays from the south were still in their early infancy; but we know nothing of the numerical strength of these different ethnic elements.

If Japan were merely a Chinese or Mongolian colony or offshoot, its whole history and its intellectual and moral life would betray the fact. Mother and daughter, in accordance with the laws of nature, would have kept pace with each other in their rise to the point of culmination and in their subsequent decline; and Japanese life would be as sterile, stagnant and crystallized today as the Chinese. A fusion of the aged and decadent natives with the Mongolian race, then also on the down grade, would only have accelerated the march toward dotage and national demise. But the Japanese nation manifested progressive tendencies from the very beginning, and from this we must infer that the young, vigorous and rejuvenating element came from the Malayan Archipelago. And, indeed, physically, intellectually and morally, the Japanese reveal a stronger affinity with the Malays than with the Mongols.

The origin and rise of the Japanese nation is a counterpart to that of the neo-Latin nations of Europe. The Italians, French and Spaniards, sprang from the fusion of aged Latin with young Teutonic elements; and the Japanese originated from an amalgamation of the old and decadent Mongolian race with the infantile Malay. On the Mediterranean shores the young Teutonic blood formed the active and shaping force, rejuvenated the Latins and built up the new nations; and in the "Land of the Rising Sun" the juvenile Malay blood rejuvenated the aging Mongolian race, and moulded the young nation. The infusion of old Roman blood into the veins of the young Teutonic race hastened the latter's development; and the admixture of Chinese had the same effect on the new Japanese nation. The peculiar mixture of blood made the neo-Latins the vanguard of modern European civilization; and a similar fusion made the Japanese the pioneers of a future Malay civilization.

The infancy of the Japanese people is enveloped in almost impenetrable darkness. They could not write their own history from the beginning, and no civilized nation stood near its cradle to record the events of its early life. The early Chinese chroniclers reported nothing about Nippon and its inhabitants. The Chinese came first in contact with the Japanese in the third century of our era, and from that time on we have some reliable history of that nation. Japanese myths, legends, traditions and archaeological monuments furnish only meager information concerning early Japan.

The Buddhist missionaries from China, who overran Japan from the fourth to the seventh century, A. D., gave a strong impulse and stimulus to Japanese intellectual life. Epic poetry and hero-worship, the first articulate expression of the adolescent national soul, began to flourish. The "Kojiki" was written in 712, and the "Nihouki" appeared in 720 A. D. They are the national epics of the Japanese, and are to that people what the Mahabharata was to the Hindus, the Iliad to the Greeks and the Edda to the Teutons. The former was written in the ancient Japanese tongue, but in Chinese characters; and the latter was composed in Chinese. Both constitute a collection of ancient myths, fables, legends and traditions, of the deeds and adventures of old Japanese deities and heroes. They are of very little historical value, although some historical truths are undoubtedly encysted in them; but they sketch in faint outline the slow progress of the nation throughout its infancy.

We learn from these epics that a mythical period of the gods preceded a legendary age of the national heroes. The gods grew more human as the nation advanced. The gods and the myths were creations of the nation. They were indigenous to the soil. The genesis of the gods was the same in Japan as elsewhere. These deities began their existence as a vast multitude of spirits or "Kami" dwelling in animals, trees, rocks, springs, seas, mountains, thunder, lightning, storm, sun, moon, stars, man in fact, in almost every object and phenomena of nature. In the battle for existence and supremacy, the "Kami" inhabiting the most striking and awe-inspiring objects and phenomena, were victorious, and captured the largest number of devout worshipers. And as the people, in their social and political evolution, advanced from the individualistic successively to the family, the clannish, the tribal and the national stage, the religious development kept pace with the political, and the tutelary deity of the leading individual, family, clan and tribe, became ultimately the supreme god, and the other divinities had to content themselves with subordinate position, or were eliminated entirely.

National union had already been attained in the eighth century, when the epics were written, and when the Mikado ruled over all the tribes of the islands. The mythology of the people was forced to conform to this condition, and the Mikado traced his descent to the supreme national god, which was originally evidently only the tutelary deity of his family or of some noted ancestor.

The legendary history of Japan began with the emperor Jummu, who is said to have reigned about 660 B. C. An unbroken chain of emperors followed down to the advent of the Buddhist missionaries in the third century of our era. Nearly all were remarkable for longevity, virtue and inventive genius. The nation was in its infancy and highly progressive. Many discoveries, epoch-making inventions and valuable improvements, were made in that age, and, as was the universal custom formerly, the crowned heads received the credit for them. Agriculture was promoted, swamps were drained, canals were dug, reservoirs for irrigation were constructed, roads were built, warehouses for the storage of grain were erected, silk culture and weaving were introduced, pottery was manufactured, shipbuilding and commerce were fostered, a crude system of writing was invented, poetry was cultivated, a religious cult was instituted, mythologies were systematized, temples were built, laws were codified, a uniform system of weights and measures was devised and adopted, and architects, artisans, physicians, musicians, astronomers, astrologers and chronologers are spoken of in the ancient chronicles, indicating an advanced and much differentiated state of society.

The social, political and economic condition of Japan during the first centuries of our era resembles very much the condition of contemporary Teutonic Europe. And we find, furthermore, that the evolution of civilization in Japan, in the farthest East of the Old World, is, in all its stages, surprisingly analogous to the development of Teutonic and semi-Teutonic culture in the extreme West. The mythologic and heroic age, the epic literature, the introduction of strange gods, an alien cult, extraneous learning and the authoritative rule of foreign priests and classics, the consequent stunting of national intellectual development, the spread and character of feudalism, the rise and fall of knighthood, the poetry of chivalry, the revival of national thought, independence and intellectual life, the emancipation from alien tutelage, and the final extraordinary activity in all the fields of human thought and action, as we have found them in the intellectual development of Europe, are duplicated in Japan. Nearly all the great intellectual and moral movements of the West found their contemporaneous counterparts in the Far East. The national life of the Japanese people began simultaneously with that of the Teutons, and almost contemporaneously ran through all the phases of infancy, childhood, and youth to manhood.

Early Japanese culture was indigenous to the country. No foreign influence shaped and directed it. Communication with the older and higher civilization of China was first opened in the third century of our era, when an army of Buddhist priests invaded the islands and made Chinese influence paramount. The missionaries from Ching. represented a higher culture. They became the tutors of young Japan, and gave its unfolding life a new form, coloring and direction. They engrafted their ancient ideas and ideals of art, literature, philosophy, science, religion, government, manners and customs on the young Japanese sapling. The Buddhist invasion almost smothered the nascent national ideas. Chinese models and patterns became the rage for upward of a thousand years. The Chinese system of writing was adopted; the native language was adulterated by a mass of Chinese words; the Confucian code of ethics was received; Shintoism, the old, native religion, was forced to the rear by Buddhism; the Chinese language became fashionable among the savants and the upper social classes; the vernacular was the despised Cinderella; and the Chinese classics were accorded supreme authority in everything. Japanese national life, in the shadow of the overspreading Chinese tree, was stunted and deformed and could not unfold itself in a free, vigorous, normal and symmetrical manner. The Japanese had the same mournful experience with China that the Teutons had with Rome, Athens and Jerusalem.

But the young and vigorous national spirit, with its native ideals and aspirations, could not be extinguished entirely. The intellectual life of Nippon flowed in two distinct and parallel currents. The one was deeply tinged by the strong influx of Chinese learning and the Buddhist cult; the other, fed exclusively from native fountains, glided along clear, pure and limpid. It was the counterpart of the dualism of Teutonic Europe from the introduction of the Roman religion and civilization down to the Reformation.

The Japanese nation passed from childhood into early youth at the time when Buddhism took root in the soil of Nippon. With childish confidence and admiration it welcomed the alien cult and culture, which gave to its intellectual life a strong impulse and stimulant. The old folk-songs, myths, legends, fables and traditions were collected and edited in the form of the "Kojiki" and "Nihouki," Shintoism was tenaciously kept alive among the common people. Some poets began to address their countrymen in the native tongue; but the government, the nobility, the scholars and the chroniclers, preferred to use the Chinese language. That age resembled the period of Charlemagne and Alfred, when native folk-songs were collected and gradually fused into grand epics, and when Latin was the language of priests, princes, historians, judges and savants.

A vast number of epic and lyric songs and romances was produced during the five centuries next succeeding the eighth. The "Myriad of Leaves," a compilation of the popular poems of the eighth century; the "Mangoshiu," a collection of folk-songs anterior to the tenth century; the "Tosa Diary," a charming, classic narrative of a journey through Japan in the ninth century; and the "Genje Monogatari," a delightful romance by Murasaki Shikib, an aristocratic lady of the tenth century, deserve special mention as representative works of Japanese literature at that state of national development. It was the Japanese era of the Troubadours, Trouveres and Minnesingers.

Japan had its Medieval Age simultaneously with Europe. Feudalism had been inaugurated some centuries before, and was now the dominant social and political institution. Knighthood flourished. The history of Nippon, from the tenth to the sixteenth century, presents little but the weary, monotonous annals of incessant and sanguinary feuds of powerful and ambitious vassals among themselves, and with the weak, decaying central power of the Mikado. Mighty feudal families the Yoritomos, the Hojos, the Ashikagos and others battled fiercely with each other for the possession of the shogunate, an office which carried with it the real, while the Mikado, the ruler by divine right, enjoyed merely nominal authority.

This interminable, anarchistic turmoil had a depressing effect on national prosperity and the growth of intellectual life. The people were exhausted, and this age was almost devoid of great men, except those engaged in the aristocratic pursuits of war and politics. But the national mind was not entirely idle. Considerable literary activity was manifested, but it was almost exclusively confined to the nobility. The literature produced, consisting of ballads, romances, love songs, lyrics, elegies and epigrams, was courtly, artistic and genteel; was addressed to the ear rather than to the heart, and lacked the force, spontaneity, imagination and idealism of the old native, popular poetry.

But even this poetry of chivalry indicated that the poets were growing insubordinate, and less willing to follow slavishly the classical models of China. They showed symptoms of an approaching revolution against absolute authority. The national soul became conscious of its growing strength and longed to assert its individuality and independence.

The sixteenth century, in Japan as well as in Europe, ushered in the dawn, the springtime, the youth and early manhood of the nation. At both extremes of the Old World it introduced a new era of great intellectual activity and creative power. The period of exhaustion and temporary decline brought on by the strifes and commotions of feudalism, came to an end. Japan advanced from youth into early manhood. The age of youthful imagination was passed, and reason enthroned. Three great generals and statesmen Nobunaga, Hildeyoshi and Ieyasu the central figures in the stirring events that transpired between 1560 and 1605 A. D., solidified the nation, broke the power of the feudal lords, reformed and reorganized the administration, opened the road to distinction to the commons, weakened the tribal spirit, strengthened the national idea, restored order, fostered literature, art and learning, promoted the public improvements and raised the island kingdom to a condition of internal strength and external power, such as it had never known before.

Christianity obtained a foothold in Japan at that time. The Jesuit Francis Xavier was successfully engaged in missionary labors in 1549 A. D. The foreign religion was received with the proverbial tolerance of the Japanese. Religious persecution was unknown in Nippon until the advent of the Christian missionaries. Buddhism, Confucianism and Shintoism had dwelt together without friction for centuries. The missionaries sowed the seed of religious intolerance and enmity. They treated the beliefs and worship of the natives with haughty contempt, and even endeavored to alienate the loyalty of their proselytes from their native to a foreign ruler. This conduct excited suspicion and hostility, and generated a fear of conquest, as it is a well-known fact that the missionaries with colored races are usually the vanguard of conquering armies.

But the Christian missionaries of Japan had to deal with a youthful, vigorous, self-conscious and aspiring nation in the full flush of youth or early manhood, and not with an infantile race as in Africa, nor with races in their dotage as in America and continental Asia. The Japanese apprehended the danger which a change of religion would work in their character, civilization, progress, social institutions, and political independence, and the Christian worship was prohibited in the early part of the seventeenth century.

Made cautious by the unpleasant experience, the Japanese adopted a policy of almost complete isolation during the two centuries and a half next ensuing. Intercourse with foreign countries was only permitted through a much restricted commerce with the Dutch, but some progressive ideas, nevertheless, filtered through this narrow and obstructed channel.

Ieyasu founded the hereditary shogun dynasty of the Tokugawas, which actually ruled Japan from 1603 to 1868. This dynasty isolated Japan; gave it order, peace and prosperity; and collected, husbanded, organized and disciplined its physical, intellectual and moral forces, for its high mission in the Far East. It fostered education and promoted art, agriculture, industry and literature. The nation unfolded its intellectual powers quietly. Great scholars Mabuchi (1697-1769), Motoori (1730-1801), and Hirata (1776-1843), and a host of statesmen, artists and authors, rose to foster a national civilization, strengthen the national spirit, and inaugurate a propaganda for a national religion and cult. Foreign influence, even that of China, was reduced to a minimum; and public attention was directed to the old, native, social, religious and political institutions, so long neglected. The Japanese people had arrived at full maturity, and were determined to create their own civilization and to shape their own destiny.

The nation stood near its zenith. It had entered the stage of its greatest originality and of its highest inventive, creative and expansive power. It had spent its childhood and youth under the tutorship of China, but it was never fully mongolized. The striving and working of the native spirit in government, art, literature, religion, philosophy, ethics and social institutions is always clearly discernible under the foreign varnish. Depending entirely upon itself, and keeping completely aloof from all foreign influence, this nation would have evolved a civilization of its own, not much inferior to that of the West.

In making this comparison we must bear in mind that the Japanese nation is somewhat younger and entered a little later upon the phase of greatest originality and inventive power than the foremost nations of Europe; that its civilization in the sixteenth and seventeenth century was not much behind that of Europe; that Europe and America shot ahead in an unparalleled spurt during the eighteenth and nineteenth centuries, when invention followed invention in quick succession; and that Japan stood absolutely alone and unaided in its work, while at least eight great European and American nations assisted each other in the upbuilding of western civilization. Many sticks will create a larger, brighter and warmer blaze than one, or a few.

Invention is the true test of civilization, and where have the great inventions of the last two centuries originated? In England, Anglo-Saxon America, Germany, Scandinavia, northern France, northern Italy and the Netherlands. The Slavic nations, the Balkan peoples, the people of southern Italy, southern France, of Spain, Portugal and Latin America, have kindled but few new lights and in this respect are certainly not superior in culture to the Japanese, who did invent everything pertaining to their own civilization.

Japan's age of seclusion came to an abrupt termination in 1853, when Commodore Perry, of the American navy, opened a breach in the wall of its exclusiveness, through which the political and commercial emissaries of all civilized nations crowded into the interior. A new era dawned for Nippon. The enlightened and progressive statesmen were quick to recognize the superiority of many occidental ideas, methods and inventions, and the people were unusually alert in adopting and utilizing them. Native students were sent abroad, foreign teachers were invited, the decrees against Christianity were revoked, foreign goods, machines and implements were imported, foreign officers were employed to organize and drill the army, a navy was built after foreign models, dress and social forms were shaped after foreign patterns, and a government was instituted which, in its main features, is a copy of the political constitutions of Europe and America.

Proud, self-confident, optimistic, progressive, intensely patriotic, conscious of her high mission, and utilizing all the achievements of modern civilization, Japan challenged China and Russia that blocked her way of progress and expansion, and in a series of gigantic battles defeated them in quick succession, and with one bound took her place in the front rank of civilized and progressive nations.

The Japanese nation is yet on the ascent, and undoubtedly has a great future before it. It is intensely progressive and with avidity grasps all new and practical ideas of reform.

The transformation of that nation within the last four decades is phenomenal and without parallel in the world's history. But the change was only superficial after all, like the change of garments or of tools. The "inner man," the character of the nation, was not affected. The Japanese may adopt hundreds of practical inventions, but in the world of ideas, conceptions, aspirations and ideals, they will progress along the lines marked out for them by the character of their race. Their opportunity is great and they will accomplish much. They are strong in the homely virtues of industry, frugality, patriotism, courage, fortitude and subordination virtues upon which all national greatness is founded. They are clear-sighted, of calm temperament, cool judgment, almost devoid of religious superstition, and peculiarly adapted to scientific pursuits.

It is providential that two great peoples, the Teutonic and the Japanese, so different in race and character, should grow up unknown to each other at the two extremes of the Old World; pass simultaneously through the phases of infancy, childhood and youth, and through all the intellectual and moral movements that accompany a nation's progress; and when fully matured meet face to face for the first time, and instantly recognize each other's worth, and jointly proceed to build up a better, broader and more symmetrical civilization.

There was great danger that our Aryan civilization would become one-sided. A "white peril" really menaced the world. The Aryan cherished the belief that his ideas and ideals only were right and all others wrong. Now Japan is demonstrating the truth that a non-Aryan, colored race can grow up sound and strong, in body, mind and morals, and evolve a civilization of a high order, without Aryan tutelage or guardianship. This fact will widen our intellectual horizon and broaden our sympathies.

Symptoms are not wanting that political thought also is undergoing a metamorphosis in Japan. The present form of government is an anomaly. The Mikado represents the primitive patriarchal, but the parliament is the exponent of advanced, democratic ideas. A conflict between the new and old is unavoidable, and is already in its incipient stage. Democratic ideas and ideals begin to permeate the masses. The superstitious awe that envelops and protects throne and altar is vanishing. The prospect of eventual democratic triumph in Japan is good, so that in this respect, also, the Japanese will be on a par with the most advanced nations.

21. The Malays.

The Malayan race is evidently yet in the phase of childhood. It is progressive and has a great future. It is scattered over a vast expanse of islands, extending from Madagascar to the Eastern Islands in the Pacific. But in spite of this great dispersion, a certain uniformity in physical types, languages, customs, social institutions and religious beliefs and rites is clearly discernible. The center of gravity of the race, and probably also its original home, is the large island of Sumatra.

The Malay, as a general rule, is indolent, easy-going, improvident, quiet, reserved, taciturn, docile, polite, ceremonious, vacillating, treacherous, daring, adventurous, musical, credulous and superstitious attributes commonly associated with a race's childhood. The different dialects are still in the various stages of agglutination. The native religions are of a very primitive character, and consist of the beliefs in tutelary personal, familiar, and tribal deities and in a host of spirits, ghosts and demons, inhabiting the more striking objects and phenomena of nature, and in the faith in witchcraft, charms, spells, magic and sorcery.

Native Malayan culture is generally of a low, primitive order. Hunting, fishing, trading and navigation are the chief pursuits. Agriculture is crude and limited in extent, and art and industry remain in a rudimentary state. No literature exists, except a mass of folk-songs and folklore, handed down orally from generation to generation.

Some nationalities, such as the Hovas of Madagascar, the Battas of Sumatra and the Tagalos of the Philippines, have made considerable progress. They are successful stock-raisers, farmers and planters; live in large, settled and orderly communities, with organized governments, hereditary chiefs or kings, popular assemblies, codes of law; and have created the rudiments of a native literature. While advanced far beyond the uncivilized tribes, even they manifest all the symptoms of youth.

It seems that a Neolithic race of a very low and primitive culture preceded the Malays on these islands. This strange race left behind many mysterious monuments menhirs, dolmens and gigantic monoliths in the human form, but which bear no resemblance to cither Malayan or Mongolian types. This race was mostly exterminated or absorbed and assimilated by the Malays, but scattered fragments of it, standing on the lowest rungs of the ladder of evolution, are still found in the wild, inaccessible, mountainous interior of Sumatra, Borneo, Java, Formosa and the Philippines.

The Malayan race has absorbed and assimilated Negritos, Papuans, Mongols and wild aborigines, extensively, and this amalgamation has caused a great variety of types, dialects, and customs, of social, political and religious institutions, and of cultural progress. Upon the whole, the race is young and progressive, but it will require many centuries of normal growth before it attains full maturity.

It was the fusion of young Malayan with aged Mongolian blood on Nippon, from which sprang the young and progressive Japanese nation.

The admixture of old blood from China, Korea or Manchuria, with the infantile Malayan from Sumatra, Borneo or Formosa, accelerated the onward march of the Japanese. Semi-Malayan Japan is the vanguard of the future Malayan civilization and power, as the semi-Teutonic Italians, Spaniards and French, were the precursors of Teutonic civilization in Europe. The tribes of purer blood, probably the Tagalos, Battas and Hovas, will reach the stages of youth and manhood several centuries later, when Japan will be on the downward grade to old age.

22. The Negro.

The African race is in its infancy. It has no history. In its cultural developments, in its social, political, religious and economic institutions, it very much resembles the condition of the Teutons at the time of Caesar. It is very backward, but it is highly progressive and has a great future before it. The day of the "dark continent" has dawned at last. The springtime of the black race has come and new life is pulsating through its numb limbs. It, too, has at last entered upon the path of progress. Aryan and Semitic explorers, traders, missionaries, soldiers and teachers, of the nineteenth century, called into life the dormant germ of progress, and gave the race the starting impulse.

Why did the black race continue in a state of lethargy and dormancy for thousands of years, while Hindus, Chinese, Egyptians, Chaldeans, Greeks, Romans and other nations, some in Africa and others in close proximity to that continent, rose, flourished and perished, is still an unsolved problem. The same question may be asked in regard to any other race or nation. Evidently, the successive appearance, rise and fall of different nations and races, is regulated by the laws of nature, not yet fully comprehended. Every race represented a phase in the life of humanity. Palaeolithic and Neolithic races represented the infancy, the Chinese and Indians the childhood; Egyptians, Semites and Chaldeans the early youth; Hindus, Iranians, Greeks and Romans, the later youth; Teutonic and semi-Teutonic nations, the prime of manhood; and the Malays and Negroes are destined to represent the human race in its decline and old age. Every race was standing behind the scenes, waiting for its cue to call it upon the stage, and to play its assigned part in the great drama of humanity. And the Negro's role is in the last act.

The African is imaginative, sensuous, indolent, improvident, unstable, passionate, cruel, musical, affectionate, loyal, faithful, docile, submissive, credulous, superstitious, enthusiastic, optimistic, cheerful, imitative, emotional, fickle and readily adapts himself to new conditions and environment. He lacks dignity, self-consciousness, perseverance and steady application; develops energy spasmodically; possesses a pliant character; and is extremely fond of play, sport and music, all characteristics of a race in its childhood. His language and dialects represent every grade between the agglutinative and inflective stages of development. He still worships anthropomorphic spirits, ghosts and demons, which dwell in the objects and phenomena of nature, and also the spirits of ancestors. Individuals, families, clans and tribes have their tutelary deities. The race has not outgrown the patriarchal and tribal state. Families, clans and tribes, are the most prominent social and political units, and are held responsible for the acts of their members.

The race is now in a transition from the tribal to the national state; it is tentatively attempting to rise to a higher level. Ephemeral leagues and confederacies are formed by voluntary coalition of tribes, and kingdoms are constructed by forcibly welding tribes together; but neither leagues nor kingdoms are lasting. The native familiar and tribal gods, where they have not been banished by Bible or Koran, in their rise and fall, share the fate of the families, clans and tribes of their worshipers.

African art, literature and science, are only rudimentary. The race has made considerable progress by its own inventions in pottery, wood-carving, metal-work, agriculture and stock-raising. It has evolved no literature beyond some folk-songs, myths and legends, handed down orally.

The advance of the African race is less pronounced in the Congo basin, where the pure Negro type still prevails, than in the eastern and northern districts of Africa, and in America, where it received a large infusion of Semitic, Berber, Latin and Anglo-Saxon blood. This blending of the older races with the young, resulted in a hastened progress of the African in South Africa, in the lake region, in Abyssinia, in the Soudan, on the Niger, in Brazil, in the West Indies and in the United States.

The race, as a whole, under normal development, cannot reach full maturity within less than fifteen centuries; but the nationalities of mixed ancestry, now slowly forming in Africa and America, will advance with accelerated pace, and reach their zenith several centuries ahead of the main body.

This completes the review. In summing up we may say that in point of age the nations and races of today may be classified as follows:

In their dotage: the American Indians, Australians, and the savage hill tribes of India and Malaysia.

In old age: all the nations of Asia, except the Japanese and Malays, and all the people of eastern and south-eastern Europe, viz: Slavs, Finns, Magyars, Greeks and Turks.

Just past their prime and on the decline: the Italians, Spaniards and Portuguese, of the Old and New World.

At or near their point of culmination and in the prime of manhood: the French, the Anglo-Saxons, the Germans, the Dutch, the Scandinavians and the Japanese.

In early youth; the more advanced nationalities of the Malays and Negroes.

In infancy: the more backward tribes and nationalities of Malays and Africans.

Age determines the progressiveness and unprogressiveness of nations and races; they advance up to their meridian, and then become sterile, decrepit and petrified.

23. The Human Race

It may not be amiss, at this time, to take a glance at the life of humanity, as it will enable us to comprehend better the age, character and mission of the various races, that ever existed, or that now occupy the earth.

As cells in individuals, and as individuals in tribes and nations; so do families, clans, tribes, nations and races rise, flourish, decay and perish within the larger organism of humanity. It is always an organism within an organism; but the identity of the larger is never affected by the coming and going of the smaller organisms. Individuals, families, clans, tribes, nations and races, while leading a separate existence, participate in the characteristic features of the successive phases of the life of humanity.

The human race, as a whole, is a living organism, and as such organism has its infancy, childhood, youth, manhood and old age, and at any time during its life, some race was, is and will be the representative of that stage of its development.

Of the early infancy of the human race, of the age when it emerged from the brute-creation, and when it had not yet created society, government, religion, art, language, tools and implements, we know scarcely anything.

From this most primitive condition, infant humanity emerged with monosyllabic languages, stone and bronze implements, pictorial writings, individual and family cults and patriarchal governments. The races of the Palaeolithic, Neolithic and bronze ages were the representatives of this phase of infancy.

Passing from infancy into childhood mankind advanced to agglutinative or polysynthetic speech, bronze and iron tools, hieroglyphic writing, megalithic monuments and tribal forms of government and religions. The American Indians, the Egyptians, the early Chaldeans and the Chinese, represented this stage, although some, in part at least, were also the representatives of the preceding stage.

The rise from childhood to youth was marked by the introduction of inflective languages, phonetic alphabets, agriculture and settled life, tools, implements and machines of iron and steel, epic and dramatic literature, speculative philosophy, art, the rudiments of science and national governments, gods and cults. The Hindus, Iranians and the Greeks and Romans, represented this phase. The Semites intervened between the Chaldeans and Aryans.

The advance from youth to manhood was characterized by an improvement in art and literature; by a more pronounced development of the national and democratic idea in government and religion; and by a phenomenal progress in inventions and the exact sciences, showing that the race, as a whole, had left the youthful stage of imagination behind, and had entered the stage of mature reason. This phase is represented by the Teutonic, the neo-Latin and the Japanese nations.

The successive color-bearers of progress and civilization came from all races, climates and continents. And although the civilizations evolved by each race or nation were tinted by national and racial character and ideas, yet, upon the whole, we discern plainly that the evolution of government, religion, language, art, literature, philosophy, science, industry and commerce, took place everywhere along parallel lines, and was governed by the same laws.

Humanity, in its social and political, and to a large degree also, in its religious evolution, as represented by the leading nations, has now reached the national stage. Nationalism has triumphed over tribalism. The individual, family, clan and tribe have been merged into the greater social unit of the nation. Thought and sentiment of every one is national. First and foremost everyone looks upon himself as an integral member of the great national organism. The national principle was the strongest destructive and constructive political force of the nineteenth century. It caused great wars, shifted long established boundaries, changed the political geography of the world, and inaugurated an epoch of violent ethnical attractions and repulsions. More than ever before did men become conscious of the strong ties of common speech, descent, history, tradition, religion, interests and aspirations, that unite them into living social and political organisms, called nations. This principle of nationalism, emanating from the foci of civilization, permeates the whole world, and its violators harvest a full crop of insurrections, rebellions and wars.

But ours is an age of unexampled progress and expansion, and mankind is not inclined to rest on the stage of nationalism. The world now presses forward further in one decade than formerly in one century. Scarcely had the human race ascended to the platform of nationalism, when it made preparation to mount, tentatively at least, to the higher level of racial union. Man became dimly conscious of the fact that he was an integral unit of an organism still higher and larger than the nation. By some irresistible force Teutons felt themselves drawn to Teutons, Latins to Latins, Slavs to Slavs, Semites to Semites, Mongols to Mongols, Malays to Malays, and Negroes to Negroes. A universal drift toward the formation of large, organically united groups of nations, based on race affinity, is evident. The new terms panslavism, panromanism, panteutonism, pangermanism, pansemitism, panmongolism and panafricanism, invented to express entirely new political ideas, are words of latest coinage. Affinity of race will surely lead to the formation of anorganically united Teutonic, Latin, Slavic, Semitic, Turanic and Mongol-Malayan group of nations.

This nascent, racial principle will grow into a powerful, dominant, political factor in the near future. It represents the next stage in the social, political and religious evolution of humanity.

After that, and speedily too, will come the last ascent, the final climb to the high plane of a common humanity and the brotherhood of man. That lofty level, of which seers, prophets, philosophers and poets have dreamt, preached and sung, will soon be reached It will mark the point of culmination in the intellectual, moral, social, political and religious evolution of the human race. The circling wave of human sympathy and love that began its existence around the individual man tens of thousands of years ago, constantly widening its sweep, as it included, one after another, the family, the clan, the tribe, the nation, the race, will at last embrace all humanity. We are nearing that goal, and will probably reach it under the leadership of the Teutonic races, and during the present era of unparalleled progress.

Many symptoms of our age point to the speedy realization of this noble ideal of a common humanity. Nations and races are preparing to abandon their former egotistical and self-sufficient isolation. The sentiment of kinship, regardless of color, race, religion or condition, was never as strong as now. Consciousness of the fact that all men are units of the grand, living organism of humanity is gaining ground. Invisible, delicate threads of sympathy are uniting man to man, without regard to distance, nationality, race or religion. Tolerance is superseding intolerance. Steamship, railroad and telegraph lines assume the functions of arteries and nerves in the grand organism, and carry nutriment, vitality, sensation and intelligence to all parts of the system. Every new thought, every original idea, every epoch-making invention, flashing up in one spot, instantly illuminates the whole earth, and is made the common property of all. Dire catastrophes; earthquakes, holocausts, inundations, wrecks, famines, epidemics and wars visiting one locality, arouse responsive sympathy, and enlist noble charity throughout the civilized world. Courts of arbitration supersede the arbitrament of the sword. International Congresses, well attended and increasing in number annually, meet at various places to promote peace, public health, industry, commerce, agriculture, public service, municipal administration, science, the exchange of ideas, religious tolerance and international law. A strong tendency toward greater uniformity in dress, manner of living, social customs, taste in art, commercial usages, industrial methods, religious ideas, and social and political institutions, is universally manifested. Surely, universal fraternization is in sight.

Our age witnesses the most brilliant efflorescence of humanity. In its expansion of intellect, wealth and power, in its broadening human sympathy, in its stupendous, feverish activity, in its originality, in its creative power, in its discoveries, in the number and value of its practical inventions, in its control of nature's laws and forces, in its application of science to the affairs of daily life, in its ethical progress, in its political and religious advance, and in the improvement of the general welfare of mankind, this era far surpasses every progressive epoch in the history of our race. There is today far more justice, truth, fairness, tolerance, charity and humanity, in the world than ever before.

All humanity is vibrating with a new life. Nearly all nations and races are drawn into the current of progress. Those irredeemably ossified by dotage will perish, but all others, even those advanced in age, will feel the pulsation of a new life. The backward, yet to some extent progressive nations and races will be revivified and galvanized into the semblance of life. They will shine in reflected light, and glow in the flame kindled by other nations. The real foci, however, of the new light will be the Teutonic nations, and in a lesser degree the semi-Teutonic nations and the Japanese.

The Teutonic race and mankind in general will reach their respective zeniths almost simultaneously. This coincidence is not accidental, but in conformity to the laws of nature. Other races, of lower organizations, have represented the infancy, childhood and youth of the human race; others, inferior in mental and moral qualities, will be the exponents of its decline; but the Teutons, the best endowed branch of the Aryan family, will properly be the representatives of its prime of manhood.

The "golden age" which is immediately before us, will be ushered in under the leadership of the Teutonic race. It will be an age of the greatest amount of peace, prosperity, power, tolerance, charity, justice and humanity, that the human race can enjoy. The elimination of the monarchical idea of rule by divine right, the triumph of democracy, the death of all the great national and racial religions and cults; the disintegration of the old rigid dogmas; the new "Ragnarok" or the passing of Brahma, Buddha, Allah and Yahweh, with a myriad of lesser gods, to the domain where the phantoms of Zeus, Apollo, Pallas, Baal, Osiris, Wotan, Thor and millions of other deities, went before; the dwindling away of cults and priesthoods; the divorce of church and state;

the separation of ethics from religion; the disappearance of the old religious systems, except among the ignorant and fossilized, and the founding of a new and universal religion among the educated and progressive, which will not be based on revelation, but on reason, and will be in full harmony with the teachings of science; the reorganization of society without privileged classes and a debased proletariat; the maintenance in full of all the social and political units, such as the individual, the family, the tribe (country, city, state and province) and the nation, and the harmonious adjustment of the rights and duties of each and all of them; a rational system of education; a just distribution of rights and duties among the citizens of the state; recognition of the right to existence, independence and freedom, of all nations without regard to color, race, religion, age and culture; fullest toleration in religious matters; and a marvelous advance in discoveries and useful inventions in the field of the natural sciences; these will be the characteristic achievements of the coming "golden age."

The future is no more a sealed book to us. The laws of nature will shape affairs in the time to come as they did in the past. Standing on the narrow boundary between the past and future, we can turn the search-light of science ahead, and in its rays discern, in dim outline, the slow approach of coming events.

We see both the Teutonic and the Human race maintain themselves for some centuries at or near their coinciding zeniths. Then inevitable decline will set in, and the Teutonic race, the representative of humanity in its prime of manhood, will enter upon the downgrade to feeble old age, like all the other races that have gone before. The symptoms of decadence will multiply from generation to generation. Originality, invention and creative power will diminish steadily; epigoni will eke out a weary existence as imitators and commentators of their great forebears; the self-luminous geniuses who had shed their effulgence over many lands, will be extinguished one after another, until the dusk of evening, the gloom of old age, settles over all Aryan nations, and over Japan.

But while the Aryans and the Japanese nation will be on the descending path to dotage, the Malay race, and close upon its heels, the African, will ascend from childhood to youth, and from youth to manhood. Led by a vanguard of nationalities that had received a strong infusion of stimulating Mongol, Semitic or Aryan blood, these dusky races will advance, take the banner of progress from the nerveless and palsied hands of the Aryan, and build up a new civilization in the Malay Archipelago, in Africa and in tropical America. The only progressive people on earth will then dwell in the equatorial regions, and the prophetic vision of Macaulay, about a civilized Maori, sitting on the fragments of London bridge, sketching the ruins of St. Paul, will become true, except that a Malay from Sumatra or Java or a Negro from the Congo or the Orinoco instead of a Maori from New Zealand, will be the archaeological student.

The civilization created by either Malay or Negro, since these races will represent humanity in its decline, will be inferior to that of the Aryan. They will be the leading races on earth at that time, but culturally they will stand on a lower level than their fair predecessors.

The Malays and Africans will eventually share the fate of all other races. They will rise to the point of culmination, remain there for a period, and will then decline, degenerate, and sink into the sterility, stagnancy and decrepitude of old age. Then every race on earth will have had its day. There will be no young and progressive race left. All will be on the descent to dotage and extinction. And when the last African nation has made the last weak effort to rise and kindle anew the flame of culture in a darkening world, and has sunk back weak and helpless with old age; then man's mission on earth will be fulfilled, and oblivion will cover up all the proud monuments which man had wrought in the course of thousands of years.

An outline sketch of the life of the human race since the dawn of history, with its representative nations or races coming successively to the front, may help to illustrate the ideas advanced in the foregoing paragraphs.

4000 B. C. At that early date we find rising civilizations on the Nile and on the Euphrates, in China, and, possibly, in tropical and subtropical America. The light of primitive culture of the aging races of the Neolithic and bronze ages was growing dim. The rest of the world dwelt in the dense darkness of infancy and barbarism. The Chinese, Egyptians, Chaldeans and Indians the races with isolated speech, pictorial writings and megalithic monuments were the representatives of humanity's childhood. They were the superior people of that age; the rest Semites, Aryans, Malays and Negroes were inferior.

3000 B. C. The nations of Egypt and Chaldea have reached the point of culmination in their lives. The pyramids, gigantic mounds, hieroglyphic records, massive temples, systematized tribal religions, orderly and complex tribal governments, rudimentary literatures and well-regulated agriculture, industry and commerce, are evidences of their comparatively high civilizations. Chinese and American Indians are still on the ascent. They and the Egyptians and Chaldeans, remain the superior races of the period. Elsewhere, in Europe, Asia and Africa, impenetrable gloom covers the land.

2000 B. C. Egypt and Chaldea are on the decline and show symptoms of decadence. China is at its zenith and probably America. The infantile Aryan and Semitic races venture to take their first hesitating steps on the course of progress. The Hindus, the vanguard of the Aryans, appear on the Indus. The foci of culture are still on the Nile, Euphrates and Peiho, but their light is growing pale.

1000 B. C. The decay and decrepitude of old age becomes more and more manifest in Egypt, Chaldea and China. The Hindu race stands at or near its zenith. The Assyrians, the precursors of the Semitic race, advance to manhood, and are ready to supplant the decadent Chaldeans and Babylonians in the hegemony of Mesopotamia. The youthful Semitic tribes and nationalities of Tyre, Sidon, Carthage, Zion, Syria, Edom and vicinity, are ripening into maturity. Infantile Hellas ventures with bold step into the field of adventure, poetry and general culture. The Teutonic nations of northern and central Europe dare not yet leave their nursery. Though grown old, feeble and unprogressive, the nation-sages of Egypt and Babylon still retain their prestige of superiority. China continues on its downward course.

500 B. C. Babylon and Egypt are sinking irretrievably into their dotage. Their light is extinguished. China petrifies in the hands of Kung-fus-tse. The Hindus exhibit signs of rapid decay and deterioration. Old age with its sterility and weakness, is settling upon the Semitic nations. Greece, closely followed by youthful Rome, is approaching maturity and manhood. They create a new and superior civilization. They are the representatives of humanity's poetic youth. A new and vigorous life begins to stir among the Teutonic nations of Europe.

1 A. D. The center of gravity of civilization has completely shifted from Africa and Asia to Europe. Egypt, Babylon, Assyria, Semitic Asia with the exception of Arabia, also Iran and India, are in a moribund condition. China is fossilized. Hellas crossed its meridian a few centuries since, and Rome stands at its zenith. Both now rule the world by their superior physical, intellectual and moral forces. The infant nations of the North pass into the early bloom of youth and venture on a contest with the adult veteran of the Tiber. And in the far East, unknown and unheeded , by the world, the young Japanese nation has left its cradle and entered upon a promising career.

500 A. D. Nearly the whole Orient is in its dotage. Greece and Rome, too, have grown old, feeble, decadent and unprogressive, and are borne down to the ground by the fierce onslaught of the youthful, vigorous and rising Teutonic nations. The young Japanese nation submits to the tutorship of sage and hoary China. A new life is pulsating through the veins of the young Arab, and spurs him on to an adventurous career.

1000 A. D. The Arab race, after an unparalleled course of conquest and progress, reaches the height of its power and culture. The foci of Cordova, Bagdad, Damascus and Cairo illuminate the world, while the lights of Athens and of Rome are extinguished, and while the young Teutonic and semi-Teutonic nations are yet preparing the kindling for their new civilization. The center of gravity of civilization again abides in the lands of the Semites. The Teutonic nations are rapidly advancing to manhood. The fusion of the youthful Teutons with the aging Romans results in the formation of the new, young, vigorous and progressive nations of Italy, Spain and France. Japan enters her heroic youth with its feudalism, chivalry and romantic poetry.

1500 A. D. The neo-Latin nations, due to the mixture of old Latin and young Teutonic blood in their arteries, advance with accelerated step. The Italians reach their zenith in the sixteenth century; the Spaniards are close upon their heels; and to the French the point of culmination is in sight. The

Teutons of purer extraction the Germans, Anglo-Saxons, Scandinavians and Dutch continue their advance to full manhood at a slower pace, and a short distance behind their half-brothers of the Mediterranean. The center of gravity of culture and power has again shifted, and the new foci of civilization spread their light from the banks of the Tiber the Ebro, the Seine, the Thames and the Rhine. The Arabs of Spain, Africa and Asia are on the down grade to old age; but they have rejuvenated India, and an evanescent Indo-Arabic civilization flashes up on the banks of the Indus and Ganges. Japan passes from youth into early manhood. The aged Slav nations are galvanized into a semblance of life by coming in contact with the strenuously active West. The Aryans, in their prime of life, venture across the Atlantic, and on the new continent find themselves confronted by a race that, unknown to the Old World, in the course of many centuries, had passed through the phases of childhood, youth and manhood, and was now wrapped in the decrepitude, sterility, feebleness and fossilization of extreme old age.

The Teutons and semi-Teutons now take rank as the superior peoples, and represent humanity in its stage of manhood.

1900 A. D. Italy and Spain crossed their respective meridians in the sixteenth century, and are now on the down grade. France reached her point of culmination at the close of the eighteenth century, and England, Germany, Scandinavia and the Netherlands, with their offshoots, stand at or near their zenith. The same is true of Japan. The aged nations and races, that are not completely incapacitated by senility, are partially resuscitated by the warmth and the light of the spreading Aryan civilization. The races absolutely fossilized with age, such as the Indian, the Australian and the savage mountain tribes of Asia and the Malay archipelago, are passing away. The infant races of Africa and the Malayan islands, under the guidance, tutelage and guardianship of Aryan, Semitic and Japanese missionaries, traders and soldiers, have entered upon the stage of history, and are taking their first lessons in civilization and progress, The noonday, the summer, the phase of manhood of the Human race is at hand, and the proud and highly endowed Aryan race is its proper representatives.

3000 A. D. Passing the narrow border between the past and the future, we observe, in dim outline, a mighty change in the picture revealed by the search-light of science. Civilization's center of gravity, and with it that of wealth and power, is again shifting southward, to the Congo, the Niger, the Amazon and the Malayan archipelago, where new and promising civilizations are springing up, while European culture is decadent from old age. All the old races the Mongol, the Tartar, the Turanian, the Indian, the Semitic, the Hamitic and the Aryan have had their day, when they were superior to all others, and were the leaders of mankind. Each was superior in its time and yet, it must be concluded that, in the general progress of humanity from infancy to manhood, the nations and races which successively represented the advance must indicate a steady growth in their intellectual and moral capacity, and that the Neolithic race was superior to the Palaeolithic, the Indians and Chinese superior to the Neolithic races, the Egyptians and Chaldean superior to the Indians and Chinese, the Hindus, Hellenes and Romans to the Egyptian and Chaldean; and the semi-Teutonic and Teutons to the Romans, Greeks and Hindus.

With thousands of years of observation and experience, man must see clearly that nations and races, black, red, yellow or white, in torrid or temperate zones, on plains or uplands, have succeeded one another in the intellectual and moral leadership of mankind, for many ages. Chance did not rule these movements. Nations and races rose, prospered and decayed, each in its proper age and place, in strict obedience to universal and immutable law. Everyone of them performed its allotted part in the grand drama of humanity.

Chapter III - Statement and Solution of Our Race-Problems

There probably never existed a people but what had to deal with a vexatious race-problem at some time during its existence. At some time they were either conquerors or conquered, and had to pass through a long era of amalgamation, friction and internal disturbances, before the confluent and heterogeneous ethnic elements could thoroughly fuse and attain a fair degree of homogeneity for the formation of a new nation or race. Such was the case with the Hindus, Egyptians, Chaldeans, Babylonians, Assyrians, Hebrews, Greeks, Romans, Persians, Arabs, Italians, Spaniards, French, Anglo-Saxons, Germans, Slavs, Magyars, Turks, Japanese and others.

With all these nations homogeneity in language, manners, types, ideas and ideals was attained long ago, mostly in the phase of childhood and youth of their respective lives, and race-problems have ceased to irritate them.

But a number of new, nascent nations are springing up in America, Australia and Africa, since the discovery of America, which are all confronted by race-problems. They are all colonies or offshoots of European nations. The Anglo-Saxons in North America, Australia and Africa, the Latins in Mexico, Central and South America, and the Dutch in South Africa, have laid the foundation of new states and planted new nations of great promise. Besides the conquering invaders and the subjugated aborigines, colonists in large numbers from every country and race on the globe flock to these newly opened lands, and in everyone of these new states or colonies, perplexing race-problems have arisen or will arise. Streams of immigrants from nations or races of the greatest variety in color, character, age, and culture, flow together in these new states, to assist in the upbuilding of the new nations. Every immigrant, every settler, becomes a factor for weal or for woe, in shaping the type, character, civilization and destiny of the new nations.

The character, and, consequently, the future history of these new nations, will depend entirely upon the nature of the mixture.

The qualitative and quantitative value, the age, character, type and numerical strength of each factor being known, we can readily forecast the fate of such new nations. If the influx of immigrants is predominantly from aged, sterile and unprogressive nations or races, the new people will be stagnant and stationary; if from young, vigorous, progressive and aspiring countries, they will advance, prosper and maintain their rank among the foremost in originality, invention and creative power.

It is, therefore, in the power, yes, it is the imperative duty of the statesmen and legislators of these new states to invite and admit immigration from progressive countries only, and to exclude immigrants from those nations which have passed into the petrifaction and decrepitude of old age. This is a solemn duty the founders and managers of new states owe to their posterity. When the new states are once fairly well settled, no matter by what people or race, their destiny is fixed, and it will be too late to correct the evil done or permitted.

The United States is a case in point. The colonies, and afterward the Union, opened wide the doors to the oppressed and distressed of all countries indiscriminately. They came, voluntarily or involuntarily; white, yellow, brown and black; and the grand doctrine of the equality of men, which is only true in a limited sense, became the fundamental principle of social and political America, and generated a brood of vexatious race-problems, the solution of which taxes the ingenuity of our statesmen and politicians to the utmost. These annoying race-problems have been the cause of endless worry, and have cost us already an inestimable sacrifice of blood and treasure; and further sacrifices of lives and property will be required unless these problems will be solved and disposed of in a rational, scientific and courageous manner.

This country was first colonized by the Anglo-Saxons, their German, Dutch and Scandinavian kindred, and a large contingent of Celts. These early colonists belonged to highly endowed, progressive and mature nations which, in the sixteenth and seventeenth centuries, or at the time when the foundation of the new American state was laid, proclaimed religious freedom; established democratic self-government in England, the Netherlands and Switzerland; instituted a liberal monarchy in Scandinavia, and advanced art, science, literature, philosophy, industry and commerce to a high degree of perfection.

It was fortunate and providential that the great, progressive Teutonic race should first people North America, almost exclusively, and lay the foundation of great, powerful, progressive and prosperous states. The American Union is phenomenally rich in natural resources, is blessed with a salubrious climate, and enjoys a splendid geographical position. Almost any race would thrive here, in a way, but the present greatness and progress of the republic in art, literature, science, inventions, discoveries, industry, agriculture and statesmanship is mainly due to the fact, that the first settlers who organized American society, and laid the foundation of the future American state, and their immediate descendants who erected the superstructure, belonged to the young, vigorous and progressive Teutonic race.

The Spanish and Portuguese colonized all of Latin America. These nations had already passed their meridian and were on the decline at the time of colonization; and Latin America, although favored with abundant resources, fine climate and an excellent geographical position, remained stationary. The Latin-American colonies never outgrew the later medieval stage of development, in which their mother countries became petrified at the time of colonization in the sixteenth and seventeenth centuries. If by any chance the Latin race had occupied North America, and the Teutonic nations had peopled the great valley of the La Plata, the conditions would be reversed; South America would today be dominated by a mighty, prosperous and highly progressive republic, and North America would present nothing but a congeries of puny, turbulent and stagnant states; liberal and progressive in their imitated form of government, but feudal and reactionary in character. The striking variance in the destiny of the two continents was due almost exclusively to the difference in age and character of the races that invaded, conquered, settled and ruled them.

From the first settlements at Plymouth, New Amsterdam and Jamestown, in the early part of the seventeenth century, down to the last quarter of the nineteenth, voluntary emigration to North America drew its recruits almost entirely from Teutonic Europe. A fair proportion came from partly teutonized Celtic lands.

The Anglo-Saxons, by dint of superior numbers, greater self-consciousness, more aggressive character, and a higher political development, naturally took the lead in the formation of the new nation, and this leadership was acquiesced in by their less numerous, aggressive and advanced Dutch, German and Scandinavian kindred. The Anglo-Saxons absorbed and assimilated the other nationalities and gave to the new nation their language, their customs, their laws, their ideals, their social, political and religious institutions, and their progressive spirit. The other nationalities never disputed seriously the hegemony of the Anglo-Saxons, but relinquished their native tongues, manners, traditions, institutions and ideals, and permitted themselves to be absorbed.

But, although English is and will remain the language of our country; although the English spirit has very largely fashioned and shaped our social, political, religious and economic institutions, yet, it must not be inferred from that that America is an Anglo-Saxon country. A complete census, taken in 1890, would have shown that the blood coursing through the veins of our white population was about one third Anglo-Saxon, one third Celtic and one third German and Scandinavian.

As the Celts of Ireland, Wales and Scotland have continuously received large infusions of Teutonic blood during many centuries, we may safely assert that the American nation toward the close of the last century was practically Teutonic in blood, age and character. The strong influx of German, Scandinavian, Dutch and Celtic elements will undoubtedly exert a considerable modifying influence in shaping the physical, intellectual and moral character of the future American nation, and cause a notable differentiation from the pure Anglo-Saxon type; but there will be, on that account, no perceptible deviation from the cultural line of march, as laid out by the Anglo-Saxon founders of the republic.

The American nation, formed by colonization, is new but not young. There is quite a distinction between these two terms, and in dealing with the history of this nation or of any other similarly started into life, we must not lose sight of this important fact A nation springing from colonization begins its life at the stage at which the mother country stood at the time of the colonization; be it that of infancy, youth, manhood or old age. The mother countries which colonized the American colonies and the Union Great Britain, Ireland, Germany, the Netherlands and Scandinavia had reached full maturity and stood in the prime of manhood at the time of the separation, and the new offshoot nation began its life or national existence in that phase. It had neither childhood nor youth with the characteristic traits of these phases in literature, art, society and form of government. Its childhood and youth were spent at the old homes on the shores of the German Ocean; and it will live only through the stages of manhood and old age. All the Teutonic nations on both sides of the Atlantic, in Australia and Africa, will march abreast through the remaining stages of their lives.

With her democracy triumphant under Cromwell; with much democratic self-government in the church; with the center of gravity of her intellectual life shifting from the field of youthful, exuberant imagination to that of reason, from poetry to science and practical affairs, the England of the seventeenth century entered the phase of manhood, and the same is true of her offshoot, transplanted to America. As in old England, so here, the men of calm reason, the scientists, the inventors, the statesmen, the practical men of affairs, and not the poets, the men of imagination, took the lead in the intellectual work.

The two Anglo-Saxon countries advanced along parallel lines. With Cobden, Bright and Gladstone; with Dickens, Thackeray and Eliot; with Tyndall, Huxley and Darwin; with Mill, Buckle and Spencer; the English nation reached the point of culmination of its life, about the middle of the last century; and at about the same time, her thriving American scion, with Emerson, Prescott, Motley, Webster, Clay, Longfellow, Lincoln, Bancroft, Morse, McCormick, Edison, Clemens, and a host of able statesmen, inventors and editors, crossed its meridian. After them the decline set in on both sides of the Atlantic. It is scarcely perceptible, but, after careful investigation, it may be discerned that the poets, philosophers, historians, and statesmen, of the present day, do not measure up fully to the standards set up by those of the preceding generation. The fact cannot be disguised that American ideals have been lowered of late. Enormous wealth and the luxury and power in its train, is the goal toward which our youths are crowding. To become a famous but poorly paid scientist, author or artist, has little attraction for the rising generation. Money is the universal dream. No Bancrofts, Motleys, Prescotts, Beechers, Emersons and Longfellows, but the great Captains of industry, commerce, finance and transportation the Vanderbilts Goulds, Astors, Carnegies, Rockefellers, Morgans, Hills and Harrimans are the true representative

Americans of the present materialistic and degenerate age, the embodied ideals of our generation. It certainly requires talent and genius to amass vast fortunes in the manner these men have done, but to place them in the same class with Emerson, Webster, Clay, Longfellow and Motley indicates a pronounced lowering of ideals.

There are other signs of decadence. Corruption is rife in the land. The cardinal virtues of honesty and truthfulness, upon and around which individual and national character and greatness are built, become neglected, and sham and mock virtues are cultivated as substitutes. The constitution is made a fetish, and expounded to hinder the normal development of the public sense of justice and right. Religious thought is fossilizing and loses its capacity to adjust itself to the great discoveries of science. The democratic spirit has become lethargic. We are steadily drifting away from the old democratic moorings of "equal rights for all, and privileges for none." We are fostering privileged classes, and privilege begets aristocracy. The wealth of the nation is rapidly being centralized in the hands of the few, and political power accompanies wealth. The kings of transportation, dukes of finance, counts of commerce and barons of industry organize all the powerful leagues, combines and trusts, and divide the territory and the people of the Union among themselves, as did the feudal lords of the Middle Ages parcel out the states. Democracy cannot flourish where the national wealth is very unequally distributed. Political power is concentrating dangerously in the national executive. Society is drifting swiftly toward degenerating luxury and extravagance. Individualism is carried to excess. Cynical and irreverent disregard of authority is spreading. Sensationalism, nervousness and hysteria, in literature, in religion, in politics, in fashions and even in reforms, have superseded the cool, calm, steady and sane methods with which affairs were conducted by preceding generations. These symptoms and many others that might be enumerated, indicate that the Anglo-Saxon portion of the American nation has passed its zenith, and has entered upon the down grade.

The achievements of the American people during the eighteenth and nineteenth centuries, in opening a vast continent, and in building up a civilization of the first order, were phenomenal. But it necessitated exhaustion of the physical, mental and moral forces, and a somewhat premature decline and old age.

Fortunately Germany, Switzerland, Scandinavia and the Netherlands, being slightly younger than the Anglo-Saxon nations, sent their heavy contingents of immigrants to the United States during the last century. They were recruited from the physically, intellectually and morally soundest and most progressive strata of European society. The effect of this immigration, when it once becomes thoroughly absorbed and assimilated, is to rejuvenate the American people to some extent, and to maintain them at or near the zenith for a longer period. It can be observed already that the states which received a comparatively large influx of this immigration are, in their social, political, religious and economic institutions, the most progressive.

Under the leadership of the Anglo-Saxons, all the Teutonic and Celtic elements fuse readily, and no race problem can arise between them.

A radical change in immigration came in the last quarter of the nineteenth century. While the current from Teutonic and Celtic countries was ebbing fast during the last decades of the last century, a broad, deep and booming stream of an entirely new and different immigration began to pour into the territory of the Union. Russia, Poland, Bohemia, Slavonia, Hungary, Roumania, the Balkan states, Greece, southern Italy, Turkey and Asia Minor began to send their emigrants by the millions to our hospitable shores.

This class of immigrants, as a general rule, belongs to nations and races in their decline, and which are, for that reason, unprogressive, stagnant and ossified in their ideas, habits and ideals. A visit at the old homes of these immigrants will soon convince anyone of this truth. The people of eastern and south-eastern Europe are very backward in art, science, literature, religion, government, agriculture, industry and commerce. They do not originate, invent or create anything of note. They contribute scarcely anything to the general stock of useful knowledge. Whatever of civilization is found among them is either imported from their more advanced neighbors, or is an inferior imitation. They do not possess the initiative nor power of progress; and if left entirely to their own resources, they would speedily revert back to semi-barbarism.

The backward condition of these peoples is not due to the retarding influence of despotic rulers or fanatic priests, hostile to progress. Why do they submit to political and religious tyranny? At the close of the Middle Ages the people of all Europe were oppressed alike. There was 'as much political despotism and authoritative clerical rule in England, France, Germany and Scandinavia, as in Russia, Hungary or the Balkan peninsula, But the Germans, English, French, Spaniards, Italians and Scandinavians, in contrast with their sluggish, semi-Asiatic eastern neighbors, were alert, aspiring and progressive, and by hard, persistent and indomitable fighting, obtained and secured what freedom and civilization they enjoy. These nations belonged to a youthful, vigorous, progressive and optimistic race, bound to advance in the face of all obstacles, and, on the contrary, the semi-Mongolic and semi-Tartaric Slavs, Finns and Magyars of the East, belonged to races which had crossed their meridians many centuries ago, had sunk helplessly into the decrepitude and senility of old age, and were incapacitated for progress and the realization of higher ideals.

As a general rule, we may affirm that all nations and races have those social, political, religious and economic institutions, which they deserve; which are best suited to their age, character, condition and culture, respectively; and which secure to them the greatest amount of prosperity, civilization and happiness which they can attain and enjoy. The nations and nationalities of the European east and southeast, in their thoughts, manners and institutions, were crystallized at an early stage in the progress of the human race; they cannot create a modern civilization; they can only imitate one to some extent; they are old and barren; they cannot appreciate, enjoy and manage successfully a democratic form of self-government; and they will never grow up to it. Organize a republic today in Russia, Poland, Bohemia or Hungary; anarchy would wipe it out tomorrow; and brutal despotism would follow the day after. These nations politically never developed beyond the more primitive stage of kingship. They are born subjects. They still adhere to the old superstition that princes and priests are endowed with superhuman attributes, and are their natural rulers by divine order. With them authority, civil or religious, must still be embodied in the person of a prince or a priest; and they cannot rise to the conception of the rule by self-imposed, impersonal law, the fundamental principle of democracy.

The mere transposition across the Atlantic of these nationalities does not change their character or age. What they are at their homes they will be here. They bring their fossilized ideas, habits and ideals with them and cannot abandon them. It is in the blood. A sterile and petrified Russian, Slavonian, Magyar, Greek, Turk, Italian, or Syrian will never change into a progressive American.

Of course, a highly progressive nation of ninety million souls can absorb, digest and assimilate a few millions of such decadent and stagnant ethnic material without much injury; but when the influx of such an inferior element swells to the magnitude of nearly a million souls per year, and continues twenty or thirty years, the effect will be highly detrimental; a marked deterioration in the type, character and spirit of the American nation must result; and the danger-signal must be sounded.

In obedience to the law of the parallelogram of forces, this strong Slavic, Semitic, semi-Mongolic and semi-Tartaric immigration will deflect the course of American progress and civilization from the normal, in the exact proportion of its numerical strength to that of the whole people. It will retard progress, hasten the advance of premature old age, and lower and change the ideals and standards of American thought and action. This is inevitable.

To check this swelling flood before it reaches the danger point of a disastrous inundation is a duty the Americans owe to themselves, to their posterity and to civilization. If this immigration cannot be stopped or reduced very materially by general legislation, let special laws be passed as was done in regard to Chinese. All the reasons and arguments that led to the Chinese Exclusion Act can be used with equal force for the exclusion of immigrants from eastern and south-eastern Europe, and from continental Asia. All Asiatics, with the exception of the Japanese and Malays, and all the nationalities that occupy a broad zone in Europe along the Asiatic border, and which are chiefly of Mongolian, Tartar, Turanic and Semitic origin, are in their dotage and incapable of progress and a high civilization. They are all unprogressive Asiatics; only a few nationalities living near the Asiatic border in Europe are covered with a thin and translucent varnish of western culture. Now, here is an inconsistency. The Chinese, a fossilized Asiatic race, pure and simple, formerly entered our Pacific harbors, direct from Canton or Shanghai, which is now prohibited; and other Asiatics, equally unprogressive, equally alien, after having made successive halts on their long journey, on the banks of the Volga, Dnieper, Danube and Vistula; and after having absorbed and assimilated some progressive Teutonic material on their westward march; and after having copied and adopted a few of the externals of western culture; are admitted indiscriminately at our eastern ports. Our gates are closed to the Asiatics of the east of that continent; but the poorly disguised Asiatics of the west of Asia and their descendants in eastern Europe, find the open door. Why this inconsistent policy? One Asiatic is as unfit and undesirable for American citizenship as another, excepting always, of course, the progressive Japanese. All ought to be excluded, or, at least, be permitted to enter the United States only in limited numbers.

And it is no particular hardship or injustice to exclude these peoples. The countries they inhabit are rich in undeveloped resources. They have abundant room for expansion at home, if they will only develop their resources. The Slavs hold possession of all northern Asia, a vast domain, very sparsely settled, and capable of furnishing happy and prosperous homes for a hundred million or more of energetic, industrious, intelligent and progressive settlers. To a large degree this is also true of Asia Minor, the valleys of the Tigris and Euphrates, and of all Central Asia. That is the proper field for the Slavic race, if it has the capacity, to invade and conquer a continent, and to fill it with the institutions of a civilization of its own creation. That this great race stolidly neglects to improve such splendid opportunities, spread out invitingly at its very door, and prefers to emigrate across a wide ocean to a distant continent, to follow in the wake of another race which has transformed a wilderness into a garden, and built up a proud civilization, argues strongly for its general unfitness, and its lack of initiative and progressive spirit. The Anglo-Saxons, Germans, French and Scandinavians, if they had been as favorably situated as the Russian Slavs and their kindred have been for centuries, would have overrun the steppes and plains and mountains of northern and western Asia generations since, and carried their language, customs, laws and civilization triumphantly to the Pacific and to the arid tablelands of Central Asia. The Slav never had the sagacity to see his great opportunity, nor the energy to improve it.

This incapacity, due to extreme old age, the race carries with it to America. Its presence, in large numbers, will cause a pronounced deterioration of American national character, and bring American civilization to a lower level. It is high time that this immigration be stopped completely or be reduced to a minimum. This race problem can now be settled without much friction; it will be impossible to dispose of it without serious trouble a few decades hence.

The Chinese problem is definitely solved. These orientals are excluded by law. The census of 1900 shows the presence in the United States of only 119,505 Chinese. There is no prospect that the Chinese will ever become a factor worth consideration in the upbuilding of the American nation, either within the Union or, possibly, within its outlying possessions.

With the Japanese the case is entirely different. Keeping in view their limited number, the inviting field for colonization, near their home, and the age, the character, the progressive spirit, the self-consciousness, the just and sensitive pride, the high sense of honor, the natural ambition, and the creditable civilization of the Japanese, the agitation against them is unreasonable, unstatesmanlike and fraught with danger.

The Japanese cannot be placed in the same class with the other Asiatics. They resent it and have a right to do so. Besides the Teutonic, Celtic and semi-Teutonic nations, the Japanese are the only progressive and cultured people that come and ask for admission. It should be granted to them freely. Japan has a population of only about fifty million souls, and the neighboring countries of Korea, Manchuria and the Malay Archipelago offer splendid opportunities for her expansion and colonization. There the Japanese can work and colonize among their own kindred. They could not if they would, and would i?ot if they could, rush to the United States in numbers large enough to create a serious race problem. The few thousands that come to this country the census of 1900 snows only 85,986 souls enter with the purpose of studying our improved methods in everything that belongs to civilization. Most of them return soon with a store of knowledge to be utilized for the benefit of their native country. Only a few remain to be absorbed and assimilated, and, as they are clean, quiet, peaceable, industrious, frugal, intelligent and progressive, they are a far better acquisition than the bulk of the immigration we receive from Russia, the lower Danube, the Balkan, Asia Minor and southern Italy.

If we discriminate against them and in favor of inferior races, their proud and sensitive spirit will resent such treatment. Such a policy is certain to involve us in serious trouble. The panic fright of the "yellow peril," especially in regard to the Japanese, is unbecoming to Americans.

But a race problem of growing magnitude looms up for us in the vicinity of Japan, and she may be forced to take a hand in its solution.

The "Philippines came into our possession as a result of the war with Spain. The population of these islands, about ten millions in number 7,635,426 according to the last census belongs chiefly to the Malay race. Some tribes or nationalities, like the Tagalos, have made considerable progress in civilization; others, and particularly the hill tribes of the interior, are still low barbarians.

The Malays, as we have seen in a previous chapter, form a young, progressive and well-endowed race. This whole race, with the exception of the Japanese, is yet in the phase of childhood, or early youth. The Japanese, as a result of the fusion of the young Malay race with the aged Mongolian, took an earlier start on the path of progress than their kindred nationalities, advanced with accelerated pace and formed the vanguard of a Malayan civilization and power, which is yet of the future.

Some Malayan nationalities, such as the Hovas of Madagascar, the Battas of Sumatra, the Tagalos of the Philippines, and others, due to the more or less extensive admixture of Chinese, Japanese, Hindu and European elements of higher age and culture, advance with hastened steps on the path blazed for them by the Japanese. They are the representatives of the race's later childhood, verging upon youth. The main body of the race advances with slower pace, and will not reach full maturity in less than fifteen or twenty centuries.

The Filipinos, due to the quickening infusion of Chinese, Japanese, Spanish and American blood, advance rapidly, and may be expected to reach their zenith in the course of four or five centuries. Time must be allowed for fusion, the attainment of homogeneity and normal growth. The Filipinos are children still, but almost ready to pass into the phase of youth. They are yet in that stage of development when genuine kingship is the most suitable form of government. With a profound sense of awe and reverence they voluntarily subordinate themselves to rulers and priests, whom they deem of superior origin and gifted with semi-divine powers. Socially, politically and religiously, they have scarcely left the tribal state. Their condition resembles that of the Germans at the beginning of the Christian era.

The islands came into our possession by an "act of Providence" as with much cant and hypocrisy, so usual in such cases, we tried to soothe our protesting conscience, and convince the world of our noble purpose. Forthwith we hastened to bestow upon these benighted islanders the great blessings of our civilization and of our superior social, political and religious institutions. We thought that what was good for us must be beneficial to them. It was an egregious blunder.

This attempt to forestall nature will meet with signal failure. To raise the temperature of the incubator much above the normal, in the hope of stimulating and shortening the hatching process, will only spoil the eggs. We labor under the sad mistake that by sending a host of teachers, preachers, soldiers, traders, clerks, judges, legislators and governors, to these islands, we will be able to expand a child into an adult at once, or to transform, in a generation or two, a nation in its childhood into one that has attained maturity, and is fit for our mature civilization and our republican form of government. We clothe this child-nation in the habiliments fitted to the large stature of a full-grown people, and stubbornly refuse to recognize the ridiculous misfit.

We cannot colonize the islands; the tropical climate forbids it. We may hold them for centuries, but their population will always be alien in race, language, religion, custom, sentiment, traditions and aspirations. The Filipinos will never be Americans in thought and feeling. They will instinctively resent the introduction among them of foreign speech, manners, religion, laws and form of government, even if they be intrinsically much superior to their own, and even if they be forced upon them with noble and benevolent intention. Our institutions are simply unsuited to the age, condition and racial character of the natives. And this contrast will deepen and become more pronounced as decades and centuries pass, and as the Filipinos advance in age and culture.

To force an alien cult and a foreign civilization upon any people always works hardship and generates unrest, discontent, insurrection and rebellion. No people of spirit will quietly submit to it. The "golden rule" applies to nations as well as to individuals.

Under these circumstances we must expect nothing but ever recurring disturbances and uprisings. The Filipinos are naturally and justly longing for the freedom and independence which will permit them to shape their destiny in harmony with their own ideas, ideals, aspirations and racial character. It is certainly no concern of ours what form of government, cult and culture they adopt or create, if it suits them. Ours is not the quixotic mission to compel the world to conform to our standards of thinking and living.

This desire and incessant struggle for freedom and independence will increase from generation to generation, in spite of all our efforts to suppress them. The native race will steadily advance in age and civilization, and some day, not far distant, will rise in its might and strike a successful blow for its liberty and independence and, covered with disgrace, we will be forced to relinquish our hold upon these islands. We will certainly find our "Teutoburg" there.

And in their struggle for independence the Filipinos will be effectively seconded by the Japanese. Affinity of blood and race, and political and economic interests will force the Japanese to interfere. All the nationalities of the Malay Archipelago, as they progress in age and culture, will become more and more conscious of the ties of blood that unite them all into one great living organism. Japan will then be accepted as the natural leader and champion of the whole Malay race, and will have to battle for its existence, and for the common interests of all Malays. Japan must play the same role in the Malayan world, that Sparta played in ancient Greece, and that Prussia played in Germany. Whenever the situation of the Filipinos is ripe for a wide-spread, well-organized rebellion against the authority of the United States, Japan will be bound to aid and abet the movement.

Let the diplomats of Washington and Tokyo exchange vows of eternal friendship, as much as they please, but we must not forget the fact that the force of circumstances is superior to all human intentions and promises. They transform friends into bitter enemies in an instant. Our possession of the Philippines is fraught with grave danger, and some day it will involve us in a disastrous war with Japan and her Malay allies.

Such a war, waged for the rule over a distant and foreign nation, may be a war to advance the pet schemes of a cabinet, of a coterie of politicians and exploiters, or of misguided religious enthusiasts, but it will never be popular in America. With the disapproval of the national conscience; fighting at long range against a foe, struggling for liberty and independence, and backed by a mighty race, growing stronger with every decade and century; such a war will be a national calamity to us.

Furthermore, the possession of the Philippines and the other recent acquisitions, which we cannot colonize with our own people, is bound to exert a demoralizing influence on our nation. We were forced to increase our army and navy enormously since we yielded to the temptation to become a proud world-power, and to rule over subject nations. The military spirit, when unduly fostered, is always antagonistic to democratic ideas. In the camp and the barracks and on board the men of war, the principle of absolute and unquestioning obedience is taught. They are the schools where monarchical and aristocratic tenets are propagated. They breed imperialism. A warlike republic, engaged in wars of foreign conquest, is paving the way for the advent of Caesarism.

And then, we are compelled to send an army of officials to these islanders, to teach them, and to make, interpret and administer the law for them. The rule mostly an irresponsible rule of a superior over an inferior race, invariably demoralizes them both, but emphatically the former. Such a policy wrecked Rome, brought premature old age to Spain, saps the vitality of the British nation, and will inject its insidious poison into our body politic. The men and women who, for any length of time, enjoy nearly absolute control over an inferior race, become aristocratic or autocratic at heart, and are rendered unfit for democratic citizenship.

If wisdom rule our nation we will relinquish our control over the Philippines as speedily as possible. Delay is fatal. Every year strengthens the ties between the two countries. A few decades more of our rule, with the natural growth there of our commercial, industrial, religious and political interests, will make it as difficult and dangerous to let go as to hold on.

Three solutions of the Philippine problem offer themselves to us:

First: We can grant independence to the Filipinos, retaining only a protectorate over them, in so far as to protect them from foreign conquest. This is their right to demand, and our duty to concede. Disturbance, commotion, turmoil and even temporary anarchy, may result; it does not matter; the law of nature must be obeyed, and we can afford to stand by, a well-meaning, disinterested and philosophical spectator, abiding the time when order shall grow out of chaos. Let them shift for themselves and mould their own destiny, as all nations that ever amounted to anything were compelled to do. Violent fermentation will clarify ideas, ideals and institutions. The Filipinos are even now far enough advanced to dispense with the service of foreign tutors and guardians. Some day, after much friction, turmoil, riot and fermentation, some men, some tribe or some nationality, will rise among them, attain supremacy; restore order; lead the people on the road to progress, prosperity and contentment; and secure to them such social, political and religious institutions as will be in full harmony with their age, environment and racial character. If we really wish them well, that is the policy toward them which we should adopt. We must abandon the erroneous and dangerous idea that it is our mission to shape their institutions and destiny in conformity to our ideals. We must bear in mind that the Filipinos represent a race, fundamentally different from ours, but young, vigorous, gifted and progressive; and that they will and must advance along lines laid out for them by nature, and which cannot fully coincide with the road we are pursuing. A good gardener will treat every plant according to its nature and habits. He will be a failure if he treats all alike. That is a lesson the nations should heed who exercise control over people varying from them in type, age and character.

Secondly: We might transfer the islands to Japan. They are a large and growing white elephant on our hands. The Japanese nation, as the next of kin to the Filipinos, is entitled to the guardianship, if guardianship be needed. Being of the same race, but farther advanced in age and culture, its rule or leadership would redound to the advantage of the Filipinos. It would at least be in accord with their age, aspirations and racial character; secure for them order, peace, prosperity and progress, and relieve us of a grave responsibility.

Thirdly: Listening to the alluring and mischievous counsel of ambition, pride, avarice and misguided philanthropy, we may retain our hold upon the islands; pursue a policy hostile to nature's unbending laws; and invite disaster and dishonor. The Philippine Archipelago is for us a box of Pandora. It is wiser to give it away than to hold and open it.

To the south of us we encounter a race-problem, as yet in its nascent stage, but promising to grow to menacing dimensions. It is the manifest destiny of the American Union to extend its sway southward to Panama, and even beyond. The people of Mexico, Central America and the West Indies, as well as of all Latin America, are evidently unfit for orderly, republican self-government. Insurrections and rebellions are chronic with them. A weak government invariably invites revolution. They are not content unless they are ruled by a strong hand. Order, peace and prosperity are only enjoyed when a strong personality like President Diaz of Mexico firmly holds the reins of government. The moment such a man steps down and out, and a weaker man, be he ever so good, just and fair, succeeds him, perennial insurrection raises its head again.

This condition is an everlasting source of annoyance and trouble to the government of the United States. Time and again, to restore some kind of order it is forced to interfere in the external and internal affairs of these puny and turbulent states. In a large measure we are already ruling this stormy region, and, eventually, at no distant day, it will become a part of our dominion, either as autonomous States of the Union, or as territories governed by the Congress and the President.

When that happens we will have another troublesome race-problem on our hands. The population of these countries is of divers origin, and consists of Indians, Negroes, Latins, a thin sprinkling of other European nationalities, and a large but indefinite number of persons of various mixture. The torrid climate forbids any extensive immigration of actual colonists and laborers from the United States. The Aryan race cannot successfully colonize the tropics. The Indians constitute the substratum of the population of Mexico and Central America. It is estimated that about eighty per cent of the blood coursing in the veins of these people, is Indian, and the remainder Aryan or Negro. The Indian race is decrepit and in its dotage. Old age has robbed it of all capacity for progress. It is a true representative of Humanity's infancy, and became petrified at that stage. It can only prosper and live contentedly under primitive patriarchal and tribal institutions of its own creation. Every attempt to lift it up to the level of our modern civilization must fail, and will only result in its confusion, demoralization, hardship and final extinction. It is a physical impossibility to transform the Indian into a progressive citizen of a republic.

The Spaniards, who, heretofore, have constituted the thin layer of an aristocratic and ruling class in the Latin possessions of America, belong to a nation that crossed its meridian during the sixteenth century, and has been aging fast ever since. They, also, are stagnant and unprogressive. They conquered all of Latin America, except Brazil, a century before the Anglo-Saxons and Dutch began their settlement of North America; but the states they founded made no progress from their own initiative. They brought with them to the New World the crystalized ideas, ideals and institutions of medieval feudalism, and tenaciously adhered to them.

The Anglo-Saxons, abhorring amalgamation with the aborigines, drove them before them, and, advancing step by step into the interior, divided the lands into small freeholds, built up a country of free homes, and laid everywhere the solid foundations of free, civilized, expanding, progressive and powerful communities. The Spaniards, on the contrary, overran the entire continent in one or two generations, subjected the natives to peonage, fused with them, and resided on their vast grants like feudal lords.

All the states of Latin America have now copied the social and political institutions of the American Union; but it is a misfit. It is a hollow shell. The form is there, but the spirit to animate it is wanting. Democratic self-government is not suited to the age and character of the people. An ideal monarchy, in fact if not in name a government by a strong, just, fair, firm, benevolent and respected personality is the form of government best adapted to the Indians, Negroes, half-breeds and Creoles of Latin America.

The African race constitutes an important, in places a dominant, factor in large parts of Latin America. As we shall treat more at large of this race when considering the Negroes of the United States, suffice it here to say that, while the Indians, half-breeds and Spaniards, are too old and ultra-conservative for a progressive democracy, the African race is too young. Every experiment with these races for the purpose of making good, law-abiding, republican citizens of their members will result in utter failure.

Three races the Indian in its dotage, the Latin just past its manhood, and the African in its childhood; all three radically contrasting in type, age and racial character occupy that vast tropical and sub-tropical region to the south of us, which we may be called upon at any moment to possess and rule.

It will be a perplexing problem. Since fusion, which goes on unabated, cannot produce a fair degree of homogeneity within many generations to come, we must deal with each race separately and in accordance with its nature.

If, as seems inevitable, we are forced to annex Central America, the West Indies and Mexico, they will come into the Union either as autonomous states or as territories. As states they will always be a source of annoyance, perplexity and expense, since the people have no capacity for democratic self-government in city, county or state. If they come in as territories, some new, un-American system of government; some system, republican in form, but monarchical or autocratic in essence, will have to be devised for them.

It will be an extremely difficult task, as we will have to deal with highly heterogeneous elements. What is good, wise and salutary legislation for one race is very apt to be bad and injurious to the other. Uniform laws applying indiscriminately to the childhood, manhood and old age of nations are sure to work mischief in some quarters.

And then, the American Union would present the strange spectacle of a powerful country, where one half of its dominion would be settled by highly progressive, civilized Aryans, enjoying and perpetuating democratic self-government; and the other half peopled by alien, half-civilized, turbulent, partly childish and partly senile races, governed by a host of officials, eager and unscrupulous in their acquisition of power and wealth. The demoralizing effect on our body politic would be stupendous. The anomaly would strain and wreck our institutions. No nation did every enjoy with impunity the irresponsible control and exploitation of weaker and inferior races.

Our wisest policy in regard to those countries would be to be content with our present domain, and to resist firmly every impulse of misguided philanthropy and every tempting ambition to control or annex them. Let these bellicose states and races fight out their quarrels among themselves as best they may, our role being simply that of a referee, to see that fairness prevails, and that no outsiders interfere. Let them shift for themselves, as best they may, through revolution, anarchy and chaos. They must pass through a process of fermentation anyhow. Some day homogeneity will be attained, and some man, some nationality, will take the lead and enforce order, and secure to that region such social, political and religious institutions as are adapted to the age, culture, environment and character of the new race. That is the only rational way of treating these peoples. We must have patience, and use tact. It is the height of folly to think that in a brief space of time these inferior and heterogeneous masses can be so transformed that they will appreciate, enjoy and perpetuate a high civilization and democratic self-government.

Last, but not least comes the question: What shall we do with our Negroes? This problem overshadows all others. It is of such a magnitude, that its solution, be it one way or the other, will involve the destiny of the American Union for all time to come. The Negroes are with us ten millions strong. They must be either absorbed and assimilated by the body politic or expelled. Either process will be extremely difficult and fraught with danger. It is a perplexing inheritance left us by our ancestors. If the slave traders of former days, the planters and the rulers of the American colonies, could have foreseen the result of the importation of the African, they would have hesitated long before they would have inflicted such a grievous wrong upon their posterity.

The Negroes were brought here in large numbers as slaves. They thrived and multiplied under extremely adverse conditions. Today there are over ten millions of colored people in the United States, and what to do with them is the great problem which, above all others annoys, perplexes and alarms our statesmen. The civil war, the first equation, so to speak, in the solution of the problem, necessitated the sacrifice of the lives of half a million of our most promising young men, crippled and disabled about four times as many; caused a pension list which, forty years after the war, costs us more than one hundred and fifty million dollars annually; destroyed an incalculable amount of property; and left a vast region a nearly barren waste.

Race problems are very expensive affairs. The first attempt to solve the Negro question actually put the existence of the Union in jeopardy, and the only fruit of the tremendous sacrifice is the abolition of slavery. The Negro cannot be bought and sold like chattels, but his condition is not much improved; he is still a pariah. We are almost as far from the final solution as we were fifty years ago. Indeed, the emancipation and enfranchisement of the Negro has rather increased the complexity of the problem.

The African is here with us, and he will either stay or leave voluntarily or involuntarily and seek a new home somewhere else. If he remain with us he will naturally select the southern states as his permanent abode, since the climate and general conditions there are more favorable to his well-being than those of the North. The Negro is at present mainly an agricultural laborer, and the great alluvial plains of the South, where the great staples of cotton and sugar are raised, are his natural domicile. There he will prosper; there he already outnumbers the whites; and there will be the future center of gravity of his race.

If the Negro abide with us, what will be the final outcome? A slow, gradual and thorough fusion of the two races is unavoidable. No race antipathy, no draconian laws, no rigid and harsh social decrees, will prevent amalgamation. No two races, however strongly contrasting, did ever occupy the same territory without ultimate fusion; and America will furnish no exception to the universal rule. Love and lust hold in contempt the social and legal barriers erected between the races. As a fact, the blending of the Aryans and Negroes went on undisturbed during the palmy days of slavery, it continues unabated since the emancipation, and it will go on unchecked in the future. It is estimated that out of the ten millions of colored people in the United States, only about three millions are Africans of pure descent; the rest carries more or less Aryan blood in its veins. The two races already shade off so gradually toward each other, that it is difficult to draw a distinct line of demarcation between them.

The colored race, in this fusion, enjoys all the advantages in regard to numbers and intellectual force. The cruel and uncompromising spirit of caste assigns all persons with a trace of African blood in their veins to the despised colored race; and the infusion of Aryan blood improves the intellectual power of the Negro race, and hastens its advance in age and culture. Its leaders owe their prominent and commanding position to their Aryan ancestors.

The colored man is essentially a farm hand, a menial laborer; he is practically barred from entering the field of the learned profession, and even of skilled labor, except in so far as they pertain exclusively to his own race. The result has been to make common labor odious in the South. The white race has been transformed into an aristocratic social stratum, where common labor in field, street or shop, is looked upon as degrading, and only the so-called genteel pursuits are permitted to its members. Being removed from intimate contact with the soil, like the fabled Antaeus of old, it deteriorates physically, intellectually and morally, as all aristocracies do. Labor, and especially labor in the field, is the perennial fountain for the rejuvenation of nations, and the Negro of the South monopolizes almost all its blessings.

The Aryan race of the South, on account of its aristocratic tendencies, is degenerating, and the young, robust, virile and progressive colored race, enjoying all the benefits of common labor, is rising. The social position of the colored race will improve in proportion as it advances in age, and as it acquires wealth, education and positions of influence and power. Race prejudices and antipathies will gradually fade away, and the border line between the two races will become blurred and obliterated. The more virile and vigorous, and eventually the numerically stronger, colored race will steadily absorb and assimilate the Aryan of the South. And after a few centuries of uninterrupted and wide-spread fusion, Aryans and Negroes of pure descent will disappear generally, and a fairly homogeneous yellow race will occupy that vast region enclosed by the Atlantic, the Gulf, the Rio Grande, the Ohio and the Potomac.

The process of the blending and fusing of two very heterogeneous ethnic elements is invariably accompanied by violent agitations, fermentation, disorders, turmoil, anarchy and a marked lowering of civilization. It will be so in the South. The colored men, precociously developed by an education suited to an adult race, and instigated thereto and encouraged by zealous, short-sighted philanthropists of the North, will persistently and with growing emphasis, demand their rights as citizens and human beings, and the white race will stubbornly defend its privileges. Frightful clashes will be unavoidable under such conditions. The South will never enjoy a full measure of tranquillity, progress, prosperity and civilization, until fusion has resulted in homogeneity, and a yellow race has achieved preponderance over the white through its superior numbers, vigor, wealth, culture and social position. To that goal are we drifting with accelerated velocity.

We emancipated and enfranchised the Negro slaves half a century ago, and foolishly imagined we had settled the race question for all time to come. It only made matters worse. The whole white race of the South was up in arms against what was called "Negro rule"; and in this struggle it gradually gained the sympathy and aid of the North. As a result the colored man was practically disfranchised again, and reduced to the condition of a pariah. In some respects his new status is worse than slavery.

But this condition is evanescent and cannot endure under our form of government. Slaves, peons and pariahs are out of place in a democracy. The downtrodden and oppressed must at least have an opportunity to rise from their low condition. This the Negro will endeavor to do. A race in its dotage and in the decrepitude of old age may resignedly submit to bondage; but a young, vigorous and progressive race, like the African, will be restive under oppression and incessantly tug at the fetters of servitude until they break. We are not dealing with an old and senile race, but with one young, strong, progressive and rising. It cannot be held down forever. Full enfranchisement must again come to the colored man.

But the African is at present absolutely unqualified for the enjoyment of the rights, and for the exercise of the duties of full American citizenship. He may obtain a high education, accumulate wealth, and attain social distinction, but he belongs to a race which is yet in its infancy. He lacks that ripeness of mind, judgment and character, which only comes with age, and which is the result of centuries of continuous and steady growth. Cramming a child with book knowledge does not confer upon it the clear and safe judgment of maturity. Dressing an infant in the habiliments of an adult does not make him a mature man. Democratic self-government is the political efflorescence of Aryan civilization. It is the keystone in the arch of a nation's or race's social and political life. It is the product of a long and tedious political evolution. Only nations, standing at or near their zenith, can institute, enjoy and perpetuate it. It is a blessing to nations in their prime, but a veritable curse to those in their infancy or old age. Of all the nations and races on earth, only the Teutons, the Japanese and a part of the neo-Latins, are fit and ripe at present for a republican form of government; all the others, young or old, will fare better under monarchical, autocratic or oligarchic rule.

It will require ages of slow, constant and normal growth before the Negro will attain to the stature of a genuine republican. It took the gifted Aryan nations some fifteen or twenty centuries, to pass from infancy through youth to manhood; from patriarchism through tribalism and kingship to democracy; and it is folly to expect that the Negro race will advance faster, and compress the normal development of many centuries into the space of a few generations. A hot-house development, such as we are forcing on the Negro, will only work incalculable mischief. We must be patient and calmly await the result of slow and normal evolution. Haste will be fatal.

Only personal rule by chief or king is suited to the present or infant phase in the life of the African race. Negro republics, after the model of the United States, have been established and guarded with fostering care in Africa and America, but every attempt has been a. signal failure. If our colored people could be transposed to some large, sparsely settled and well favored region, and there, fully equipped with all social, political, religious and economic means that go to make up American civilization, and be enjoined to begin their own independent national existence without alien tutors, masters or guardians, and to shape their own future as would suit them best, they would not be able to maintain this culture and these free institutions for two generations; but through disorder, riot, chaos and anarchy, would immediately slide back into kingship, voodooism and semi-barbarism. They would degenerate until, in their downward course, they would reach conditions suitable to the childhood phase of national or racial evolution.

The Negro, for these reasons, is a menace to our free institutions. As his race is still in its infancy, he is naturally a monarchist at heart, and will blindly and loyally follow a leader who has gained his confidence and inspired him with awe and respect. The colored voter, for this reason, unquestionably, unfalteringly and unswervingly follows his political boss, and thus forms a veritable praetorian guard in our party politics. This guard, governed by monarchical instinct, already holds the balance of power in a number of leading states, and, in the hands of ambitious and unscrupulous politicians, can and does decide the fate of the Union. There is real danger to the republic when two millions of voters can be marshalled and directed in favor of the disguised monarchical principle of personal rule against the republican idea of government by impersonal law.

The erection of the proud and lofty structure of American civilization is due chiefly to the unreserved adoption of the principles of democracy; but the presence of the Negro is undermining the edifice. Under all forms of government, there is and always must be a party for and a party against privileges. The struggle for or against privileges runs through all the internal history of all nations and races since the dawn of history. Privilege has been from the beginning and now is the apple of discord in our republic. Indeed, baneful privileges will sprout and flourish in the midst of free, democratic institutions, as noxious weeds grow most luxuriantly where noble cereals thrive the best. Genuine democracy must always be the defender of popular rights, and the uncompromising opponent of privileges enjoyed by a few or a class. Its main strength, for that reason, must be derived from the wage-earners and the poorer middle classes. These, if they fully comprehend their own interests, must be true democrats.

But American Democracy has been hopelessly disorganized and demoralized ever since slavery became a powerful social, political and economic institution. The so-called Democratic party, during the first half of the last century, drew its chief support from the South, and the opulent slaveholders shaped its policy and directed its course. But slavery gradually transformed the democratic whites of the South into aristocrats. That metamorphosis is inevitable where a superior and an inferior race meet in the same territory and settle down side by side; the superior race will form an aristocracy. The two races stood and still stand to each other in the relation of adult and child, of master and apprentice, of guardian and ward, of tutor and pupil, of lord and servant. The fair Aryans of the South strove and fought successfully for special privileges, and acquired all the good and bad characteristics of old aristocracies courage, pride, high sense of honor, extravagance, courteous manners, aversion to common labor, contempt of laborers, and a taste for the pursuit of only such occupations as were considered genteel. The place of the menial and wage-worker in the South was filled by the African slave; true democracy was practically without a representative south of Mason and Dixon's line.

This anomaly in our party politics the control of a democratic party by an aristocracy has completely demoralized the Democracy of America. This condition prevailed in ante-bellum days, and it has not changed since the day of the emancipation of the slaves; the only difference being between an opulent and haughty aristocracy before the war and a less affluent one since. The spirit is and must be the same and cannot be eradicated as long as the two races dwell together and a stratified society remains. The white man, rich or poor, is a veritable aristocrat; and the colored man, out of touch with democracy, where he naturally belongs, is forced indirectly to aid the party of privileges. The colored laborer, even in the North, is forced into this anomalous position.

Almost every colored workingman thus eliminates a democrat from our social and political structure, and to that extent enhances the power of the party of privileges. If white workingmen filled the places of the colored laborers and there are two millions of them then, and then only, would we have a true, strong, aggressive, well organized and triumphant American democracy, South as well as North. And America sadly needs it. Privilege is undermining our free institutions. Privilege is the cause of dangerous accumulations of wealth and power in the hands of a few. Privilege creates an aristocracy. Privilege may be a temporary benefit, but it is a permanent curse. The democratic principle: "equal rights for all, privileges for none" is the only principle which can assure us the highest intellectual and moral development of our people, and perpetuate our free political institution. But the success of this principle is put in jeopardy by the presence of the Negro, who cannot grow up to the stature of a true democrat for some centuries to come, and who will be either a pariah of no importance, or a servile retainer of some privileged person or class.

If the African remain with us, a yellow race will ultimately inhabit the South. Unavoidable fusion will be quickened by the present large influx of Slavs and Latins, who are much less imbued with race-pride, race-prejudice and race-antipathy than Teutons and Celts. The yellow race of America, springing from the blending of the juvenile Negro race with the Latin and Slavic races who are in their decline, and with the Teutonic and Celtic in their prime, will hasten through its phase of infancy, and begin its racial or national life at the stage of early youth.

To illustrate: Applying the age of the individual to the life of a nation or race, we may set down the age of the young African race at about four years, and the average age of the mature Teutons, Celts, Latins and Slavs at forty. A fusion of the white and black races, in equal parts, in obedience to the law of the parallelogram of forces, will result in a yellow race at the youthful age of twenty-two years. This new race would have no childhood, but commence its separate racial existence in the bloom of youth, and thence pursue its normal course through youth and manhood to old age.

This young, vigorous and progressive yellow race, advancing with accelerated pace, due to the strong infusion of older Aryan blood, may be expected to reach full maturity, or the point of culmination in its life, about eight centuries hence. It will then enjoy the period of its greatest inventive and creative force and of political power and expansion, which are invariably associated with a nation's prime of manhood. Not until then will it be ripe for a republican form of government. Before it reaches that stage, it will have to pass through the phases of true chieftainship and kingship, the characteristic political features of nations in their childhood and youth. The civilization which this race will create and develop will betray its dual origin; it will be partly Aryan and partly African in character.

Two races, separated by the Ohio and the Potomac, speaking a common language, living under one government, but deeply contrasting in color, type, age, character, traditions, sentiment, ideas, ideals and aspirations, will ultimately occupy the United States if we allow matters to drift as they may. The Aryan race of the North stands now near its zenith, and will remain there for a few centuries to come, at the best; but, in accordance with the laws of nature that govern the rise and fall of nations and races, its decline, its descent to the feebleness, sterility and stagnancy of old age will come ultimately.

Nothing will prevent it; it is only a question of time. In the meantime, and while the Aryan race is slowly entering upon the downward grade, the AfroAryan race of the South, youthful, virile, progressive, optimistic and aspiring, will advance steadily in age and culture, and eventually overtake the degenerating Aryan. The colored race of the South will then have absorbed and assimilated the white element, and attained a fair degree of homogeneity. Much friction between the two races north and south of the Ohio will result, destructive race conflicts will be inevitable, and ultimately there will be either a complete separation of the two races, with the cleavage along ethnical lines, or the younger, more vigorous and at that time more progressive yellow race, will dominate the whole.

If that ever should come to pass and it must come in obedience to the laws of nature our republican institutions are doomed. The Aryan race, in its decline, sliding from the democratic heights toward Caesarism, and the yellow race, in its ascent, still within the monarchical zone, will unite in seeking refuge from disorder, riot and anarchy, under the scepter of a king; and that king may be an Afro-Aryan. Surely this race problem is a question of life or death to the Aryan race of the South; a question of progress or retrogression to the whole American nation.

However, if contrary to all expectations, the Negro race should distribute itself throughout the whole Union, and its ten millions become gradually absorbed and assimilated by the eighty millions of Aryans, then the American nation of the future will have from ten to twenty per cent, of African blood coursing through its veins, and, according to our present standard, must be classed as a colored people.

If this prospect is not pleasing to the American people, they must take hold of the other horn of the dilemma; they must resort to the elimination of the Negro. There is no other alternative. The colored people will not leave voluntarily, although that is clearly in their own interest. The immediate future offers them in this country nothing but degradation, humiliation, injustice and oppression; nothing but the lot of menials, serfs, outcasts and pariahs. But the race is yet too young, and for this reason, too destitute of initiative, self-consciousness, self-dependence and race pride, to venture on such a course. It has no Moses to lead it out of bondage through a forbidding desert to the promised land. Its own leaders value the applause of their condescending white superiors far higher than the approval of their own people. The average Negro manifests no desire to leave this country, and fusion is his most cherished ideal. The race is still in its infancy and wants to be led and ruled. For the present it must remain the ward of the Aryan, and Have his fate decided for him. The exodus of the colored people, if it ever come, will take place only by strong persuasion.

It will not be necessary to resort to drastic and inhuman measures to attain this end. We must bear in mind that this country is also the Negro's land of birth, and that his rights as a citizen and human being must be respected.

Violence must be avoided. Extensive deportation is cruel, unjust and impractical. All efforts aiming &t elimination must be educational. Every American, white or colored, must be made to see that this race problem is forcing a crisis upon this nation, in the solution of which is involved its future character, civilization and welfare. All ought to be made to recognize the fact that this nation has a mission to carry Aryan civilization to the highest perfection; that it is the duty of this generation to transmit to posterity unimpaired its free institutions; and that this cannot be done if it invites general deterioration by absorption and assimilation of ethnic elements on a large scale which are either too old or too young for our civilization and institutions. All ought to be convinced that the condition of the colored race in the near and distant future will be very much improved if it is separated and segregated from the white race, and compelled to work out its own destiny and create its own civilization in some suitable territory now owned by the United States, or to be acquired for that purpose. It is absolutely necessary that all should see clearly what is before us on the diverging roads, in order that a wise choice be made.

If, after due deliberation, the people come to the conclusion that it is best to leave matters as they are and let them shape themselves as best they may, then we ought to accept our fate cheerfully and philosophically, break down the barriers between the races, elevate the African intellectually, morally, politically and socially, shorten the period of transition from heterogeneity to homogeneity, and thus avert much of race conflicts, strife, riot, bloodshed and general demoralization. If, however, it be decided by the people, and especially by the Negro race, or a large part thereof, that segregation is in the best interest of the two races, then every effort should be made, every aid given, to make the colonization of the Negro a success.

It can be carried out without undue hardship. Tropical and sub-tropical America offer many very inviting fields for the colonization of the colored race. It will not be difficult for us to secure ample territory for that purpose on the West Indian Islands, in Central America, or in the valleys of the Orinoco or the Amazon. The land is very fertile and the Negro is naturally adapted to the climate of the torrid zone. The region is sparsely settled by the Indian, an aged, decrepit and perishing race, by Africans, and by Latins who manifest no strong aversion to amalgamation with the Negro. Neither Indians nor Latins will be able to block the advance of the African race. That vast region of tropical and sub-tropical America can never be successfully colonized by Aryans; only the Negro can prosper there. That is the proper arena where the Afro-American race can work out its own destiny.

The cost of the Negro's colonization will be trifling as compared with the expense of his retention, and must not deter us. We must bear in mind that, if we had fully comprehended the Negro-question in all its bearings, fifty years ago, and, in order to settle it finally, at any cost, had paid full value for every slave; had borne the expense of the Negro's deportation to some suitable foreign land; had fitted him out with farms, houses, tools, implements, machines, schools and churches; and had even paid the expense of his government for decades; even then, the outlay would have been trivial as compared with the stupendous material damage sustained by the Union through the Civil War, not to mention the incalculable sacrifice of the blood, limbs and health of the flower of the country. That Civil War should be a lesson worth heeding. It was unnecessary. Some foresight, some comprehension of the working of natural law in the history of nations, some sense of justice, fairness and tolerance, some willingness to sacrifice before an appeal to arms, would have prevented it. Let the present generation be wiser through the terrific experience of the preceding.

The colonization of the Negro race in tropical and subtropical America would be of great advantage to it. Here, in the Union, nothing awaits it but the humiliation of pariahs, for generations to come; there it can lay the foundation of young, progressive, independent, prosperous and powerful nations. Stern necessity brings out what is best in nations as well as in individuals. Placed before the alternative "root, hog, or die," the race would achieve great things. Forced to shift for itself, it would acquire that initiative and self-reliance, so necessary to success, and which it can never attain in its present dependent condition as servant, pupil, apprentice or ward of the dominant Aryan race.

The colored people with us are ten millions strong. Latin America contains several millions more. These numbers would soon double and treble in the new home of the race. These millions, with a strong infusion of quickening Aryan blood in their veins, would readily absorb and assimilate all alien elements, young or old, Indian, Teutonic, Slav or Latin; and out of this fusion would gradually spring a new, young, virile, progressive and homogeneous Afro-American race or nation.

This race would speak the English language and link itself commercially, industrially and culturally to the great Anglo-Saxon group of nations. It would serve an apprenticeship and a term of tutelage under American masters and tutors, for a limited time; for we would be compelled to exercise a kind of protectorate over the new colony. But, in the course of some generations or centuries, the Afro-American race would pass from childhood into youth, celebrate its real emancipation, and begin to evolve its own social, political and religious institutions, in harmony with its environment, age and character. The civilization it would create would not be a faithful copy of ours; no more than ours is a servile imitation of that of ancient Greece and Rome, our former tutors. Its literature, art, religion and form of government would bear chiefly the impress of the African genius.

That race, at its tropical home, would have to pass through the successive phases of childhood and youth into manhood; through tribalism and chieftainship into nationalism and kingship; through tribal and national into racial cults and religions; before it would be ripe and mature enough to comprehend, appreciate, create and enjoy a high civilization with democratic self-government.

The infusion of older Aryan and Indian blood into the veins of this Afro-American race would accelerate its pace of development, and, like the Japanese of the Malayan world, and like the semi-Teutonic Italians, Spaniards and French of Europe, it would form the vanguard of the great African race, and reach its zenith some centuries in advance of their kindred nations of purer blood, larger mass and slower evolution in Africa.

In about one thousand years hence this brown or yellow race would have extended its sway over all tropical and subtropical America. It would then have reached its prime of manhood and stand near the point of culmination in its life. It would then pass through an era of great originality, and of inventive, creative and expansive power; and would evolve a brilliant Afro-American civilization. It would establish famous centers of commerce, industry, art, literature, learning, wealth and political power in Mexico, Central America, on the West Indian Islands, and on the banks of the Orinoco and the Amazon. By reason of the approaching age of the Aryan races, the centers of wealth, power and culture could shift from the Hudson and Mississippi to tropical America, and beacon lights of a new, Afro-American civilization could flash up from the Antilles, the Orinoco and the Amazon, and dusky savants from these regions would explore the dust-covered ruins of St. Louis, Chicago and New York.

Led by the Afro-American vanguard, the African nationalities of mixed Negro, Semitic, Hamitic and Aryan extraction, occupying the Soudan, the lake region and South Africa, would advance in close pursuit, to be followed some centuries later by the gross of the race in the Congo basin, of purer descent and slower evolution. The African race would then be at its zenith and surpass all other contemporary races in culture and power. It would encircle the earth in a broad zone along both sides of the equator. But, as the representative of humanity past its prime and on its decline, its civilization would be inferior to that of the Aryans which had preceded it.

This is what the Negro race may be expected to achieve, if it exchanges servitude for independence; and with such bright and inviting prospects in view, it ought not to be difficult to convince its leaders that voluntary emigration is the best policy to be pursued; and to call out from among the colored people a Moses who will lead them out of bondage into a land of great promise.

And then, when the African has been eliminated from our population; when our gates have been closed against further immigration of stagnant, decadent, unprogressive and undesirable ethnic elements from Asia and from eastern and south-eastern Europe; a new era of unexampled progress will dawn upon the United States. Teutons and Celts will rush to the sunny South, and take the place of the departed Negro. Labor will be ennobled again. The aristocratic spirit of class and caste will disappear, and the democratic principle, which must always look for its main support to the ranks of the wage-workers, will triumph South as well as North. The South, so long handicapped by slavery, aristocratic proclivities and the institutions of caste, will rise and contribute her full share to American civilization. The South will not only produce soldiers and statesmen, but bring forth her quota of authors, scientists, artists, merchant princes, captains of industry and transportation, inventors and philosophers. The American people, from Maine to the Rio Grande, from Key West to Puget Sound, will form one great, highly endowed, progressive, homogeneous Aryan, or rather Teutonic nation, which, having solved aright its vexatious race problems, will march onward and upward with firm and steady stride to the highest level of civilization attainable by the human race in our era. And whatever of decline, decadence and the feebleness of old age the distant future may have in store for us, we will have fulfilled our mission; we will have acted well our part in the grand drama of humanity.

THE END.